D1053126

PSYCHOLOGY OF TERRORISM, CONDENSED EDITION

Coping with the Continuing Threat

Edited by Chris E. Stout

Contemporary Psychology

Westport, Connecticut
London

Library of Congress Cataloging-in-Publication Data

Psychology of terrorism : coping with the continuing threat / [edited by] Chris E. Stout.—Condensed ed.

    p. cm.

    Includes index.

    ISBN 0–275–98207–6 (alk. paper)

    1. Terrorism--Psychological aspects. 2. Terrorism--Prevention. I. Stout, Chris E.

HV6431.P797 2004

303.6'25—dc22   2004004633

British Library Cataloguing in Publication Data is available.

Library of Congress Catalog Card Number: 2004004633
ISBN: 0–275–98207–6
ISSN: 1546–668X

First published in 2004

Praeger Publishers, 88 Post Road West, Westport, CT 06881
An imprint of Greenwood Publishing Group, Inc.
www.praeger.com

Printed in the United States of America

The paper used in this book complies with the Permanent Paper Standard issued by the National Information Standards Organization (Z39.48–1984).

10 9 8 7 6 5 4 3 2 1

Copyright Acknowledgments

The editor and publisher gratefully acknowledge permission to excerpt passages from the following sources:

Excerpts from "Combating Terrorism: Some Responses from the Behavioral Sciences," by Susan E. Branson. Copyright © 2002 by Susan E. Branson. Reproduced with permission of American Psychological Association.

Excerpts from "Promoting Resilience in Response to War and Terror," by Ronald F. Levant. Copyright © 2003 by Ronald F. Levant. Reproduced with permission.

Appendixes A, B, C taken from *Prudent Preparation*. Copyright © 2002 by the National Strategy Forum. Reproduced with permission.

To my parents, Carlos L. and Helen E. (Simmons) Stout, to my wife and soulmate, Dr. Karen Beckstrand, to my mother-in-law, Mary Louise (Wentz) Beckstrand, and to my children and heroes, Grayson Beckstrand Stout and Annika Beckstrand Stout.

You all have taught me and continue to teach me so very much.

CONTENTS

SERIES FOREWORD

As this new millennium dawns, humankind has evolved—some would argue has devolved—exhibiting new and old behaviors that fascinate, infuriate, delight, or fully perplex those of us seeking answers to the question, "Why?" In this series, experts from various disciplines peer through the lens of psychology telling us answers they see for questions of human behavior. Their topics may range from humanity's psychological ills—addictions, abuse, suicide, murder, and terrorism among them—to works focused on positive subjects including intelligence, creativity, athleticism, and resilience. Regardless of the topic, the goal of this series remains constant—to offer innovative ideas, provocative considerations, and useful beginnings to better understand human behavior.

Series Editor

Chris E. Stout, Psy.D., MBA
University of Illinois, College of Medicine
Illinois Chief of Psychological Services

Advisory Board

Bruce E. Bonecutter, Ph.D.
University of Illinois at Chicago

ACKNOWLEDGMENTS

As with the first four volumes of this project, *Volume I: A Public Understanding*; *Volume II: Clinical Aspects and Responses*; *Volume III: Theoretical Understandings and Perspectives (with a special section on the Roles and Impacts of Religions)*; and *Volume IV: Programs and Practices in Response and Prevention*, we covered a wide breadth and great depth of examination of this complex topic. The set is a testament to the great contribution of a rich and diverse set of authors and perspectives. I shall always be grateful to those involved in its production.

There is also the behind the scenes involvement by proxy of one's family that also comes into play in projects of this scale. My children, Annika and Grayson, have been understanding in seeing more the back of my head while I was clacking away at my keyboard at all hours, and maintaining a never-ending willingness to navigate the maze of files and papers on the floor of my study in order to give me a hug good morning or request a bedtime story. Likewise, my partner and wife, Dr. Karen Beckstrand, has helped to triage household crises, provide useful critiques of chapter drafts, and has been my anchor through all manner of ups-and-downs.

Debora Carvalko, my editor, continues to be my best critic and mentor. This and other recent titles are truly with thanks to her—the technical as well as inspirational. And, as with the first project, this work would have been no more than an idea without the intellectual productivity and excellent work of the contributing authors herein. To you all, I am very grateful. My sincere thanks to each of you.

Chris E. Stout
Kildeer, Illinois

INTRODUCTION

Chris E. Stout

The topic of "terrorism" has sprung forth into the American public's consciousness with perhaps unparalleled robustness from the formerly obscure workings of some think tanks, governmental intelligence agencies, political science departments in universities, and plot-lines of Hollywood screenwriters. Today it is ubiquitous. As of this writing, an unscientific Google search yields 1,410,000 hits for the combined search terms "America" and "terrorism." An order of magnitude more, I suspect, than would have been yielded before September 11, 2001. Perhaps a positive side-effect is a greater American awareness of what was an already growing global problem.

Recently, prior to beginning work on this volume, the war in Iraq was commencing. As a result, I fielded a number of media contacts and provided interviews. In doing so, I was always asked what could be done in preparation here in the United States to better manage related stresses—increased anxiety resulting from heightened terrorism alerts, media blitzes of imbedded reporters' coverage, topsy-turvy markets, and what became the basis for many jokes, parodies, and now has evolved to the level of cliché—duct tape and plastic wrap for personal protection on the home front.

A bit to my surprise, I also found that there are still a number of lecture attendees, newspaper reporters, and television anchors who wonder how it is that terrorists come to be and what, if anything, can be done in response or prevention. The combination of all these ques-

tions and my desire at taking a crack at starting to answer them led
to the creation of this book. This is a distillation of about 1,200 pages
of some of the best thinking from some of the best informed about
one of the most difficult topics we are currently dealing with, as well
as new material specifically addressing ideas as to what can be done.
This is primarily a much condensed form of my four-volume work for
Praeger, *The Psychology of Terrorism*, published in 2002.

Intro __ As I have stated before, terrorism is a complex issue that does not
respond well to reductionism, so I again apologize if somehow this
book looks like it tries to simplify these complexities. I don't believe
any book or book-set can teach the reader everything he or she ever
wanted to know about terrorism in five easy pieces. Instead, my goal
with this book is to provide one book in which there is a thematic
sampling of diverse perspectives and approaches within a context of
application.

_ There simply is no single psychology of terrorism, no unified field
theory if you will. Some have suggested that "psychologies of terrorism" may be a more apt term. I wouldn't find much to argue with
such a suggestion. Like before, my goal is not to provide some ho-
mogenized or sterile rendition of information. Although there is no
unifying perspective per se in this book, I hope that this book may act
as a unified *source* of perspectives. To borrow from one of my favorite
disclaimers, the editors of *Foreign Policy* state in every issue: the content herein does "not represent any consensus of beliefs. We do not
expect that readers will sympathize with all the sentiments they find
here . . . but we hold that while keeping clear of mere vagaries (we)
can do more to inform . . . public opinion by a broad hospitality to di-
vergent ideas than it can by identifying itself with one" perspective.
And to paraphrase, although I do not accept responsibility for the
views expressed in any chapter, what I do accept is the responsibility
for giving them a chance to appear. I expect we will learn much more
about these issues as we all become more aware and wise.

As with the initial four volumes, the skills, expertise, and academic
pedigree of the contributing authors are unparalleled. Their titles include U.N. Humanitarian Affairs Officer, Assistant to the Under-
Secretary-General for Peacekeeping, and Assistant to the Special
Representative of the Secretary-General to the former Yugoslavia
and to NATO Beale Fellow (Harvard), a boursier de la Confédération
Suisse; American Psychological Association Fellow; past presidents
of Psychologists for Social Responsibility, the Society of the Study of
Peace, Conflict and Violence, and the International Society for

Political Psychology; United Nations Development Program for Women, the USAID Rwanda Rule of Law Project; and co-director of the Solomon Asch Center for the Study of Ethnopolitical Warfare. The authors are graduates or faculty from the University of Pennsylvania, Columbia University, Harvard University, Southwest Texas State University, Bryn Mawr College, the Civitan International Research Center at the University of Alabama, the Institute for Mental Health Initiatives at George Washington University, the University of Illinois College of Medicine, and the University of Massachusetts.

This book starts with a powerful work by Rick McCauley that puts modern terrorism into context, along with the psychological issues involved in understanding the perpetrators of terrorism, including the motivations and strategies. He then deals with the U.S. response to terrorism, including issues of fear and identity shift in reaction to the events of September 11. My dear friend and generally extraordinary person, Henry Breed, provides a wonderfully written perspective on how U.N. Peace Operations could be more rapid and effective as a tool against terrorism. John M. Davis instructs readers in the ways international psychology's professional societies offer a mechanism for understanding and predicting the development of international terror activities and the dilemma of managing secrecy of security and intelligence with the clandestine operations of terrorists and their organizations. International psychological associations may provide the nexus or the scholarly point of convergence between these adversarial actors.

"As the world gets smaller—with CNN, the Internet, and transportation advances—different cultural groups have more contact with each other. With this comes the opportunity for greater understanding, but also greater conflict. Our enhanced technology requires an enhanced psychology." Such is the wise perspective from Stephen D. Fabick in his chapter, which addresses not only the problems resulting from transitory power imbalances and blind tribal loyalties, but offers a pragmatic model of understanding ingroup aggrandizement and outgroup dismissal and disdain, along with an applied mechanism for creating positive change. Timothy Gallimore's work likewise provides insight for understanding and methods for intervention, but his focus is on the emotional sequelae of unresolved trauma and its causal role in subsequent violence. Ervin Staub's approach is to intervene early in the development of children with methods that are relevant in the raising of caring children who become caring, helpful, and altruistic. He considers issues of caring for others' welfare, experiential learning, and resultant understanding in the context of various obstacles that can concomitantly contribute to violence, if not terrorism. These include: poverty, injustice, repressed political systems, and culture change. The idea of learning skill sets that generalize, or "scale," beyond just adaptive responses to terrorism is a better use of resources, and may in the long run provide the additional benefits of improved general psychological functioning and emotional well-being. Such is the case with the increasingly popular area of resilience. Edith Henderson Grotberg's work is a detailed and actionable example of developing resilience. She also details the International Resilience Research Project that she pioneered in 22 countries worldwide. Her authority and wisdom is provided in the context of application and intervention.

It is with great pleasure that the reach of these authors' works may now extend even further. Knowledge of these critically important issues is everyone's responsibility today.

CHAPTER 1

Using Psychology to Counter Terrorism at the Personal and Community Level

Chris E. Stout

This chapter is meant to serve as a brief examination of differing perspectives on the causes of terrorism, a review of psychology's offerings in dealing with terrorism (including public preparation, counter-terrorism, and response), as well as a source of content and resources on what steps individuals and groups of individuals (e.g., families, communities, businesses) can take to be better prepared in this so called new "era of terrorism."

There is a fine line of knowing how much and what types of information are optimal for keeping the public up to date without causing a panic or instilling information fatigue. Perhaps psychology can offer some guidance. We know, for example, that issuing nonspecific alarms is counter-productive because such actions tend to make people more paranoid and less mindfully alert. Perhaps taking a sober approach to what individuals can do to be better prepared for the uncertainty of these times vis-à-vis the terrorist pall would be helpful. That is the goal of this chapter—to offer realistic considerations of how the complex mechanisms of terrorism may play out (but without alarmist the-sky-is-falling hyperbole), to consider approaches of preparation, and to provide a rich variety of resources, some of which are as close as the Internet or one's local library. Accurate risk-assessment combined with appropriate preparation can go a long way to mitigate fears and anxieties.

Differing Perspectives on the Causes of Terrorism

As stated, this area shall be touched upon only briefly as there are many contradictory opinions and little consensus. Nevertheless, a brief review of these differences may help in setting a context for appreciating the complexity of the issue of terrorism. (For readers interested in more detail, please review Stout's [2002] *The Psychology of Terrorism*, Vols. I–IV.)

For most, it is difficult to understand how someone can commit a terrorist act; so we are quick to consider psychopathology as the cause. Of course, the complex nature of terrorism amplifies the manifold motivations. There are frustratingly few, if any, simple answers. Scott Atran's "Genesis of Suicide Terrorism" in *Science Magazine* (2003) offers that

> Contemporary suicide terrorists from the Middle East are publicly deemed crazed cowards bent on senseless destruction who thrive in poverty and ignorance. [However,] recent research indicates they have no appreciable psychopathology and are as educated and economically well-off as surrounding populations. A first line of defense is to get the communities from which suicide attackers stem to stop the attacks by learning how to minimize the receptivity of mostly ordinary people to recruiting organizations.

Clark McCauley offers an excellent examination of this topic in chapter 2 in this volume.

Some theorists have focused on the so called "abuse of wealth" theory, which considers wealth to be the world's number one problem at the moment—stimulating more desires of greed and driving the accumulation of possessions rather than yielding increased happiness, contentment, or satisfaction. This is juxtaposed with the concern that wealthy nations are not using their riches to deal with global problems of hunger, illness, or poverty. Indeed, it is difficult for some nonradical and nonreactionary citizens of moderate income, social class, and education living in developed countries to cope with the embarrassingly garish displays by others of their wasteful consumerism. Many see materialism run amok along with the concomitant (if not co-morbid) pretentiousness that accompanies such selfish vulgarity. Although it may not be the generalizable case, it certainly appears that many people are obsessed with hedonistic (but nevertheless rationalized) motivations that border on the obscene—huge, costly, and ironically unsafe utility vehicles that will never be taken off-road that are outfitted with a myriad of gizmos and consume immense amounts of fossil fuel; passions for ever larger "McMansions" in gated communities; overly thin, bleached blonde and bronzed "trophy wives" perpetually chatting to their clones on mobile phones; the list and clichés go on and on. This level of steroidial keeping-up-with-the-Joneses gives the appearance of gargantuan self-absorption.

The risk in considering such appearances as somehow causing or justifying a terrorist attack against such countries, political structures, or economic systems smacks of a simple-minded paradigm of blaming the victim. But there may be lessons to be learned from this as well. (See later in this chapter the approaches of a more ethical distribution of wealth and Judeo-Christian mores.)

There are also concerns about unworkable or at least unenforceable international laws such as the Kyoto Protocol, Interpol, the Geneva Convention, the Declaration of Human Rights, and nonproliferation agreements. And it would seem that U.N. peacekeeping is no longer a viable option in many international flashpoints. Similarly, there is a growing concern that there is a lack of understanding among cultures, and that few attempts are being made to find common ground, especially in times of conflict. This lack of understanding and common ground could then lead to major impasses in the future, for example, between the United States and China, or between China and India. Without a framework of careful diplomacy, problems will turn into major face-downs with potentially catastrophic consequences.

Susan E. Brandon, Senior Scientist, Science Directorate at the American Psychological Association, compiled an impressive document titled, *Combating Terrorism: Some Responses from the Behavioral Sciences* (2002), to provide examples of how current psychological science can be applied to issues related to terrorism, that is—preparedness, response, recovery, and mitigation.

Brandon's prologue notes that the work is

> intended to illustrate the manner in which policy and planning regarding terrorism and counter-terrorism strategies might be informed by what is known about the limitations and capabilities of human behavior. The solution to the challenges posed by terrorism will not be found only in technological fixes. Rather, our best defenses and offenses depend on psychological variables: the psychology of decision-making, surveillance, and fear; perceptual and motivation variables in security systems, human factors considerations in human/machine interactions, and so on.

The document is sizable and not reproducible herein; interested readers are encouraged to review the document in toto on the

American Psychological Association's Web site. Some questions
raised include

> What kind of a person becomes a follower in a terrorist group? What
> kind of a person is likely to be a leader in such a group? What can be
> done to reduce the motivation of others to engage in terrorist violence
> against the United States and its allies? How do we make judgments
> about the likely causes of a particular event? How can we maintain at-
> tention and observant behavior in luggage screeners? How can we
> train people to act effectively in situations that involve high risk, with-
> out exposing them to danger during the training procedures? What
> will the public do in the instance of a large-scale attack, and how can
> we be best prepared? What can be done to help people cope with the
> ongoing threat of terrorism? What are likely to be the greatest risks
> from radiological incidents?

A sample of their findings that are of particular interest follow
(Brandon, 2002):

What kind of person becomes a follower in a terrorist group?
(p. 5)

If the movement sees itself as acting in the name of the proper authorities, and preserving or restoring the established values and conventions of a society, the followers are apt to be right-wing authoritarians.
"Right-wing" as used here means an individual who submits to those
whom he considers the established/proper authorities. Religious fun-
damentalists in many faiths are right-wing authoritarians. The Right-
Wing Authoritarianism (RWA) scale assesses how submissive,
aggressive and conventional a person is. This test has been shown to be
reliable across time and valid in cultures both inside and outside North
America. As a group, "high RWAs" tend to be very prejudiced and aggressive. Their motivations to attack come from fear of what they perceive to be a dangerous, disintegrating, and increasingly immoral
world; their fear-based impulse to attack is released by a powerful self-
righteousness. These individuals tend to be quite dogmatic in their beliefs and steadfast in their resolve, with markedly inconsistent and
compartmentalized thinking. (Altmeyer, 1996)

What kind of person is likely to be a leader in such a group?
(p. 5)

Usually they are right-wing authoritarians who also score highly not
only on the RWA but also on the "Social Dominance Orientation Scale"
(Pratto, 2001). Social dominators are highly prejudiced, power-hungry
individuals with a strong drive to dominate others and with little moral

restraint. They may be either reactionary or revolutionary; however, they gravitate to right-wing groups because members in these groups are gullible. Skilled social dominators present whatever image will bring them power, without necessarily believing in what they say they stand for. For example, they tend to agree that it is more important to look religious than to actually be such, and are likely to strongly believe in letting other people die for "the cause," and profess their own willingness to do so too, but have little intention of actually letting that happen. (Altmeyer, 1998)

Implications for counter-terrorism (p. 5)

We can understand some of the precipitating causes that make people more likely to join terrorist groups to the extent that we can assess those who are terrorists independently of their particular cultural and political contexts. For example, educational institutions that develop and maintain very strict fundamental religious beliefs or very strict Marxist-Leninist doctrine are equally likely to be places where young people can be recruited into terrorist groups. We also can increase the rate at which such individuals are identified because of how personality variables are likely to cluster together. For example, because individuals who score high on authoritarianism also are highly prejudiced in terms of attitudes about race, ethnicity, and sex, these prejudices can be a way of identifying individuals who are more vulnerable to joining terrorist groups.

What can be done to reduce the motivation of others to engage in terrorist violence against the United States and its allies? (p. 11)

From the perspective of *Terror Management Theory* (Pyszczynski, Solomon, & Greenberg, 2002), aggression, human conflict, and war are rooted, at least in part, in the threat posed by those with different beliefs and values to the psychological security and protection from anxiety that are provided by one's own beliefs and values. Although economic, military, and other concerns certainly play an important role in international conflict, this theory proposes that it is the ideological threat posed by a worldview different from one's own that rouses the passions necessary for people to risk their own lives in an attempt to destroy those who pose such psychological threats. According to this view, therefore, terrorist violence is rooted in the failure of a culture to meet the psychological and physical needs of its members, and the displacement of the fear and anger that results from this thwarting of needs onto a more powerful culture whose beliefs and values pose a threat to one's own cultural worldview.

A large number of experiments, conducted in nine different countries, have found that:

1. reminders of mortality increase the tendency to apply stereotypes and view others in simple closed-minded ways (Greenberg, Simon, Solomon, Chanel, & Pyszczynski, 1992; McGregor et al., 1998),

2. prejudice and intergroup hostility is heightened by conditions that undermine one's self-esteem and faith in one's own cultural worldview (Solomon, Greenberg, & Pyszczynski, 2001),

3. the tendency to respond negatively toward those different from oneself can be reduced and sometimes eliminated by values from one's culture that promote tolerance and respect for others, and

4. because people use their affiliation with close others and members of their culture to assuage their existential fears, such individuals are especially influential in influencing attitudes, values, and behavior tendencies.

Implications for counter-terrorism (p. 11)

Proximity to physical danger or threat, vulnerability to sickness, disease, and malnutrition, or participation in groups that encourage high-risk behaviors, all should increase peoples' commitment to their own cultural view, decrease their tolerance and acceptance of others outside their culture, and make them distance themselves from people who display emotions that they fear in themselves (such as anger or anxiety). Changes in cultural context that decrease fear of death would be expected to decrease stereotypic thinking and make an individual more open to adopting alternate worldviews.

Communication campaigns that use core cultural values to motivate individuals to oppose terrorism are more likely to be effective than those that either ignore or oppose such values. Reducing the appeal of terrorism and hostility toward the United States might be best accomplished by encouraging respected moderate local community leaders to speak out against such activity. (Pyszczynski et al., 2002)

An Examination of Risks

"Anthrax is not contagious, fear is!" This is one of my favorite quotes. It was made by Rear-Admiral. Brian W. Flynn, Ed.D., (Fmr.) Asst. Surgeon General U.S. Public Health Service, during his 2001 presentation "Terrorism and Mental Health," at the National Health Policy Forum. I think the quote truly speaks to the core of terrorism, and it offers clues to dealing in a better way with the threat of terrorism. Psychological preparedness can markedly mitigate the actual as well as emotional impact of an event or the chronic worry associated with threats of such. This is not to suggest that denial, passive acceptance, or becoming jaded or dulled is a coping strategy, indeed, quite the contrary. It is this author's belief that having a realistic knowledge of risks and responses better prepares individuals and communities. Let's examine those of current concern.

Chemical Risks?

Peter Huber (2003, p. 73) notes that there should be little concern over chemical attacks as their "acute effects are felt only when concentrations are high. Dilution and dispersal are near-perfect remedies. And long term effects are far less grave." The scenario with a chemical attack would most likely be an evacuation of a building or neighborhood rather than some grid-locked urban center. There were no evacuations in 1978 for the Love Canal or in 1982 for Times Beach. It is the resultant panic that would likely cost most lives and injuries. But if people realize the problem is contained, then the high-risk panic should not manifest.

Radiological Risks?

It is actually unlikely that much risk of harm exists for U.S. nuclear power plants to be good targets as the security and systems back-ups have been in place for a number of years, and have been further evaluated and enhanced as of late. So, a dirty bomb or a conventional explosive or incendiary device used to disperse a small amount of cesium or the like would be a more realistic threat, as individuals could obtain such material from a multitude of medical and industrial facilities within the United States. If such a device were detonated, it would likely cause the specific area to be quarantined, but the greater damage likely would be psychological—induced fear that what happened could happen again. Or, a circumstance in which no one could visit the Washington Memorial because it became a hot-zone could cast a pall on the nation's pride and ego. No one died when Three Mile Island became hot (Huber, 2003).

What are likely to be the greatest risks from radiological incidents? (Brandon, 2002, p. 45)

The greatest impact of radiation accidents has been from human reactions to the accident, rather than from exposure to radioactive substances. These have not been panic reactions as much as behaviors that occurred because of a lack of information. For example:

Three Mile Island, Pennsylvania (1979): Feed water to steam generators of a nuclear power reactor stopped, resulting in a loss of
cooling of the reactor core. Very little radioactivity was eventually
released to the environment. However, psychological effects have
been documented, resulting from inaccurate estimates of very
large radiation release levels, and the emotional political response
and media coverage, which projected fetal health outcomes.
(Agency for Toxic Substances and Disease Registry, 1999)

Chernobyl, USSR (1986): Within 30 months of an accident in a
nuclear reactor, the death toll was 30; about 15,000 people were
unable to work because of exposure-related illnesses, 12,000 children received large doses to the thyroid, and 9,000 persons were
exposed in utero. Other health-related aftereffects were radiopho-
bia, an increase in stress-related illnesses due to fear of radiation
and dislocation of people; poor diets due to stringent safeguards
against potentially contaminated food, the aborting of as many as
200,000 healthy fetuses because of fears of radiation exposure, and
increases in alcoholism. (Agency for Toxic Substances and Disease
Registry, 1999)

Implications for counter-terrorism (Brandon, 2002, p. 45)

It is predicted that the use of radioactive materials in small explosive
devices ("dirty bombs") within the U.S. probably would kill relatively
few people. The damage would be primarily from people acting in the
absence of good information and subsequent economic impact.
Current media coverage of threats from such attacks are likely to focus
on the ill-effects of an attack, while not providing any way for the
reader to learn how to gauge the effects of an attack, nor what to do
should such an attack occur. This only increases the likelihood of panic
behavior that otherwise would not occur and that could be avoided al-
together.

Biological Risks?

Debora MacKenzie, author of the article "Bioarmageddon" (1998,
p. 42), offers two differing responses to the same bio-terrorist attack:

It begins with a threat. A terrorist group declares that unless its demands are met within 48 hours, it will release anthrax over San
Francisco. Two days later, a private plane flies across the Bay, spreading an aerosol cloud that shimmers briefly in the sunlight before disap-
pearing.

Scenario one: Thousands are killed in the panic as 2 million people
flee the city. Another 1.6 million inhale anthrax spores. Antibiotics are

rushed in, but the hospitals are overwhelmed and not everyone receives treatment. Most of the country's limited stock of anthrax vaccine has already been given to soldiers. Emergency crews provide little help as there are only four germ-proof suits in the whole city. More than a million of the Bay Area's 6.5 million residents die.

Scenario two: In the two days before the attack, citizens seal their doors and windows with germ-proof tape. They listen to the radio for instructions, their gas masks, drugs, and disinfectants ready. Few panic. When sensors around the city confirm that the cloud contains anthrax spores, hospitals receive the appropriate antibiotics and vaccines. Trained emergency teams with germ-proof suits and tents set up in the places where automated weather analyses show the deadly cloud will drift. With advance preparation and rapid response only 100,000 people die.

These scenarios are predicated on the point that there is a warning provided, and that it is considered valid. It is doubtful that any terrorist would be so polite, or that the method of disbursal would be dramatic or even noticed. Thus, it becomes incumbent for us to increase our systems of surveillance. Fortunately, at the time of this writing, the Centers for Disease Control and Prevention are instituting such a national system, but the system will only monitor the manifest result of an outbreak, not an initial release. For that, diagnostic technologies run by the Defense Advanced Research Projects Agency (DARPA) are able to distinguish the first symptoms of anthrax, plague, and many other potential agents of bioterrorism, many of which resemble flu symptoms. Such is additionally important in the differential diagnosis of true positives and the hypochondriasis that could result from anxiety, panic, and hysteria of a publicly known release of an agent. MacKenzie (1998, p. 2) notes that "Eventually, DARPA would like to develop a detector that weighs no more than 2 kilograms, can identify as few as two particles of 20 different biological agents in a sample of air, costs less than $5000 and does not give false negatives. Such detectors could be deployed around cities to give early warning of airborne disease."

What if we are "over-engineering" solutions in the first place? Consider the June 2001 Dark Winter scenario of clouds of smallpox virus released in three shopping malls in December immediately infecting 1,000 people, then spooling up to a staggering 3,000,000 dead by February. Such makes for great press for alarmist Armageddon-is-just-around-the-corner (or microbe), however, smallpox is not very coetaneous in the first place and actually spreads slowly. So why was such a hysterical scenario considered in Dark Winter? In the Dark Winter model, there was an expectation that for every one person primarily infected, he or she would infect 10 more. In reality, the number is more likely to be less than one, and even if it were just *over* one, the spread would be easily containable (Begley, 2002).

Additional Risk Areas

Thomas Homer-Dixon (2002) warns of various risks resultant from our own developments. We now need to be wary of the clever exploitation of our society's new and growing complexities—materials engineering and advances in the chemistry of explosives along with miniaturization of electronics have made bombings more lethal and harder to detect, even when constructed by amateurs. Many recipes for bomb-making are still available for free via the Internet or public library. Many large building and hotel floor plans also remain accessible on the Internet.

Communications technologies allow for rapid and encrypted communications anywhere via satellite phones to the Internet, thus enabling great ease and speed in sharing information on weapons, attack plans, and tactics. Such technologies also simplify the surreptitious transfers of funds across borders through the ages-old Hawala system, which is especially common in Middle Eastern and Asian countries with clan-based networks. If satellite-phones are too expensive, there is off-the-shelf technology for "spread-spectrum" radios that randomly switch their broadcasting and receiving signals, thus making it almost impossible to intercept communications transmissions. Today's off-the-shelf laptop has computational power on par with what the entire U.S. Department of Defense had in the 1960s. Steganography encryption is easy to use and there are at least 140 tools available for downloading on the Internet. Although the Internet was initially designed for military use, and thus backed up, it is not too difficult to hack into a root server or router. One can also exploit newer peer-to-peer software (like the information transfer tool, Gnutella). One could then distribute millions of "sleeper" viruses programmed to attack specific machines or the network itself at a predetermined date and time.

There are tens of thousands of transmission lines strung across the United States and they are impossible to protect, yet easily accessible by a SUV. Transmission towers can easily be brought down with one well-placed explosive. Coordinate a few of those to detonate at the same time and watch the chaos spread—as long as your CNN or Internet connection isn't also knocked out, too.

Many large gas pipelines run near or through urban areas. They have huge explosive potential, which would cause great local damage and wide disruptions in the energy supply. Radioactive waste pools are perhaps the most lethal targets. Catastrophic results would occur if the waste was dispersed into the environment, but, thankfully, this would be hard to pull off, technologically. Benign technologies have great destructive power. Consider chemical plants. They are packed with toxins and flammables (and maybe explosives, too) and security for them is lax, according to a 1999 federal investigation by the Committee on Energy and Commerce.

Trains carry tens of thousands of tons of toxic material along transport corridors throughout the United States. A terrorist would simply need to check the schedule and place a piece of rail across the path of that train to cause a wreck, releasing the chemicals and causing a mass evacuation—all with zero risk to the terrorist. Rail and highway tunnels are also vulnerable as they offer choke points that make fire extinguishing extremely difficult, as occurred in Switzerland and Baltimore in 2001.

Remember the impact that foot-and-mouth disease had in the United Kingdom? To create the same impact in the United States, all someone would have to do is contaminate 20 to 30 large livestock farms or ranches. In a matter of weeks the cattle, sheep, and pig industries would grind to a halt, costing the economy tens of billions of dollars. We have a vast grain storage and transportation network in the United States. It is easily accessible and unprotected (think of the grain silos dotting the countryside as well as the many railcars on tracks and in yards). Someone could drop a contaminant into a few of these and watch it diffuse through the food system. Polychlorinated biphenyls (PCBs) would be an ideal toxin because it is easy to find (in the oil of old electrical transformers). PCBs are potent because they have trace amounts of dioxins, which are carcinogenic, neurotoxic, and disruptive of the human endocrine system. Children are particularly vulnerable to exposure. Millions could be exposed in a short time window. In January 1999, in Belgium, 500 tons of animal feed were accidentally contaminated by about 50 kilograms of PCBs from old transformer oil. Ten million people in Belgium, the Netherlands, Germany, and France ate the contaminated food products. It is expected that this single incident with *animal feed* may eventually cause about 8,000 cases of cancer.

Large System Complexities

The U.S. economy gains many of its efficiencies, and thus economies, from complex linkages of corporations, factories (especially with just-in-time manufacturing methods), and urban centers that are linked by highways, railways, electrical grids, and fiberoptic cables—all are increasingly complex and interconnected. Disproportionately large disruptions and economies of scale can quickly occur as a result of disrupting any nonlinear or systemic behavior or system such as electrical, telephone, or air traffic. Think chain reaction or what is known as "knock-on effects." Consider 9/11 and the World Trade Center. They were great symbolic targets. There was a huge amount of damage in a single strike. They took seven years to build and only 90 minutes to collapse. The destruction took with it thousands of lives, 10 million square feet of office space, more than $30 billion in direct costs, and millions of lives impacted, worldwide, forever. The terrorists achieved this using a kiloton of explosives, available for $280 per ticket and $3.50 for each box cutter.

As human beings we function within a nonlinear psychological network that is highly intricate and can be very unstable. A terrorist attack, or just the threat of an attack can result in a mix of emotions including grief, anger, horror, fear, anxiety, disbelief, and perhaps even hatred. Attacks and threats shake our individual and collective psychology by undermining basic feelings of safety and security. The zenith of terrorism is when it is simple and symbolic. This amplifies the emotional impact—if something is unimaginably cruel, then anything may be possible, and only our imaginations limit the potential horror that could befall us or our loved ones without a moment's notice. That is indeed the powerful psychology of terrorism.

Homer-Dixon notes that if someone can bring down what seems to be magnificent and bold statements of American capitalism like a house of cards as was done with the World Trade Center towers, then perhaps how we view ourselves as strong and robust may also be a false facade. Terrorists are good at exploiting the "multiplier effect." For example, many people did not like to fly even before 9/11, but since then terrorists have been able to exploit those fears of flying. In addition, insecure people may no longer buy costly items or go on big vacations, just in case. The result? Goods don't sell and business suffers. People then lose their jobs and, in turn, become more careful about their spending. Markets then constrict as a result and more businesses scale back. Scaling back causes more job losses. Job losses cause people to restrict spending, and so on, and so on. Thus, we do *ourselves* in. Powerful psychology.

Game theory may shed some light as well. Sharon Begley, science journal writer for the *Wall Street Journal*, reported in 2003 that "terrorists make rational decisions about the kind and timing of attacks, employing a substitution strategy. When U.S. airports installed metal detectors in 1973, for example, skyjackings fell to 16 a year from 70. But hostage-taking surged to 48 a year, up from 20, and assassinations to 36 a year from 20. Similarly, after U.S. embassies were fortified in 1976, attacks on American diplomatic targets fell to 20 a year from 28. But assassinations of diplomats and soldiers outside secured compounds rose to 53 a year from 20. Squeeze here, and terrorism bulges out there."

Planning Issues

Richard Friedman (2002, p. 4) of the National Strategy Forum notes that

> The public expectation that the government will respond effectively in a crisis is high. This confidence is well-warranted; government emergency response teams at all levels have shown their effectiveness many times over in the past. However, trauma creates personal confusion, fear, mistrust, and hostility. If government action is not rapid and effective—a strong possibility in the wake of a catastrophic terrorism incident—the public may become unwilling to follow government direction. Advance planning involving both the public and government can help reduce expectation to a reasonable level and show individuals what they can do to help themselves. Information is critical. People are vulnerable to inconsistent, conflicting messages. The public message should avoid false reassurances and provide individuals with options and alternatives that are feasible and helpful.

Addressing these issues is the focus of this section.

As part of his work with the Surge Capacity Workgroup of the Bioterrorism & Hospital Advisory Committee of the Massachusetts Department of Public Health, Steven E. Locke, M.D. (personal communication, November 19, 2002), noted that there are issues that need federal legislative or regulatory attention in the case of using hotels (or other alternatives to hospitals) for the housing and caring for the less seriously injured. Those organizations and businesses that provide housing and care must be held harmless or be provided with some type of indemnification due to potential litigation stemming from allegations related to problems such as contamination of buildings or accidents. Locke's concern is that without indemnification, there is the risk that local or federal government may need to "declare martial law and commandeer [those] buildings."

Friedman (2002, p. 3) offers an alternative approach to marshal law and legislative interventions:

A biological attack with an agent such as smallpox is lethal and persistent, with transmissible infection to the general public. The principal means available to government officials to prevent the spread of disease are the containment of infected persons and quarantine. Since the initial reaction of most people would be to flee the immediate occurrence area, it would be very difficult for the government to impose and enforce a quarantine. The American public is accustomed to a high degree of personal autonomy and civil liberties, and it is likely that many would disregard or resist quarantine orders.

He provides a creative solution of

an alternate approach to a widespread quarantine is family home treatment. Indeed, it may be more beneficial for individuals as well as the wider community that a mass exodus from affected areas be avoided. A household may be a better place for individuals than a hospital or temporary community shelter. During a bioterrorism event this could help break the disease cycle and reduce the burden on incident managers and first responders. With proper advance training and minimal supplies, individuals could monitor themselves for indications of exposure to disease and treat injuries at home. Also, anxiety decreases when there is a combination of good information coupled with familiar and stable surroundings. (Friedman, 2002, pp. 3–4)

From a national perspective, Debora MacKenzie (1998, p. 42) notes that following the identification of an agent, one approach would be vaccinating people before exposure, but such a course can be problematic due to limited availability of the vaccine, problematic distribution, and the lack of help for those already infected. In the United States, we have also learned that people do not wish to be vaccinated for smallpox when weighing the risks versus the benefits of doing so. Molecular science being what it is today also adds the problem of manufacturing a bug that has differing antigens or is a novel artificial pathogen to begin with, which would render the traditional vaccine useless.

The scientific countermeasure that DARPA is considering involves "developing vaccines quickly enough for them to be created, mass-produced, and distributed after an attack. The first step, which many researchers including those in the fast-paced field of genomics are now working on, involves speeding up DNA sequencing so that an unknown pathogen's genes could be detailed in a day. The resulting sequences could then be the basis for developing an instant DNA vaccine," MacKenzie (1998, p. 42) notes.

Public Worries, Fears, and Psychologies

Karen W. Arenson (2003) interviewed public school officials for the *New York Times.* She quoted one official, Robert K. Durkee, vice president for public affairs at Princeton, who stated that "The 9/11 experience has alerted everyone to the fact that there could be retaliation in this country (due to the war in Iraq), whether by individuals associated with Iraq or by others." A July 2002 poll by the National Association of School Resource Officers of 658 school-based police officers at U.S. public and private schools noted the levels of vulnerability they felt regarding a potential terrorist attack:

95% consider their school vulnerable;

79% said their schools were inadequately prepared;

55% said they had received no terrorism training;

83% said gaining access to their school is somewhat or very easy;

74% said their schools don't communicate adequately with parents on school safety, security, and crisis planning issues; and

27% reported receiving assistance in preparing for a terrorist attack from federal, state, or local agencies.

Moving beyond schools and colleges, the phenomena of Sudden Acute Respiratory Syndrome, or SARS, has also fueled worry. In an interview by Marie McCullough (2003), Priscilla Wald, a Duke University English professor who studies disease and popular culture, stated that

"Anxieties surrounding epidemics are always several things at once.... They are about the disease and the spread of the disease, but ... the threat of the disease is always refracted through the cultural anxieties that it taps into." That's why West Nile virus and the anthrax attacks were much more worrisome than, say, the flu, even though there are more than 30,000 flu-related deaths each year in the United States. Yet a Gallup poll taken in April 2002, shortly after SARS showed up in North America, found that 37 percent of American adults are worried about getting it. Americans are a bit less worried about SARS than they were about West Nile virus, but more than they were about anthrax, Gallup polls show. The psychology behind epidemics has always been a prod-uct—and shaper—of cultural fears. "Go back to the Bible or to Homer and you can see that plagues were seen as a divine judgment," Wald said. Bubonic plague, which decimated medieval populations, eventually shook their faith in God, which weakened the church's power. And if that wasn't terrifying enough, "black death" disrupted international trade, the labor supply, and feudal control of peasants.

McCullough (2003) continues:

Fear of epidemics often goes hand in hand with persecution and preju-dice. The Nazis capitalized on centuries-old anti-Semitism when they isolated Jews in ghettos on the pretense that these affluent, educated citizens carried diseases. Another famous victim of prejudice was Mary Mallon, or "Typhoid Mary," an Irish immigrant and domestic servant who was sexually active outside marriage in the early 1900s. Her case illustrated the struggle to balance public safety and individual liberty. When health officials quarantined her, she disputed their correct but unproven theory that she was a healthy carrier of the disease. After los-ing in court, she fled, assumed a new name, and infected another fam-ily that hired her. She was ultimately forced into relative isolation on an island in New York harbor.

What will the public do in the instance of a large-scale attack, and how can we be best prepared? (Brandon, 2002, pp. 31–32)

- The National Research Council report on "Making the nation safer," noted that although outright behavioral panic will be rare, it is likely to occur under special conditions such as clogged roads or entrap-ment in a building. (2002)

- Social science research has shown that panic, in the case of a disas-ter—which, by definition, is an event that generates casualties in excess of available resources—is rare. (Dynes & Tierney, 1994; Johnson, 1987)

- During the 1979 accident at the nuclear power plant at Three Mile Island, almost 40 percent of the population within 15 miles of the nuclear plant evacuated the area on their own, effectively and with-out evidence of panic. (Clarke, 1999)

- The evacuation of the World Trade towers when they were bombed in 1993 was orderly and calm, despite thousands of people trapped in dark columns filled with smoke, and preliminary reports of the evacuations that occurred on September 11 contain similar descrip-tions. (Glass & Schoch-Spana, 2002)

- The evacuation of cars and pedestrians from the Capitol Mall area in Washington, D.C., on September 11 was orderly and calm, despite massive traffic jams, temporary closing of the metropolitan trains, and radio reports of bombings at the Capitol and congressional buildings. (Personal observation by an evacuee, Susan Brandon)
- Perhaps the event in American history that is closest to an incident of WMD [weapons of mass destruction] or biological/chemical attack is the Spanish flu epidemic in 1918, where more than half a million Americans died. History shows us that people implemented disease control and treatment strategies within their communities. (Glass et al., 2002)
- Social science analyses have shown repeatedly that, in disaster, people act in accordance with their customary norms and roles—able-bodied assist the impaired, supervisors assume responsibility for those whom they supervise, and friends look out for friends. (Glass et al., 2002)

Too often, planning for biological/chemical, WMD, and other radiological attack has been myopic, assuming that emergency rescue and medical systems will be capable of managing such a disaster alone and that the public is incapable of playing a supportive or even vital role. Emergency planning has generalized the "yellow tape" approach—separating the public from the site of an accident by yellow tape—from localized accidents to large-scale disasters. (Glass et al., 2002)

Implications for counter-terrorism (Brandon, 2002, p. 32)

Planning for wide-scale WMD, biological/chemical or other radiological attacks should be guided by what we know about human behavior in such situations:

1. *Keep panic in check.* The general public should be viewed as a capable partner, so that civic institutions and neighborhood groups are used to assist with information dissemination, outbreak monitoring, and medical treatment and distribution.
2. *Plan for treatment of victims in the home.* By definition, hospitals, clinics, and even mobile medical care facilities will be incapable of handling all those who are in need. Emergency plans need to include how to disseminate information about outbreak, nutrition, sanitation, infection control, and how to care for the seriously ill. At present, we plan to create a stockpile of smallpox vaccination. Needed as well is an information stockpile (in diverse languages and aimed at diverse populations). (Glass et al., 2002)
3. *Engage the public in the planning.* Many issues can be best dealt with before an attack occurs. These include decisions about quarantine

(should children be isolated from parents?) and setting priorities for the use of scarce medical resources.

4. *Recognize the value of distributed response systems.* Mobile emergency-response teams and incident command centers will not be able to take advantage of what has been shown to be the most effective disaster response, which is the community of people who surround the victims. These are the people who have the greatest information on local customs, organizations, infrastructure and special needs, and who will act most effectively if they can respond to immediate problems and challenges in creative and individualized ways.

The types of terrorist attack that tend to currently cause the most public worry in the United States are:

Biological: Smallpox, anthrax, bubonic plague

Chemical: Choking, blister, nerve, blood agents

Radiological: Radiation bomb (or dirty bomb) or nondispersive device containing radioactive material

Explosive: Conventional bomb or other explosive device

Incendiary: Explosive designed to produce or spread fire

Nuclear: Atomic or hydrogen bomb or missile

Readers interested in learning more about the types, symptoms, and treatment for these should refer to Appendix A for more details.

In consideration of the long-term psychological impact of terrorism, what can be done to help people cope with the ongoing threat of terrorism? (Brandon, 2002, p. 40)

Terror Management Theory (TMT) is a psychological theory of how people cope with their awareness of the inevitability of death, and how a core fear of human mortality and vulnerability leads to a need for self-esteem, faith in a cultural worldview, and hostility toward those who hold different cultural worldviews. (Pyszczynski et al., 2002)

From the perspective of TMT, the recent terrorist attacks provided Americans with a massive reminder of death and the fragility of life, coupled with an attack on the psychological structures that normally protect us from fears of death and vulnerability. People's responses to the attacks have been highly similar to what has been found in over 150 experiments, conducted in at least 9 different countries, on the effects of reminders of death and threats to one's cultural worldview:

1. reminders of mortality lead people to respond more negatively to those who criticize one's country and to behaviorally distance themselves from such individuals; reminders of mortality also lead people

to respond more positively to those who praise one's country and to behaviorally approach such persons,

2. increased attraction to heroes and more reverence for cultural icons, such as American flags or crucifixes,
3. increased need for information and understanding,
4. increased desire for justice and punishment of moral transgressors,
5. a shift toward desires for security over desires for freedom,
6. increased desire to help, especially those who are part of one's own culture. (Greenberg, Porteus, Simon, & Pyszczynski, 1995)

Implication for counter-terrorism (Brandon, 2002, p. 40)

Death-related fear, and the various psychological defenses that this fear gives rise to, can be minimized by actions that increase valuing of one's culture and self-esteem, and that develop and maintain close personal relationships with family, loved ones, friends, and those who share one's beliefs and values.

What More . . . ?

Thomas Homer-Dixon (2002) suggests that we need to acknowledge our limitations and take steps to reduce our vulnerabilities related to economies and technologies, for example, loosening the couplings in our economic and technological networks, building in various buffers and circuit breakers that interrupt dangerous feedbacks, and dispersing high-value assets so they are less concentrated and thus less inviting. He thinks we should move to greater use of decentralized, local energy production and alternative energy sources to decrease user dependence on the energy grid. And, there should be increased autonomy of local and regional food-production networks so that if one network is damaged, the impact doesn't cascade on to other regions as well. Increased inventories of feedstocks (or parts for industry) would result in increased production costs due to inefficiency, but the extra security in having more stable and resilient production networks could far outweigh this cost.

The key to heightened public anxiety is the incessant barrage of sensational reporting and commentary offered by 24-hour TV news, yet there must be a balance of information sharing, censorship, and ethics. The Unabomber hated being pushed off the television stage by McVeigh, so he killed two more people following the Oklahoma City bombing. Kevorkian started videotaping his killings for CBS when Michigan stopped taking him to court.

The capacity for terrorists to be successful depends on their ability to understand the complex systems we depend upon so critically, so our capacity to defend ourselves depends on that same understanding. Pauchant and Mitroff (2002) offer a strategy—learning and deep change. In their model, all events, even tragic ones, teach us. Complex systems have both the creative aspect offering speed or efficiency and the potentially destructive side that allows for catastrophic outcomes. They note that all complex systems are susceptible to organizational error (such as the *Challenger* tragedy), human error (such as Bhopal, Chernobyl, or the Exxon Valdez), terrorism (e.g., Tylenol tampering in Chicago, the Oklahoma City bombing, and of course, 9/11). We need to respond to complexity by searching for the destructive side. For example, Johnson & Johnson modified both packaging and products after the tampering event. Safety can be increased by redesign— the Pentagon was and is a harder target than the World Trade Center. The relative amount of damage done to the two 9/11 targets should provide lessons for the design of future skyscrapers, dams, nuclear plants, and other large structures.

The Brookings Institution (2002) produced a white paper entitled *Protecting the American Homeland*. It offered suggestions for protecting key targets (p. 53):

Target	Suggested measure
Buildings and facilities with large numbers of people	Improve air intake system security at major nonfederal buildings: reduce accessibility, provide better filters, add reverse pressure–internal overpressure features.
	Selectively institute more security precautions at major buildings against conventional explosives (e.g., shatterproof glass).
National symbols	Accelerate GSA plan for federal building security.
Critical infrastructure	Protect key nodes of electricity grid.
	Place chemical sensors at reservoirs; protect and monitor reservoir grounds and pumps.
	Improve security of E-mail.

> Centralize management and databases of inspection, and bolster food safety inspections.
>
> Improve cybersecurity.
>
> Improve airport security.
>
> Improve Amtrak security at tunnels and elsewhere.
>
> Place chemical weapons sensors at public sites such as subway stations.
>
> Improve fire resiliency of major tunnels and security at major bridges.

The total, annual cost estimates for these and additional, general protection features is $8.8 billion.

Possible Post-Event Effects

Following an event, people are initially dazed, stunned, and in shock. The shock may last minutes, hours, days, or months before a more intense emotional response to the event is developed (Troiani, 2002).

- 12–25% will remain cool and collected during the actual impact of a disaster.
- 10–25% will develop post traumatic symptoms that will usually dissipate within six weeks of the incident. (Those who immediately develop post traumatic stress disorder [PTSD] will recover within three months of the trauma.)
- 15–25% of disaster victims will not display serious symptoms until three months after the trauma.
- 80% of victims of traumatic catastrophic events are able to successfully cope and recover from the trauma, but
- 10–30% are at risk for developing serious long-lasting psychological disorders.

PTSD Symptom Clusters

Emotional Symptoms:

> Restricted range of affect
>
> Dazed and/or disoriented

    Selective inattention

    Inability to visualize memories of the event

    Emotional withdrawal from ordinary life activities

Increased Arousal Symptoms:

    Insomnia

    Impaired concentration

    Hypervigilance

    Exaggerated startle response

Clinical Approach Controversies

It was long believed that the treatment of choice for those having suffered through a traumatic event or having PTSD was Critical Incident Stress Debriefing (CISD) or Critical Incident Stress Management (CISM). The *Washington Post* (2002) reported that CISD may do nothing to prevent psychiatric disorders and may actually even be iatrogenic and harmful. The *Post* described a Dutch study reported in *The Lancet* on debriefing in multiple situations that found little difference between those who get no counseling and those who just talk to friends and family. "Debriefing 'may even put some survivors at heightened risk for later developing mental health problems,' said experts at the National Institute of Mental Health who independently evaluated the technique after the Sept 11 attack in the U.S."

The *Post* noted that

> The debriefers were well-intentioned, but NIMH experts said the blanket intervention was inappropriate because most people who received counseling would have recovered on their own. Shock and grief were widespread after Sept 11, but those were considered normal reactions to tragedy and the experts said the "sensible" policy was "to expect normal recovery." Debriefing consists of individual or group sessions lasting one to three hours where survivors describe what they have been through and talk about their feelings, offered within hours or days of a tragedy, the technique seems superficially similar to established therapies that encourage people to relive traumatic memories and thereby gradually grow less sensitive to them. But debriefing usually offers no follow-ups and may simply cause people to become more distressed, researchers said.
>
> It's probably inappropriate to recommend blanket or universal emotional recall of events because of the likelihood of creating additional distress among people who may be coping just fine. A much better ap-

proach . . . would be to wait a few weeks to separate the majority of resilient people who are recovering on their own from those who are not
getting better. Special attention could be paid to survivors, families of
victims and first responders such as firefighters, who are at higher risk
for long-term problems. At that point, administering intensive treatments such as cognitive behavioral therapy to specific individuals has a
much better chance of reducing the risk of long-term trauma.
(*Washington Post*, 2002)

There is no universal standard following a traumatic event in order
to evaluate if someone needs clinical intervention or not. There is no
proverbial one-size-fits-all, nor should there be. Lt. Col. Elspeth
Cameron Ritchie, a psychiatrist and director of mental health policy
at the Defense Department, was quoted in the *Post* article, "What we
need to do is a good assessment rather than rushing in and offering
therapy." Such an issue is also important when considering cross-
cultural intervention or when doing work in cultures different from
one's own or in which one was trained.

Stevan Weine and his colleagues from the Task Force on
International Trauma Training (2002, p. 157) note that "Traumatic
stress and mental health knowledge were applied widely and enthu-
siastically, but the outcomes were not always beneficial, and in many
cases may have been hurtful (Maynard, 1999). The Red Cross's *World
Disasters Report 2000* sharply criticized international mental health
initiatives and issued the urgent call for standards to better structure
relief efforts (Walker & Walter, 2000)." The Task Force on
International Trauma Training responded to the need by developing
a set of guidelines (see Weine, et al., 2002).

Surgeon General Richard Carmona sparked controversy within the
psychological profession when he stated that psychologists had an
important role to play in helping to reduce the high levels of stress
many Americans were experiencing because of the war in Iraq, threat
of terrorism, and so on. Then-president of the American Psychological Association, Philip G. Zimbardo, responded to Carmona's
comments on the occasion of the California Psychological
Association's bestowing him with the Lifetime Achievement Award
in 2003. Zimbardo noted:

Surgeon General Carmona, who was an honored guest at this convention yesterday, made local TV news by indicating that psychologists
had an important role to play in helping to reduce the high levels of
stress that many Americans were experiencing, such as giving parents
advice to expose their families to less television viewing of the cover-

age of the war. . . . However, with all due respect, I must in good conscience challenge his specific advice and recommend just the opposite. There are two solutions to coping with the intense national stress created by our pre-emptive strike against the nation of Iraq: Emotion-Focused Coping and Problem-Directed Coping. Emotion-focused coping attempts to change oneself through activities that make one feel better, but do not change the stressor. That is the coping strategy proposed by the Surgeon General. If watching the seemingly endless war news on many major TV channels is distressing, and especially so for children, then surely watching less or none at all will moderate stress levels. Indeed, not watching can aid with denial that the United States is really destroying a nation, killing thousands of Iraqis, soldiers and civilians, and also putting our soldiers and those from Britain in harm's way—by enemy or "friendly" fire. Of course, not watching makes you less stressed but allows the war to continue without dissent or challenge from responsible citizens. Watching or not, the war wages on. Such coping deals with stress symptoms and not stress causes.

The second strategy for reducing stress is "problem-solving coping," which attempts to identify the true cause of the stress in terms of the nature of the stressor. War is one of the intense stressors we are dealing with as a nation. The mature, tough solution is not to look away from the cause but to deal with the stressor at its origin.

As was noted earlier in this chapter, there are a variety of positions, perceptions, and opinions. This chapter, as well as this book, seeks to offer a venue for differing voices.

Conclusion: Future Directions

It is one thing to build bomb-resistant, reverse-pressure buildings, develop higher-tech surveillance and security, or clever counter-biologicals, but it is another, more difficult thing to alter one's worldview. Some promote a more ethical distribution of wealth as a counter-terrorist, egalitarian approach, reminding us that in 1789 the French revolutionaries said: "Let's risk everything, since we have nothing." The Gospel of Luke says: "Every one to whom much has been given, of him will much be required." Indeed Judeo-Christian mores compel those to be one's brother's keeper, to practice the Golden Rule. The first epistle of John 3:17 offers: "How does God's love abide in anyone who has the world's goods and sees another in need and yet refuses to help? Let us love not in word or speech, but in truth and action."

The challenge before us all is to build a true culture of civil security. Perhaps psychology can offer some perspective if not guidance in doing this. If we all were more psychologically and practically prepared, we might have a better resilience and hardiness to what may come our way—be it terrorist-based; a natural disaster like a flood, earthquake, or tornado; or a personal trauma of a house fire or victimization. During the anthrax scare, there was widespread panic in the United States even though only 10 letters out of millions were found to have traces of the very containable pathogen. In contrast, New Zealanders are prepared to survive independently for three days in the event of major weather catastrophes. "Preventive diplomacy," now known as "preventive action" offers a model of good and benevolent governance and an emphasis on human rights within economic and social development. Writing in *Foreign Affairs*, Peter G. Peterson (2002), wisely suggests that U.S. public diplomacy is in need of a new paradigm that is part of a comprehensive policy, and reforms that include:

1. developing a coherent strategic and coordinating framework;
2. increasing customized, two-way dialogue in place of conventional, one-way, push-down communication;
3. expanding private-sector involvement;
4. improving the effectiveness of public diplomacy resources; and
5. increasing the assets devoted to public diplomacy.

Peterson concludes that "strong leadership and imaginative thinking, planning, and coordination are critical. Public diplomacy is a strategic instrument of foreign policy, and U.S. leaders must provide the sustained, coordinated, robust, and effective public diplomacy that America requires. Indeed, the war on terrorism demands it" (Peterson, 2002, p. 94).

Ronald F. Levant (personal communication, April 20, 2003), Ed.D., ABPP, Recording Secretary of the American Psychological Association and Dean, Center for Psychological Studies, Nova Southeastern University, reports that the APA, the American Psychological Foundation, and Verizon, Inc., are providing funding for the continuation of the APA Task Force on Promoting Resilience in Response to Terrorism.

The Task Force is developing information that is most likely to help citizens deal with the stress, anxiety, and fear caused by terrorism. The work product will present a range of information in the form of fact sheets designed for different groups in our society: children, adults, older adults, people of color, first responders, etc. To provide a scientific foundation for this effort, the Task Force reviewed the literature on psychological resilience, as well as the literature on terrorism in other countries (e.g., Northern Ireland, Israel) and on the response to natural disasters like hurricanes and earthquakes. However, it is clear that natural disasters are different from terrorism, because they lack the element of intentionally inflicting harm on innocent and defenseless civilians, that many find so abhorrently cruel. The literature suggests that several variables are associated with post-disaster psychological status. Pre-disaster psychological vulnerability (e.g., prior episodes of PTSD), degree of exposure to the traumatic event during and immediately after the disaster, and the occurrence of major life stressors (e.g., loss of home, unemployment) are associated with poorer post-disaster adjustment.

On the other hand, personality resources such as resilience or hardiness and social support are associated with better post-disaster psychological status. Stress inoculation programs and programs for dealing with acute and chronic stress and anxiety are likely to be of significant help in coping with threat of terrorist attack. However, different segments of our diverse society have different methods of coping and managing stress. Hence we need to keep the diverse needs of our pluralistic society uppermost in its mind as we develop this information. Recent data suggest that age and gender are associated with the development of PTSD following the September 11 attacks, with children and females more likely to develop symptoms. Also of interest, those who watched greater amounts of TV viewing of the attacks are more likely to develop symptoms. Very little is known about how specific ethnic groups respond to disasters and hence more research is needed in this area. One challenge for the future is to design and evaluate psychoeducational programs aimed at enhancing the factors of resilience (Confident Optimism, Productive and Autonomous Activity, Interpersonal Warmth and Insight, and Skilled Expressiveness) and hardiness (a sense of Control over one's life, Commitment as a result of finding meaning in one's existence, and viewing change as Challenge). (Reprinted with permission.)

While consulting at the United Nations via the Society of the Psychological Study of Social Issues, which holds nongovernmental organization (NGO) status with the United Nations, the author coauthored a position paper entitled "Mental Health: The Most Common Denominator" in which the point was made that mental health is on a par with biomedical factors in determining the quality of life, productivity, and mortality rates in all countries, developing, transitional, or industrialized (Stout, Okorududu, and Walker, 2000). These issues were addressed in the context of the 1995 World Summit for Social Development and resulted in what is known as the Copenhagen Declaration. Thus, psychology and the application of psychological principles can play a critical role in crafting policy.

The contribution that physical health plays in the complex interchange of world events also should be considered. Friend and colleague, Jordan Kassalow, from the Council on Foreign Relations, notes in an impressive white paper published in 2001 that

> The link from war to health is clear: wars kill and injure soldiers and civilians, but they also destroy infrastructure and social structures, in both cases with adverse effects on the population's general health. In the eastern Democratic Republic of Congo, for example, war and ill health are tightly entwined. Of 1.7 million excess deaths between August 1998 and May 2000, only 200,000 were attributable to acts of violence, and wherever the war worsened, infectious disease and malnutrition followed. Medical facilities are often singled out for attack in "new wars" because they provide valuable loot, easy victims, and a way to demoralize civilian populations. War also causes exceptional mobility, and armies, peacekeepers, and refugees act as vectors for the transmission of disease. (p. 11)

Perhaps less obvious is the reciprocal nature of this as well. Dr. Kassalow goes on to say,

> There is also evidence of the reverse effect, that of health on war. Combatants in new wars are often the socially excluded, even if they only act as proxies for more socially advantaged groups. Poor health shortens people's time horizons, making them more likely to engage in risky behavior; conversely, strong democracies with broad support from healthy populations are less likely to engage in conflict, at least with each other. It seems that one cannot easily separate issues of conflict, violence, poverty, or war from issues of health. What kills more people than war and violence? Illness. Plain and sadly simple. Illness. Infectious diseases alone killed 54 million people in 1998. If you examine the relationship between health and economics, "empirical evidence at the microeconomic level also demonstrates that improved health status is associated with economic growth. The most direct mechanism that explains this effect is the fact that improved health increases productivity and reduces worker absenteeism. Most notable, research sug-

gests that the effects of improved health are probably greatest for the most vulnerable—the poorest and the least educated. This can be explained by their dependence on work that requires manual labor. Conversely, poor health reduces economic productivity by creating labor shortages and heightening absenteeism, redirecting resources from education and infrastructure toward increased spending on health care, and reducing individual resources by diminishing savings and imposing higher health care costs, thus leading to isolation from the global economy where connectivity is the key to prosperity. For example, illness is the leading reason why families in China fall below the poverty line. . . . Ill health, however, leads to vicious spirals, aggravating insecurity and decreasing the return on all forms of investment in the future." (Kassalow, 2001, p. 11)

Psychology itself can work to broaden its own perspectives well beyond the limits of the parochial if not jingoistic viewpoint of Northern or Western hegemony. Marsella (1998) calls for a "global community psychology model" with a meta-psychology that would concern itself with:

1. recognition of the global dimensions and scale of our lives,
2. limiting the ethnocentric bias in many existing theories, methods and interventions,
3. encouraging the development of indigenous psychologies,
4. emphasizing the cultural determinates of behavior,
5. using systems, contextual and nonlinear conceptualizations of human behavior, and
6. increasing the use of qualitative, naturalistic, and contextual research methods.

Flynn (2001) noted that the major challenges for psychology and the behavioral sciences to address hinge on the fact that there has been no model or structure for truly dealing with a national disaster. Contributing and compounding this problem is that there is a scarcity of good research on risk and protective factors as well as good intervention research. In addition, training issues need to incorporate such considerations—both in traditional training programs as well as workshops for professionals already in the field. We need to expand the models of assistance for those with preexisting severe mental illnesses while also addressing the needs of other vulnerable populations such as children and first responders. Finally, we need to incorporate seamless mechanisms for tracking behavioral health impacts and outcomes of programs, and to be able to then incorporate the feedback gained and revise as need be on an on-going basis in order to develop empirically derived methods of care and preparedness.

Psychology has much to offer, but it also has much to discover.

References

Agency for Toxic Substances and Disease Registry. (1999). *Toxicological profile for ionizing radiation*. Washington, DC: U.S. Department of Health and Human Services.

Altmeyer, B. (1996). *The authoritarian specter*. Cambridge, MA: Harvard University Press.

Altmeyer, B. (1998). The other "authoritarian personality." In M. Zanna (Ed.), *Advances in Experimental Social Psychology, Vol. 30*. New York: Academic Press.

Arenson, K. W. (2003, February 26). As possible targets, universities take precautions. *New York Times*.

Atran, S. (2003, March 7). Genesis of suicide terrorism. *Science, 299(5612)*, 1534–1539.

Begley, S. (2002, November 8). New bioterror models show limited threat from small pox attack. *Wall Street Journal*, p. B1.

Begley, S. (2003, May 16). A beautiful science: Getting the math right can thwart terrorism. *Wall Street Journal*, p. B1.

Brandon, S. E. (2002, September 6) *Combating terrorism: Some responses from the behavioral sciences*. Science Directorate, American Psychological Association, www.apa.org/ppo/issues/terrorhome.html.

Brookings Institution (2002). *Protecting the American homeland*. Washington, DC: The Brookings Institution.

Clarke, L. (1999). *Mission improbably: Using fantasy documents to tame disaster*. Chicago: University of Chicago Press.

Dynes, R., and Tierney, K. (1994). *Disasters, collective behavior and social organization*. Newark: University of Delaware Press.

Flynn, B. W. (2001, October 23). *Terrorism and mental health*. Washington, DC: National Health Policy Forum.

Friedman, R. (2002). *Prudent preparation*. Washington, DC: National Strategy Forum, www.nationalstrategy.com.

Glass, T., & Schoch-Spana, M. (2002). Bioterrorism and the people: How to vaccinate a city against panic. *Confronting Biological Weapons, CID, 34*, 217–223.

Greenberg, J., Porteus, J., Simon, L., & Pyszczynski, T. (1995). Evidence of a terror management function of cultural icons: The effects of mortality salience on the inappropriate use of cherished cultural symbols. *Personality & Social Psychology Bulletin, 21(11)*, 1221–1228.

Greenberg, J., Simon, L., Solomon, S., Chanel, D., & Pyszczynski, T. (1992). Terror management and tolerance: Does mortality salience always intensify negative reactions to others who threaten the worldview? *Journal of Personality and Social Psychology, 63*, 212–220.

Homer-Dixon, T. (2002, January/February). The rise of complex terrorism. *Foreign Policy,* 52–62.

Huber, P. (2003, March 31). Panic and terrorism. *Forbes,* 73.

Johnson, N. (1987). *Response to disaster: Fact versus fiction and its perpetuation.* Lanham, MD: University Press of America.

Kassalow, J. (2001). *Why health is important to US foreign policy.* Council on Foreign Relations, http://www.cfr.org/publication.php?id=3946#.

Levant, R. F. (2003, April 20). Personal communication.

Locke, S. E. (2002, November 19). Personal communication.

MacKenzie, D. (1998, September 9). Bioarmageddon. *New Scientist, 159(2152),* 42–46.

Marsella, A. J. (1998). Toward a "global community psychology": Meeting the needs of a changing world. *American Psychologist, 53,* 1282–1291.

Maynard, K. (1999). *Healing communities in conflict.* New York: Columbia University Press.

McCullough, M. (2003, April 20). *Fear of SARS taps into other worries.* Knight Ridder Newspapers.

McGregor, H., Leiberman, J., Greenberg, J., Solomon, S., Arndt, J., Pyszczynski, T., & Simon, L. (1998). Terror management and aggression: Evidence that mortality salience promotes aggression against worldview threatening individuals. *Journal of Personality and Social Psychology, 74,* 591–605.

National Research Council. (2002). *Making the nation safer: The role of science and technology in countering terrorism.* Washington, DC: National Academy Press, prepublication copy.

Pauchant, T. C. & Mitroff, I. I. (2002). Learning to cope with complexity. *The Futurist,* 68–69.

Peterson, P. G. (2002). Public diplomacy and the war on terrorism. *Foreign Affairs, (81)* 5, 74–94.

Pratto, F., Sidanius, J., Stallworth, L., & Malle, B. F. (2001). Social dominance orientation: A personality variable predicting social and political attitudes. In Hogg, M. A. & Abrams, D. (Eds.), *Intergroup relations: Essential readings. Key readings in social psychology* (pp. 30–59). Philadelphia: Psychology Press/Taylor & Francis.

Pyszczynski, T., Solomon, S., & Greenberg, J. (2002). *In the wake of 911: The psychology of terror in the 21st Century.* Washington, DC: American Psychological Association.

Solomon, S., Greenberg, J., & Pyszczynski, T. (2000). Pride and prejudice: Fear of death and social behavior. *Current Directions in Psychological Science, 6,* 200–204.

Stout, C. E. (Ed.) (2002). *The Psychology of Terrorism,* Vols. I–IV. Westport, CT: Praeger.

Stout, C. E., Okorududu, C., and Walker, P. (April, 2000). A mental health approach to enhancing the implementation of the Copenhagen program for action (sponsored and approved by APA Division 9), for the *Second Preparatory Session of the General Assembly on the Implementation of the Outcome of the World Summit for Social Development*, position paper. New York: United Nations.

Troiani, J. (2002). *The management of the psychological consequences of terrorism.* Camp San Luis Obispo, CA: National Interagency Civil-Military Institute.

Walker, P., and Walter, J. (2000). *World disasters report: Focus on public health.* Geneva: International Red Cross and Red Crescent Societies.

Washington Post. (2002, 6 September). *Two studies raise doubts on trauma counseling's value*, washingtonpost.com.

Weine, S., et al. (2002). Guidelines for international training in mental health and psychological interventions for trauma exposed populations in clinical and community settings. *Psychiatry, 65(2)*, 156–164.

Zimbardo, P. G. (2003, April). Lifetime Achievement Award speech. California Psychological Association Annual Meeting, San Jose, CA.

CHAPTER 2

PSYCHOLOGICAL ISSUES IN UNDERSTANDING TERRORISM AND THE RESPONSE TO TERRORISM

Clark McCauley

This chapter begins with a brief effort to put modern terrorism in context. Thereafter, the chapter is divided into two main sections. The first section deals with psychological issues involved in understanding the perpetrators of terrorism, including their motivations and strategies. The second section deals with the U.S. response to terrorism, including issues of fear and identity shift in reaction to the events of September 11, 2001. I cannot offer a full review of the literature related to even one of these issues, and for some issues there is so little relevant literature that I can only point in the general directions that research might take. In using a very broad brush, I need to apologize in advance to scholars whose knowledge and contributions are not adequately represented here. A little theory can be a dangerous thing, especially in the hands of a nonspecialist in the relevant area of theory. But the events of September 11 warrant some additional risk-taking in connecting psychological research to understanding of the origins and effects of terrorism.

Terrorism as a Category of Violence

Violence and the threat of violence to control people is an idea older than history, but the use of the word *terror* to refer to political violence goes back only to the French Revolution of the 1790s. The revolutionaries, threatened by resistance within France and foreign armies at its borders, undertook a Reign of Terror to suppress the enemy within. This first violence to be called terrorism had the power of the state behind it. Terrorism today is usually associated with political violence perpetrated by groups without the power of the state. Few of these nonstate groups have referred to themselves as terrorists, although prominent exceptions include the Russian Narodnaya Volya in the late 1800s and the Zionist Stern Gang of the late 1940s. Most nonstate terrorists see themselves as revolutionaries or freedom fighters.

State terrorism was not only first, it continues to be more dangerous. Rummel (1996) estimates 170 million people were killed by government in the twentieth century, not including 34 million dead in battle. Most of the victims were killed by their own government, or, more precisely, by the government controlling the area in which the victims were living. Stalin, Mao, and Hitler were the biggest killers (42 million, 37 million, 20 million killed, respectively), with Pol Pot's killing of 2 million Cambodians coming in only seventh in the pantheon of killers. By comparison, killing by nonstate groups is minuscule. Rummel estimates 500,000 killed in the twentieth century by terrorists, guerrillas, and other nonstate groups. State terrorism is thus greater by a ratio of about 260 to 1. Worldwide, Myers (2001) counts 2,527 deaths from terrorism in all of the 1990s. Three thousand terrorist victims on September 11 is thus a big increment in the killing done by terrorists, but does not change the scale of the comparison: State terrorism is by far the greater danger.

Despite the origin of the term *terrorism* in reference to state terror, and despite the pre-eminence of state terror in relation to nonstate terror, terrorism today is usually understood to mean nonstate terrorism. Nonstate terrorism includes both anti-state terror and vigilante terror, but it is usually anti-state terrorism that is the focus of attention—violence against recognized states by small groups without the power of a state. Most definitions of anti-state terrorism also include the idea of violence against noncombatants, especially women and children, although the suicide bombing of the U.S. Marine barracks in Beirut in 1984 is often referred to as terrorism, as is the September 11 attack on the Pentagon.

Anti-state terrorism cannot be understood outside the context of state terrorism. Compared with the nineteenth century, the twentieth century saw massive increases in state power. The modern state reaches deeper into the lives of citizens than ever before. It collects more in taxes, and its regulations, rewards, and punishments push further into work, school, and neighborhood. The state culture is thus ever harder to resist; any culture group that does not control a state is likely to feel in danger of extinction. But resistance to state culture faces state power that continues to grow. It is in the context of growing state power that anti-state terrorists can feel increasingly desperate.

Much has been written about how to define anti-state terrorism, but I generally agree with those who say the difference between a terrorist and a freedom fighter is mostly in the politics of the beholder (see McCauley, 1991, and McCauley, 2003, for more on this issue). The psychological question is how members of a small group without the power of a state become capable of political violence that includes violence against noncombatants. In the remainder of this chapter, I follow common usage in referring to anti-state terrorism simply as "terrorism."

Terrorist Motivations

Individuals become terrorists in many different ways and for many different reasons. Here I will simplify to consider three kinds of explanation of the September 11 attacks: they are crazy, they are crazed by hatred and anger, or they are rational within their own perspective. My argument is that terrorism is not to be understood as pathology, and that terrorists emerge out of a normal psychology of emotional commitment to cause and comrades.

Terrorism as Individual Pathology

A common suggestion is that there must be something wrong with terrorists. Terrorists must be crazy, or suicidal, or psychopaths without moral feelings. Only someone with something wrong with him could do the cold-blooded killing that a terrorist does.

The Search for Pathology

Thirty years ago, this suggestion was taken very seriously, but 30 years of research has found little evidence that terrorists are suffering from psychopathology. This research has profited by what now amounts to hundreds of interviews with terrorists. Some terrorists are captured and interviewed in prison. Some active terrorists can be found in their home neighborhoods, if the interviewer knows where to look. And some retired terrorists are willing to talk about their earlier activities, particularly if these activities were successful.

Itzhak Shamir and Menachem Begin, for instance, moved from anti-Arab and anti-British terrorism to leadership of the state of Israel. Interviews with terrorists rarely find any disorder listed in the American Psychiatric Association's *Diagnostic and Statistical Manual of Mental Disorders.*

More systematic research confirms the interview results. Particularly thorough were the German studies of the Baader-Meinhof Gang. Although the terrorists had gone underground and their locations were unknown, their identities were known. Excellent German records provided a great deal of information about each individual. Prenatal records, perinatal records, pediatric records, preschool records, lower-school records, grade school records, high school records, university records (most had had some university education)—all of these were combed for clues to understanding these individuals. Family, neighbors, schoolmates—all those who had known an individual before the leap to terrorism—were interviewed. A comparison sample of individuals from the same neighborhoods, matched for gender, age, and socioeconomic status, was similarly studied. The results of these investigations take several feet of shelf space, but are easy to summarize. The terrorists did not differ from the comparison group of nonterrorists in any substantial way; in particular, the terrorists did not show higher rates of any kind of psychopathology.

Terrorists as Psychopaths

Some have suggested that terrorists are antisocial personalities or psychopaths. Psychopaths can be intelligent and very much in contact with reality; their problem is that they are socially and morally deficient. They are law-breakers, deceitful, aggressive, and reckless in disregarding the safety of self and others. They do not feel remorse for hurting others. As some individuals cannot see color, psychopaths cannot feel empathy or affection for others.

Explaining terrorism as the work of psychopaths brings a new difficulty, however. The September 11 attackers were willing to give their lives in the attack. So far as I am aware, no one has ever suggested that a psychopath's moral blindness can take the form of self-sacrifice. In addition, psychopaths are notably impulsive and irresponsible. The mutual commitment and trust evident within each of the four groups of attackers, and in the cooperation between groups, are radically inconsistent with the psychopathic personality.

It is possible that a terrorist group might recruit a psychopath for a particular mission, if the mission requires inflicting pain or death without the distraction of sympathy for the victims, but the mission would have to be a one-person job, something that requires little or no coordination and trust. And the mission would have to offer a reasonable chance of success without suicide.

The Case Against Pathology

Of course there are occasional lone bombers or lone gunmen who kill for political causes, and such individuals may indeed suffer from some form of psychopathology. A loner like Theodore Kaczynski, the "Unabomber," sending out letter bombs in occasional forays from his wilderness cabin, may suffer from psychopathology. But terrorists operating in groups, especially groups that can organize attacks that are successful, are very unlikely to suffer from serious psychopathology.

Indeed, terrorism would be a trivial problem if only those with some kind of psychopathology could be terrorists. Rather, we have to face the fact that normal people can be terrorists, that we are ourselves capable of terrorist acts under some circumstances. This fact is already implied in recognizing that military and police forces involved in state terrorism are all too capable of killing noncombatants. Few would suggest that the broad range of soldiers and policemen involved in such killing must all be suffering some kind of psychopathology.

Terrorism as Emotional Expression

When asked at a press conference on October 11, 2001, why people in the Muslim world hate the United States, President Bush expressed amazement and replied, "That's because they don't know us."

President Bush is not the only one to accept the idea that the September 11 attacks were an expression of hatred. "Why do they hate us?" has been the headline of numerous stories and editorials in newspapers and magazines. Despite the headlines, there has been little analysis of what hatred means or where it may come from.

Hatred and Anger

The surprising fact is that, although a few psychoanalysts have discussed hatred, there is very little psychological research focused on hate or hatred. Gordon Allport (1954) offered brief mention of hatred in writing about *The Nature of Prejudice*, and more recently Marilyn Brewer (2001) has asked "When does ingroup love become outgroup hate?" But empirical research on hatred, particularly research that distinguishes hatred from anger, is notably absent. In contrast, there is a large and well-developed research literature on the emotion of anger. Does hatred mean anything more than strong anger? An example suggests that hatred may be different. A parent can be angry with a misbehaving child, angry to the point of striking the child. But even caught up in that violence, the parent would not hate the child.

A few differences between anger and hatred show up in the way these words are used in everyday speech. Anger is hot, hatred can be cold. Anger is a response to a particular incident or offense; hatred expresses a longer-term relation of antipathy. We sometimes talk about hatred when we mean only strong dislike, as in "I hate broccoli," but even in this usage there is the sense of a long-term unwavering dislike, a dislike without exceptions, and perhaps even the wish that broccoli should be wiped from every menu.

In *The Deadly Ethnic Riot*, Donald Horowitz offers a distinction between anger and hatred that is consistent with the language just considered. Horowitz (2001, p. 543) quotes Aristotle as follows: "The angry man wants the object of his anger to suffer in return; hatred wishes its object not to exist." This distinction begs for a parallel distinction in offenders or offenses, a distinction that can predict when an offense leads to anger and when to hatred. One possibility (see also Brewer, 2001) is that an offense that includes long-term threat is more likely to elicit the desire to eliminate the offender. The emotional reaction to threat is fear. Thus hatred may be a compound of anger and fear, such that anger alone aims to punish whereas hatred aims to obliterate the threat. If hatred is related to anger, then research on anger may be able to help us understand the behavior of terrorists.

The Psychology of Anger

Explanation of terrorism as the work of people blinded by anger is at least generally consistent with what is known about the emotion of anger. In particular, there is reason to believe that anger does get in the way of judgment. In *Passions Within Reason*, Robert Frank (1988) argues that blindness to self-interest is the evolutionary key to anger. If each individual acted rationally on self-interest, the strong could do anything they wanted to the weak. Both would realize that the weaker cannot win and the weaker would always defer to the stronger. But anger can lead the weaker to attack the stronger despite the objective balance of forces. The stronger will win, but he will suffer some costs along the way and the possibility of these costs restrains the demands of the stronger.

This perspective suggests an evolutionary advantage for individuals for whom anger can conquer fear. The result should be a gradual increase in the proportion of individuals who are capable of anger. Everyday experience suggests that most people are capable of anger under the right circumstances. What are those circumstances—that is, what are the elicitors of anger?

There are basically two theories of anger (Sabini, 1995, pp. 411–428). The first, which comes to us from Aristotle, says that anger is the emotional reaction to insult—an offense in which the respect or status due to an individual is violated. The second, which emerged from experimental research with animals, says that anger is the emotional reaction to pain, especially the pain of frustration. Frustration is understood as the failure to receive an expected reward. These theories obviously have a great deal in common. Respect expected but not forthcoming is a painful frustration. For our purposes, the two theories differ chiefly in their emphasis on material welfare. Insult is subjective, asocial, whereas at least some interpretations of frustration include objective poverty and powerlessness as frustrations that can lead to anger. This interpretation of frustration–aggression theory was popular at the 2002 World Economic Forum, at which many luminaries cited material deprivation as the cause or at least an important cause of violence aimed at the West (Friedman, 2002a).

Individual Frustration and Insult

The immediate difficulty of seeing the September 11 terrorists as crazed with anger is the fact, much cited by journalists and pundits, that the September 11 terrorists were not obviously suffering from frustration or insult. Mohammed Atta came from a middle-class family in Egypt, studied architecture in Cairo, traveled to Hamburg, Germany, for further studies in architecture, and had a part-time job doing architectural drawings for a German firm. His German thesis, on the ancient architecture of Aleppo, was well received. According to Thomas Friedman's (2002b) inquiries, several others of the September 11 pilot-leaders came from similar middle-class backgrounds, with similar threads of personal success.

The origins of the September 11 terrorist-leaders are thus strikingly different from the origins of the Palestinian suicide terrorists that Ariel Merari has been studying for decades in Israel (Lelyveld, 2001). The Palestinian terrorists are young, male, poor, and uneducated. Their motivations are manifold but notably include the several thousand dollars awarded to the family of a Palestinian martyr. The amount is small by Western standards but enough to lift a Palestinian family out of abject poverty, including support for parents and aged relatives and a dowry for the martyr's sisters. It is easy to characterize these suicide terrorists as frustrated by poverty and hopelessness, with frustration leading to anger against Israel as the perceived source of their problems.

But this explanation does not fit at least the leaders of the September 11 terrorists. Whence their anger, if anger is the explanation of their attacks? Perhaps they are angry, not about their own personal experience of frustration and insult, but about the frustrations and insults experienced by their group.

Group Frustration and Insult

In the *Handbook of Social Psychology*, Kinder (1998) summarizes the accumulated evidence that political opinions are only weakly predicted by narrow self-interest and more strongly predicted by group interest. The poor do not support welfare policies more than others, young males are not less in favor of war than others, parents of school-age children are not more opposed than others to busing for desegregation. Rather it is group interest that is the useful predictor. Sympathy for the poor predicts favoring increased welfare. Sympathy for African Americans predicts support for busing and other desegregation policies. Unless individual self-interest is exceptionally large and clear cut, voters' opinions are not self-centered but group-centered.

Similarly, Kinder recounts evidence that political action, including protest and confrontation, is motivated more by identification with group interest than by self-interest.

Thus participation of black college students in the civil rights movement in the American South in the 1960s was predicted better by their anger over society's treatment of black Americans in general than by any discontent they felt about their own lives. . . . Thus white working-class participants in the Boston antibusing movement were motivated especially by their resentments about the gains of blacks and professionals, and less by their own personal troubles (Kinder, 1998, p. 831).

Group identification makes sense of sacrifice from individuals who are not personally frustrated or insulted. The mistake is to imagine that self-sacrifice must come from personal problems, rather than identification with group problems. This mistake rests in ignorance of the fact that many post–World War II terrorists have been individuals of middle-class origins, people with options. The Baader-Meinhof Gang in Germany, the Red Brigade in Italy, the Weather Underground in the United States—these and many other post–WWII terrorist groups are made up mostly of individuals with middle-class origins and middle-class skills honed by at least some university education (McCauley & Segal, 1987). Explaining self-sacrifice as a result of personal problems is no more persuasive for terrorists than for Mother Teresa or U.S. Medal of Honor winners.

The power of group identification is thus the foundation of intergroup conflict, especially for large groups where individual self-interest is probably maximized by free-riding, that is, by letting other group members pay the costs of advancing group welfare that the individual will profit from. Here I am asserting briefly what I elsewhere argue for in more detail (McCauley, 2001).

The explanation of terrorist sacrifice as a fit of anger overcoming self-interest can now be reformulated in terms of anger over group insult and group frustration. The potential origins of such anger are not difficult to discern.

Insult and Frustration as Seen by Muslims (and Others)

From Morocco to Pakistan lies a belt of Muslim states in which governments have police and military power but little public support. The gulf between rich and poor is deep and wide in these countries, and government is associated with Western-leaning elites for whom government, not private enterprise, is the source of wealth. Political threat to the state is not tolerated; imprisonment, torture, and death are the tools of the state against political opposition. As the Catholic Church in Poland under communism came to be the principal refuge of political opposition, so fundamentalist Muslim mosques are the principal refuge of political opposition to government in these states.

In this conflict between Muslim governments and Muslim peoples, the United States and other Western countries have supported the governments. When the Algerian government was about to lose an election to the Islamic Salvation Front in 1992, the government annulled the election and Europeans and Americans were glad to accept the lesser of two evils. Western countries have supported authoritarian governments of Egypt, Jordan, and Pakistan with credits and military assistance. U.S. support for Israel against the Palestinians is only one part of this pattern of supporting power against people.

Al-Qaeda is an association of exiles and refugees from the political violence going on in Muslim countries. Long before declaring *jihad* against the United States, Osama bin Laden was attacking the house of Saud for letting U.S. troops remain in the holy land of Mecca and Medina after the Gulf War. Fifteen of the September 11 terrorists came originally from Saudi Arabia, although most seem to have been recruited from the Muslim diaspora in Europe. The United States has become a target because it is seen as supporting the governments that created the diaspora. The United States is in the position of someone who has stumbled into a family feud. If this scenario seems strained, consider the parallel between Muslims declaring *jihad* on the United States for supporting state terrorism in Muslim countries, and the United States declaring war on any country that supports terrorism against the United States.

It is important to recognize that it is not only Arab and Muslim countries in which U.S. policies are seen as responsible for terrorist attacks against the United States In an IHT/Pew poll of 275 "opinion-makers" in 24 countries, respondents were asked how many ordinary people think that U.S. policies and actions in the world were a major cause of the September 11 attack (Knowlton, 2001). In the United States, only 18 percent of respondents said many people think this; in 23 other countries, an average of 58 percent said most or many people think this. In Islamic countries, 76 percent said most or many think this, and even in Western European countries, 36 percent said most or many think this. Americans do not have to accept the judgments of other countries, but they will have to deal with them.

Anger or Love?

If group identification can lead to anger for frustrations and insults suffered by the group, it yet remains to be determined if there is any evidence of such emotions in the September 11 terrorists. Our best guide to the motives of those who carried out the attacks of September 11 is the document found in the luggage of several of the attackers. Four of the five pages of this document have been released by the FBI and these pages have been translated and interpreted by Makiya and Mneimneh (2002). I am indebted to Hassan Mneimneh for his assistance in understanding this document.

The four pages are surprising for what they do not contain. There is no list of group frustrations and insults, no litany of injustice to justify violence. "The sense throughout is that the would-be martyr is engaged in his action solely to please God. There is no mention of any communal purpose behind his behavior. In all of the four pages available to us there is not a word or an implication about any wrongs that are to be redressed through martyrdom, whether in Palestine or Iraq or in 'the land of Muhammad,' the phrase bin Laden used in the al-Jazeera video that was shown after September 11" (Makiya et al., 2002, p. 21). Indeed, the text cites approvingly a story from the Koran about Ali ibn Talib, cousin and son-in-law of the Prophet, who is spat upon by an infidel in combat. The Muslim holds his sword until he can master the impulse for vengeance—an individual and human motive—and strikes only when he can strike for the sake of God.

Rather than anger or hatred, the dominant message of the text is a focus on the eternal. There are many references to the Koran, and the vocabulary departs from seventh-century Arabic only for a few references to modern concepts such as airport and plane (and these modern words are reduced to one-letter abbreviations). To feel connection with God and the work of God, to feel the peace of submission to God's will—these are the imperatives and the promises of the text. Invocations and prayers are to be offered at every stage of the journey: the last night, the journey to the airport, boarding the plane, takeoff, taking the plane, welcoming death. The reader is reminded that fear is an act of worship due only to God. If killing is necessary, the language of the text makes the killing a ritual slaughter with vocabulary that refers to animal sacrifice, including the sacrifice of Isaac that Abraham was prepared to offer.

Judging from this text, the psychology of the September 11 terrorists is not a psychology of anger, or hatred, or vengeance. The terrorists are not righting human wrongs but acting with God and for God against evil. In most general terms, it is a psychology of attachment to the good rather than a psychology of hatred for evil. Research with U.S. soldiers in World War II found something similar; hatred of the enemy was a minor motive in combat performance, whereas attachment to buddies and not wanting to let them down was a major motive (Stouffer et al., 1949). This resonance with the psychology of combat—a psychology usually treated as normal psychology—again suggests the possibility that terrorism and terrorists may be more normal than is usually recognized.

Terrorism as Normal Psychology

The trajectory by which normal people become capable of doing terrible things is usually gradual, perhaps imperceptible to the individual. This is among other things a moral trajectory, such as Sprinzak (1991) and Horowitz (2001) have described. In too-simple terms, terrorists kill for the same reasons that groups have killed other groups for centuries. They kill for cause and comrades, that is, with a combination of ideology and intense small-group dynamics. The cause that is worth killing for and dying for is not abstract but personal—a view of the world that makes sense of life and death and links the individual to some form of immortality.

The Psychology of Cause

Every normal person believes in something more important than life. We have to, because, unlike other animals, we know that we are going to die. We need something that makes sense of our life and our death, something that makes our death different from the death of a squirrel lying by the side of the road as we drive to work. The closer and more immediate death is, the more we need the group values that give meaning to life and death. These include the values of family, religion, ethnicity, and nationality—the values of our culture. Dozens of experiments have shown that thinking about death, their own death, leads people to embrace more strongly the values of their culture (Pyszczynski, Greenberg, & Solomon, 1997).

These values do not have to be explicitly religious. Many of the terrorist groups since World War II have been radical-socialist groups with purely secular roots: the Red Brigade in Italy, the Baader-Meinhof Gang in Germany, the Shining Path in Peru. Animal rights and saving the environment can be causes that justify terrorism. For much of the twentieth century, atheistic communism was such a cause. Thus there is no special relation between religion and violence; religion is only one kind of cause in which individuals can find an answer to mortality.

What is essential is that the cause should have the promise of a long and glorious future. History is important in supporting this promise. A cause invented yesterday cannot easily be seen to have a glorious and indefinite future. The history must be a group history. No one ever seems to have had the idea that she or he alone will achieve some kind of immortality. Immortality comes as part of a group: family group, cultural group, religious group, or ideological group. A good participant in the group, one who lives up to the norms of the group and contributes to the group, will to that extent live on after death as part of the group. The meaning of the individual's life is the future of the cause, embodied in the group that goes on into the future after the individual is dead.

The Psychology of Comrades

The group's values are focused to a personal intensity in the small group of like-minded people who perpetrate terrorist violence. Most individuals belong to many groups—family, co-workers, neighborhood, religion, country—and each of these groups has some influence on individual beliefs and behavior. Different groups have different values, and the competition of values reduces the power of any one group over its members. But members of an underground terrorist group have put this group first in their lives, dropping or reducing every other connection. The power of this one group is now enormous, and extends to every kind of personal and moral judgment. This is the power that can make violence against the enemy not just acceptable but necessary.

Every army aims to do what the terrorist group does: to link a larger group cause with the small-group dynamics that can deliver individuals to sacrifice. Every army cuts trainees off from their previous lives so that the combat unit can become their family; their fellow-soldiers become their brothers and their fear of letting down their comrades becomes greater than their fear of dying. The power of an isolating group over its members is not limited to justifying violence. Many nonviolent groups also gain power by separating individuals from groups that might offer competing values. Groups using this tactic include religious cults, drug treatment centers, and residential schools and colleges. In brief, the psychology behind terrorist violence is normal psychology, abnormal only in the intensity of the group dynamics that link cause with comrades.

Some commentators have noted that the September 11 terrorists, at least the pilot-leaders, spent long periods of time dispersed in the United States. How could the intense group dynamics that are typical of underground groups be maintained in dispersal? There are two possible answers. The first is that physical dispersal is not the same as developing new group connections. It seems that the dispersed terrorists lived without close connections to others outside the terrorist group. They did not take interesting jobs, become close to co-workers, or develop romantic relationships. Although living apart, they remained connected to and anchored in only one group, their terrorist group.

The second possibility is that group dynamics can be less important to the extent that the cause—the ideology of the cause—is more important. As noted earlier, the pilot-leaders of the September 11 terrorists were not poor or untalented; they were men with a middle-class background and education. For educated men, the power of ideas may substitute to some degree for the everyday reinforcement of a like-minded group. Indeed, the terrorist document referred to above is a kind of manual for using control of attention to control behavior, and this kind of manual should work better for individuals familiar with the attractions of ideas. Probably both possibilities—a social world reduced to one group despite physical dispersal, and a group of individuals for whom the ideology of cause is unusually important and powerful—contributed to the cohesion of the September 11 perpetrators.

The Psychology of Cult Recruiting

Studies of recruiting for the Unification Church provide some insight into individual differences in vulnerability to the call of cause and comrades (McCauley et al., 1987). Galanter (1980) surveyed participants in Unification Church recruiting workshops in southern California, and found that the best predictor of who becomes a member was the answer to a question about how close the individual feels to people outside the Unification Church. Those with outside attachments were more likely to leave, whereas those without outside connections are more likely to join. This is the power of comrades. Barker (1984) surveyed participants in Unification Church recruiting workshops in London, and found that the best predictor of who becomes a member was the answer to a question about goals. Those who said "something but I don't know what" were more likely to join. This is the power of cause, a group cause that can give meaning to an individual's life. Terrorist groups, like cult groups, cut the individual off from other contacts and are particularly attractive to individuals without close connections and the meaning that comes with group anchoring. Only those who have never had the experience of feeling cut off from family, friends, and work will want to see this kind of vulnerability as a kind of pathology. The rest of us will feel fortunate that we did not at this point in our lives encounter someone recruiting for a cult or terrorist group.

The Psychology of Crisis

The psychology of cause and comrades is multiplied by a sense of crisis. Many observers have noted an apocalyptic quality in the worldview of terrorists. Terrorists see the world precariously balanced between good and evil, at a point where action can bring about the triumph of the good. The "end times" or the millennium or the triumph of the working class is near, or can be made near by the right action. Action, extreme action, is required immediately, for the triumph of the good and the defeat of evil. This "10 minutes to midnight" feeling is part of what makes it possible for normal people to risk their lives in violence.

Consider the passengers of the hijacked flight that crashed in western Pennsylvania. The passengers found out from their cell phones that hijacked planes had crashed into the World Trade Center. They had every reason to believe that their plane was on its way to a similar end. Unarmed, they decided to attack the hijackers, and sacrificed their lives in bringing the plane down before it could impact its intended target, which was probably the Pentagon or the White House. When it is 10 minutes to midnight, there is little to lose and everything to gain.

The sense of crisis is usually associated with an overwhelming threat. In the case of the September 11 terrorists, the threat seems to be a fear that fundamentalist Muslim culture is in danger of being overwhelmed by Western culture. The military and economic power of the West, and the relative feebleness of once-great Muslim nations in the modern era, are submerging Muslims in a tidal wave of individualism and irreligion. Note that it is attachment to a view of what Muslims should be and fear for the future of Muslims that are the emotional foundations of the terrorists. They do not begin from hatred of the West, but from love of their own group and culture that they see in danger of extinction from the power of the West.

Similarly, the United States, mobilized by President Bush for a war against terrorism, does not begin from hatred of al-Qaeda but from love of country. Mobilization includes a rhetoric of crisis, of impending threat from an evil enemy or, more recently, an "axis of evil." Americans' anger toward al-Qaeda, and perhaps more broadly toward Arabs and Muslims, is not an independent emotion but a product of patriotism combined with a crisis of threat.

The Psychology of the Slippery Slope

The sense of crisis does not spring full-blown upon an individual. It is the end of a long trajectory to terrorism, a trajectory in which the individual moves slowly toward an apocalyptic view of the world and a correspondingly extreme behavioral commitment. Sprinzak (1991) has distinguished three stages in this trajectory: a *crisis of con-*

fidence, in which a group protests and demonstrates against the prevailing political system with a criticism that yet accepts the system's values; a *conflict of legitimacy,* in which the group loses confidence in reform and advances a competing ideological and cultural system while moving to angry protest and small-scale violence; and a *crisis of legitimacy,* in which the group embraces terrorist violence against the government and everyone who supports the government. Whether as an individual joining an extreme group, or as a member of a group that becomes more extreme over time, the individual becomes more extreme in a series of steps so small as to be near invisible. The result is a terrorist who may look back at the transition to terrorism with no sense of having ever made an explicit choice.

Psychology offers several models of this kind of slippery slope (see McCauley et al., 1987, for more detail). One is Milgram's obedience experiment, in which 60 percent of subjects are willing to deliver the maximum shock level ("450 volts XXX Danger Strong Shock") to a supposed fellow subject in a supposed learning experiment. In one variation of the experiment, Milgram had the experimenter called away on a pretext and another supposed subject came up with the idea of raising the shock one level with each mistake from the "learner." In this variation, 20 percent went on to deliver maximum shock. The 20 percent yielding cannot be attributed to the authority of the experimenter and is most naturally understood as the power of self-justification acting on the small increments in shock level. Each shock delivered becomes a reason for giving the next higher shock, because the small increments in shock mean that the subject has to see something at least a little wrong with the last shock if there is something wrong with the next one. A clear choice between good and evil would be a shock generator with only two levels, 15 volts and 450 volts, but the 20 percent who go all the way never see a clear choice between good and evil.

Another model of the terrorist trajectory is more explicitly social-psychological. Group extremity shift, the tendency for group opinion to become more extreme in the direction initially favored by most individuals, is currently understood in terms of two mechanisms: relevant arguments and social comparison (Brown, 1986, pp. 200–244). Relevant arguments explain the shift as a result of individuals hearing new arguments in discussion that are biased in the initially favored direction. Social comparison explains the shift as a competition for status in which no one wants to fall behind in supporting the group-favored direction. In the trajectory to terrorism, initial beliefs and commitments favor action against injustice, and group discussion and ingroup status competition move the group toward more extreme views and more extreme violence.

The slippery slope is not something that happens only in psychology experiments and foreign countries. Since September 11, there have already been suggestions from reputable people that U.S. security forces may need to use torture to get information from suspected terrorists. This is the edge of a slope that leads down and away from the rule of law and the presumption of innocence.

Terrorism as Strategy

Psychologists recognize two kinds of aggression, emotional and instrumental. Emotional aggression is associated with anger and does not calculate long-term consequences. The reward of emotional aggression is hurting someone who has hurt you. Instrumental aggression is more calculating—the use of aggression as a means to other ends. The balance between these two in the behavior of individual terrorists is usually not clear and might usefully be studied more explicitly in the future. The balance may be important in determining how to respond to terrorism: As argued above, emotional aggression should be less sensitive to objective rewards and punishments, while instrumental aggression should be more sensitive.

Of course, the balance may be very different in those who perpetrate the violence than in those who plan it. The planners are probably more instrumental; they are usually thinking about what they want to accomplish. They aim to inflict long-term costs on their enemy and to gain long-term advantage for themselves.

Material Damage to the Enemy

Terrorism inflicts immediate damage in destroying lives and property, but terrorists hope that the long-term costs will be much greater. They want to create fear and uncertainty far beyond the victims and those close to them. They want their enemy to spend time and money on security. In effect, the terrorists aim to lay an enormous tax on every aspect of the enemy's society, a tax that transfers resources from productive purposes to anti-productive security measures. The costs of increased security are likely to be particularly high for a country like the United States, where an open society is the foundation of economic success and a high-tech military.

The United States is already paying enormous taxes of this kind. Billions more dollars are going to the FBI, the CIA, the Pentagon, the

National Security Agency, and a new bureaucracy for the director of homeland security. Billions are going to bail out the airlines, to increase the number and quality of airport security personnel, to pay the National Guard stationed at airports. The costs to business activity are perhaps even greater. Long lines at airport security and fear of air travel cut business travel and holiday travel. Hotel bookings are down, urban restaurant business is down, all kinds of tourist businesses are down. Long lines of trucks at the Canadian and Mexican borders are slowed for more intensive searches, and the delays necessarily contribute to the cost of goods transported. The Coast Guard and the Immigration and Naturalization Service focus on terrorism and decrease attention to the drug trade. I venture to guess that the costs of increased security and the war on terrorism will far outrun the costs of losses at the World Trade Center and the reparations to survivors of those who died there.

Political Damage to the Enemy

In the longer term, the damage terrorism does to civil society may be greater than any dollar costs (see McCauley, in press-a). The response to terrorism inevitably builds the power of the state at the expense of the civil society. The adage that "war is the health of the state" is evident to anyone who tracks the growth of the federal government in the United States. With every war—the Civil War, World War I, World War II, the Korean War, the Vietnam War, the Gulf War, and now the war against terrorism—the power of the government has grown in directions and degrees that are not relinquished after the war has ended. During World War II, for example, the income tax, which previously had applied only to high-income people, was imposed even on low-income people. The federal government also introduced withholding to make it easier to collect tax money. After the war, income taxes and tax withholding remained as a normal part of American life (Higgs, 1987).

Polls taken in years preceding the terrorist attack on September 11 indicate that about half of adult Americans saw the federal government as a threat to the rights and freedoms of ordinary Americans. No doubt fewer would say so in the aftermath of the recent attacks, a shift consistent with the adage that "war is the health of the state." But if more security could ensure the safety of the nation, the Soviet Union would still be with us. It is possible that bin Laden had the Soviet Union in mind in an interview broadcast by CNN. "Osama bin Laden told a reporter with the Al Jazeera network in October that 'freedom and human rights in America are doomed' and that the U.S. government would lead its people and the West 'into an unbearable hell and a choking life'" (Kurtz, 2002).

Mobilizing the Ingroup

Terrorists particularly hope to elicit a violent response that will assist them in mobilizing their own people. A terrorist group is the apex of a pyramid of supporters and sympathizers. The base of the pyramid is composed of all those who sympathize with the terrorist cause even though they may disagree with the violent means that the terrorists use. In Northern Ireland, for instance, the base of the pyramid is all who agree with "Brits Out." In the Islamic world, the base of the pyramid is all those who agree that the United States has been hurting and humiliating Muslims for 50 years. The pyramid is essential to the terrorists for cover and for recruits. The terrorists hope that a clumsy and overgeneralized strike against them will hit some of those in the pyramid below them. The blow will enlarge their base of sympathy, turn the sympathetic but unmobilized to action and sacrifice, and strengthen their own status as leaders at the apex of this pyramid.

Al-Qaeda had reason to be hopeful that U.S. strength could help them. In 1986, for instance, the United States attempted to reply to Libyan-supported terrorism by bombing Libya's leader, Muammar Qaddafi. The bombs missed Qaddafi's residence but hit a nearby apartment building and killed a number of women and children. This mistake was downplayed in the United States but it was a public relations success for anti-U.S. groups across North Africa. In 1998, the United States attempted to reply to al-Qaeda attacks on U.S. embassies in Africa by sending cruise missiles against terrorist camps in Afghanistan and against a supposed bomb factory in Khartoum, Sudan. It appears now that the "bomb factory" was in fact producing only medical supplies.

A violent response to terrorism that is not well aimed is a success for the terrorists. The Taliban did their best to play up U.S. bombing mistakes in Afghanistan, but were largely disappointed. It appears that civilian casualties resulting from U.S. attacks in Afghanistan had, by February 2002, added up to somewhere between 1,000 and 3,700 deaths, depending on who is estimating (Bearak, 2002). Although Afghan civilian losses may thus approach the 3,000 U.S. victims of September 11, it is clear that U.S. accuracy has been outstanding by the standards of modern warfare. Al-Qaeda might still hope to profit by perceptions of a crusade against Muslims if the United States extends the war on terrorism to Iraq, Iran, or Somalia.

U.S. Reaction to September 11: Some Issues of Mass Psychology

In this section I consider several psychological issues raised by the U.S. reaction to the terrorist attacks of September 11. Has the United States been terrorized? What kinds of identity shifts may have occurred after September 11?

Fear after September 11

There seems little doubt that the events of September 11, soon followed by another plane crash at Rockaway Beach, did make Americans less willing to fly. In early 2002, air travel and hotel bookings were still significantly below levels recorded in the months before the attacks. Beyond fear of flying, there is evidence that Americans became generally more anxious and insecure. Some law firms specializing in preparation of wills and trusts saw a big increase in business after September 11. Gun sales were up in some places after September 11, suggesting a search for increased security broader than against the threat of terrorism. Owning a gun may not be much help against terrorists, but, at least for some individuals, a gun can be a symbol and reassurance of control and personal safety. Pet sales were also reported up in some places. Again, a pet is not likely to be much help against terrorists, but, at least for some individuals, a pet may be an antidote to uncertainty and fear. A pet offers both an experience of control and the reassurance of unconditional positive regard (Beck & Katcher, 1996).

It is tempting to interpret a big decrease in air travel as evidence of a big increase in fear, but it may be that even a small increase in fear can produce a large decrease in willingness to fly. When the stakes are high, a small change in risk perception can trigger a large decrease in willingness to bet. Indeed, decreased willingness to fly need not imply any increase in fear. Some may have already been afraid of flying, and found September 11 not a stimulus to increased fear but a justification for fears—or for acting on fears—that had been previously ridiculed and suppressed. Thus there may be only a minority with increased fear of flying after September 11. Myers (2001) offered four research generalizations about perceived risk that can help explain increased fear of flying after September 11. We are biologically prepared to fear heights, we fear particularly what we cannot control, we fear immediate more than long-term and cumulative dangers, and we exaggerate dangers represented in vivid and memorable images. All of these influences can help explain fear of flying, but only the last can explain why fear of flying increased after September 11. Fear of heights preceded September 11, every passenger gives up control on entering a plane, and the immediate risk of climbing onto a plane is little affected by four or five crashes in a brief period of time.

Myers notes, however, that the risks of air travel are largely concentrated in the minutes of takeoff and landing. This is a framing issue: Do air travelers see their risk in terms of deaths per passenger mile—which makes air travel much safer than driving—or do they see the risk as deaths per minute of takeoff and landing? With the latter framing, air travel may be objectively more risky than driving.

Still, Myers may be correct in focusing on the importance of television images of planes slicing into the World Trade Center, but the importance of these images may have more to do with control of fear and norms about expressing fear than with the level of fear. Myers reports a Gallup poll indicating that, even before September 11, 44 percent of those willing to fly were willing to admit they felt fearful about flying. It is possible that this fear is controlled by a cognitive appraisal that flying is safe, and the images of planes crashing interfere with this appraisal. This interpretation is similar to the "safety frame" explanation of how people can enjoy the fear arousal associated with riding a roller coaster or watching a horror film (McCauley, 1998b).

If the safety frame is disturbed, the fear controls behavior and, in the case of air travel, people are less willing to fly. One implication of this interpretation is that, for at least some individuals, government warnings of additional terrorist attacks in the near future would make no difference in the level of fear experienced—vivid crash images may release the latent fear no matter what the objective likelihood of additional crashes.

Acting on the fear experienced is a separate issue. It is possible that warnings of future terrorist attacks affect the norms of acting on fear of flying, that is, the warnings reduce social pressure to carry on business as usual and reduce ridicule for those who are fearful about flying. Fear of flying is an attitude, and there is no doubt that social norms have much to do with determining when attitudes are expressed in behavior (Ajzen & Fishbein, 1980).

Indeed, the impact of government warnings and increased airport security are very much in need of investigation. President Bush was in the position of trying to tell Americans that they should resume flying and that new airport security made flying safe again, even as security agencies issued multiple warnings of new terrorist attacks. These warnings had the peculiar quality of being completely unspecific about the nature of the threat or what to do about it. The possible downside of such warnings is suggested by research indicating that threat appeals are likely to be repressed or ignored if the appeal does not include specific and effective action to avoid the threat (Sabini, 1995, pp. 565–566). Even the additional airport security may be of dubious value. It is true that many Americans seemed reassured to see Army personnel with weapons stationed in airports, although the objective security value of troops with no training in security screening is by no means obvious. But if there is any value to the framing interpretation of increased fear offered above, then adding military security at airports may actually increase fear. Vivid images of armed troops at airports may be more likely to undermine than to augment the safety frame that controls fear of flying.

Differences in security procedures from one airport to another can also contribute to increased fear. A journalist from Pittsburgh called me not long after new security procedures were introduced at U.S. airports. His paper had received a letter to the editor written by a visitor from Florida, a letter excoriating the Pittsburgh airport for inadequate security. The writer had been frightened because she was asked for identification only once on her way to boarding her return flight from Pittsburgh, whereas she had been stopped for identification five times in boarding the Florida flight to Pittsburgh.

Fear of flying is not the only fear to emerge from September 11. Survivors of the attacks on the World Trade Center (WTC), those who fled for their lives on September 11, may be fearful of working in a high-rise building and afraid even of all the parts of lower Manhattan that were associated with commuting to and from the WTC. Many corporate employees who escaped the WTC returned to work in new office buildings in northern New Jersey. In these new settings, some may have been retraumatized by frequent fire and evacuation drills that associated their new offices and stairwells with the uncertainties and fears of the offices and stairwells of the WTC. For these people, the horror of the WTC may have been a kind of one-trial traumatic conditioning experiment, with follow-up training in associating their new workplace with the old one. Their experience and their fears deserve research attention.

A small step in this direction was a December conference at the University of Pennsylvania's Solomon Asch Center for Study of Ethnopolitical Conflict. The conference brought together eight trauma counselors from around the United States who had been brought in to assist WTC corporate employees returning to work in new office spaces. A report of lessons learned from this conference is in preparation, but a few issues can already be discerned. Perhaps most important is that the counselors were selected and directed by corporate Employee Assistance Programs with more experience of physical health problems than of mental health problems. Thus the counselors were all contracted to use Critical Incident Stress Debriefing techniques with every individual and every group seen; at least officially, no room was left for a counselor to exercise independent judgment about what approach might best suit a particular situation.

Similarly, the counselors were understood as interchangeable resources, so that a counselor might be sent to one corporation on one day and a different corporation the next day, even as another counselor experienced the reverse transfer. The importance of learning a particular corporate culture and setting, the personal connection between individual counselor and the managers that control that setting, the trust developed between an individual counselor and individuals needing assistance and referral in that setting—these were given little attention in the organization of counseling assistance. It appears that the experience of counselors working with WTC survivors has not yet been integrated with the experience of those working with survivors of the Oklahoma City bombing (Pfefferbaum, Flynn, Brandt, & Lensgraf, 1999). There is a long way to go to develop anything like a consensus on "best practice" for assisting survivors of such attacks.

In sum, fear after September 11 includes a range of fear reactions, including fear of flying by those with no personal connection to the WTC, more general fears and anxieties associated with death from uncontrollable and unpredictable terrorist attacks, and specific workplace fears among those who escaped the WTC attacks. These reactions offer theoretical challenges that can be of interest to those interested in understanding the relation between risk appraisal and fear (Lazarus, 1991), as well as to those interested in the commercial implications of public fears.

Cohesion after September 11: Patriotism

All over the United States, vehicles and homes were decorated with the U.S. flag after September 11. Walls, fences, billboards, and Emails were emblazoned with "God Bless America." It is clear that the immediate response to the attacks was a sudden increase in patriotic expression. The distribution of this increase across the United States could be a matter of some interest. Was the new patriotism greater in New York City and declining in concentric circles of distance from New York? Was it greater among blue-collar than white-collar families? Was it greater for some ethnic groups than for others? Was it greater in cities, possibly perceived as more threatened by future terrorist attacks, than in suburbs and small towns?

The attacks of September 11 represent a natural experiment relevant to two prominent approaches to conceptualizing and measuring patriotism. In the first approach, Kosterman and Feshbach (1989) distinguish between patriotism and nationalism. Patriotism is love of country and is generally accounted a good thing; nationalism is a feeling of national superiority that is accounted a source of intergroup hostility and conflict. In the second approach, Schatz, Staub, and Lavine (1999) offer a distinction between *constructive* and *blind* patriotism. *Constructive* patriotism refers to love of country expressed as willingness to criticize its policies and its leaders when these go wrong; *blind* patriotism refers to love of country coupled with norms against criticism—"my country right or wrong." Constructive patriotism is here accounted the good thing and blind patriotism the danger.

Thus, both approaches distinguish between good and bad forms of patriotism, and both offer separate measures of the good and bad forms. That is, there is a scale of patriotism and a scale of nationalism, and a scale of constructive patriotism and a scale of blind patriotism. In both approaches, there is some evidence that the two scales are relatively independent. Some individuals score high on patriotism, for instance, but low on nationalism. Similarly, some individuals score high on constructive patriotism but also score high on blind patriotism (an inconsistency that seems to bother those answering questions less than it bothers theorists).

What happened to these different aspects of patriotism among Americans after September 11? As increased cohesion is known to increase conformity and pressure on deviates, one might expect that patriotism, blind patriotism, and nationalism increased, whereas constructive patriotism decreased. Another possibility is that scores on these measures were unchanged after September 11, but identification with the country increased in relation to other directions of group identification. That is, Americans rating the importance of each of a number of groups—country, ethnic group, religious group, family, school—might rate country higher in relation to other groups.

It seems likely that both kinds of patriotism increased, both scores on the patriotism scales and ratings of the relative importance of country. If so, additional questions can be raised. Did nationalism and blind patriotism increase more or less than the "good" forms of patriotism? Was the pattern of change different by geography, education, or ethnicity?

Cohesion after September 11: Relations in Public

News reports immediately after September 11 suggested a new interpersonal tone in New York City. Along with shock and fear was a new tone in public interactions of strangers, a tone of increased politeness, helpfulness, and personal warmth. Several reports suggested a notable drop in crime, especially violent crime, in the days after the attacks.

It would be interesting to know if these reports can be substantiated with more objective measures of social behavior in public places (McCauley, Coleman, & DeFusco, 1978). Did the pace of life in New York slow after the attacks? That is, did people walk slower on the streets? Did eye contact between strangers increase? Did commercial transactions (e.g., with bus drivers, postal clerks, supermarket cashiers) include more personal exchange? Did interpersonal distance in interactions of strangers decrease? This research will be hampered by the absence of relevant measures from New York in the months before September 11, but it may not be too late to chart a decline from levels of public sociability and politeness that may still have been elevated in early 2002.

Cohesion after September 11: Minority Identity Shifts

A few reports have suggested that minority groups experienced major changes of group identity after September 11. Group identity is composed of two parts: private and public identity. Private identity is how the individual thinks of him- or herself in relation to groups to which the individual belongs. Public identity is how the individual thinks others perceive him.

Public Identity Shift for Muslims and Arabs

The attacks of September 11 produced an immediate effect on the public identity of Arabs, Muslims, and those, like Sikhs, who can be mistaken by Americans for Arab or Muslim. Actual violence against members of these groups seems mercifully to have been rare, with 39 hate crimes reported to the New York City Police Department in the week ending September 22, but only one a week by the end of December (Fries, 2001). Much more frequent has been the experience of dirty looks, muttered suggestions of "go home," physical distancing, and discrimination at work and school (Sengupta, 2001). Many Arab Americans and Muslims say they have been afraid to report this kind of bias.

American reactions to Muslims and Arabs after September 11 pose a striking theoretical challenge. How is it that the actions of 19 Arab Muslims can affect American perceptions of the Arabs and Muslims that they encounter? The ease with which the 19 were generalized to an impression of millions should leave us amazed; "the law of small numbers" (Tversky & Kahneman, 1971), in which small and unrepresentative samples are accepted as representative of large populations, has not been observed in research on stereotypes. Indeed, the difficulty of changing stereotypes has often been advanced as one of their principal dangers.

Of course, not every American accepted the idea that all Arabs are terrorists, but even those who intellectually avoided this generalization sometimes found themselves fighting a new unease and suspicion toward people who looked Arab. Whether on the street or boarding a plane, Americans seem to have had difficulty controlling their emotional response to this newly salient category. It seems unlikely that an attack by nineteen Congolese terrorists would have the same impact on perceptions of African Americans. Why not?

One possible explanation of the speed and power of the group generalization of the September 11 terrorists is that humans are biologically prepared to essentialize cultural differences of members of unfamiliar groups. Gil-White (2001) has suggested that there was an evolutionary advantage for individuals who recognized and generalized cultural differences so as to avoid the extra costs of interacting with those whose norms did not mesh with local norms. This perspective suggests that we may have a kind of default schema for group perception that makes it easy to essentialize the characteristics of a few individuals encountered from a new group. To essentialize means to see the unusual characteristics of the new individuals as the product of an unchangeable group nature or essence. Previous familiarity with the group, a pre-existing essence for the group, could interfere with this default, such that African terrorists would not easily lead to a generalization about African Americans.

It would be useful to know more about the experience of Muslims and Arabs in the United States after September 11, not least because those experiencing bias may become more likely to sympathize with terrorism directed against the United States. Interviews and polls might inquire not only about the respondent's personal experience of bias, but about the respondent's perception of what most in his or her group experienced. As elaborated above, the motivation for violence may have more to do with group experience than with personal problems.

Public Identity Shift for African Americans

The attacks of September 11 may also have produced an effect on the public identity of African Americans. Their sharing in the costs and threats of terrorist attack may have strengthened their public status as Americans. Several African Americans have suggested that the distancing and unease they often feel from whites with whom they interact was markedly diminished after September 11. The extent and distribution of this feeling of increased acceptance by white Americans could be investigated in interviews with African Americans. Again, the distinction between personal experience and perception of group experience could be important in estimating the political impact of September 11 on African Americans.

Finally, there is an issue of great practical importance in understanding the public identity of Muslim African Americans as a minority within a minority. This group is likely to have faced conflicting changes after September 11, with increased acceptance as African Americans opposed by decreased acceptance as Muslims. The distinctive attire of African American Muslims, particularly the attire of women of this community, makes them readily identifiable in public settings. With the attire goes a community lifestyle that also sets this minority apart from other African Americans. Thus public reactions to Muslim African Americans should be very salient in their experience, and this experience could be determined by researchers with entrée to their community. Again, the distinction between personal experience of the respondent and perceived group experience may be important.

One way of learning about shifts in the public identities of minorities is to study changes in the mutual stereotyping of majority and minority. Stereotypes are today generally understood as perceptions of probabilistic differences between groups, differences that may include personality traits, abilities, occupations, physique, clothing, and preferences (McCauley, Jussim, & Lee, 1995). Thus, researchers might ask both minority and majority group members about whether and how September 11 changed their perceptions of the differences between majority and minority.

Perhaps even more important for understanding the public identity of minorities would be research that asks about *metastereotypes*. Metastereotypes are perceptions of what "most people" believe about group differences. Although they are little studied, there is some evidence that metastereotypes are more extreme than personal stereotypes, that is, that individuals believe that most people see stronger ingroup–outgroup differences than they do (Rettew, Billman, & Davis, 1993). The public identity of the minority might thus be measured as the average minority individual's perception of what "most people" in the majority group see as the differences between minority and majority. Related metastereotypes might also be of interest: the average minority individual's perception of what most minority members believe about majority–minority differences, the average majority member's perception of what most majority members believe about these differences, and the average majority member's perception of what most minority members believe about these differences.

The attacks of September 11 and their aftermath offer a natural experiment in conflicting pressures on public identity. Research on public identities of minorities could enliven theoretical development even as the research contributes to gauging the potential for terrorist recruitment in groups—Muslim Arabs in the United States, Muslim African Americans—that security services are likely to see as being at risk for terrorist sympathies. In particular, public identity shifts for Muslim African Americans will be better understood by comparison with whatever shifts may obtain for African Americans who are not Muslim.

Private Identity Shifts

Private identity concerns the beliefs and feelings of the individual about a group to which the individual belongs. The most obvious shifts in private identity are those already discussed as shifts in patriotism. Patriotism is a particular kind of group identification, that is, identification with country or nation, and increases in patriotism are a kind of private identity shift. This obvious connection between national identification and patriotism has only recently become a focus of empirical research (Citrin, Wong, & Duff, 2001; Sidanius & Petrocik, 2001).

Here I want to focus on shifts in private identities of minorities. As with public identity shifts, the three minority groups of special interest are Muslim Arabs living in the United States, African Americans, and Muslim African Americans. For each group, research can ask about changes since September 11 in their feelings toward the United States and feelings toward their minority group. What is the relation between changes in these two private identities? It is by no means obvious that more attachment to one identity means less attachment to others, but in terms of behavior there may be something of a conservation principle at work. Time and energy are limited, and more behavior controlled by one identity may mean less behavior controlled by others. There is much yet to be learned about the relation between more particularistic identities, including ethnic and religious identities, and overarching national identity.

Group Dynamics Theory and Political Identity

Public reaction to terrorist attacks is strikingly consistent with results found in research with small face-to-face groups. In the group dynamics literature that began with Festinger's (1950) theory of informal social influence, cohesion is attachment to the group that comes from two kinds of interdependence. The obvious kind of interdependence arises from common goals of material interest, status, and congeniality. The hidden interdependence arises from the need for certainty that can only be obtained from the consensus of others. Agreement with those around us is the only source of certainty about questions of value, including questions about good and evil and about what is worth living for, working for, and dying for.

It seems possible that identification with large and faceless groups is analogous to cohesion in small face-to-face groups (McCauley, 2001; McCauley, 2003). A scaled-up theory of cohesion leads immediately to the implication that group identification is not one thing but a number of related things. Research has shown that different sources of cohesion lead to different kinds of behavior. Cohesion based on congeniality, for instance, leads to groupthink, whereas cohesion based on group status or material interest does not lead to groupthink (McCauley, 1998a).

Similarly, different sources of ethnic identification may lead to different behaviors. Individuals who care about their ethnic group for status or material interest may be less likely to sacrifice for the group than individuals who care about their group for its social reality value—for the moral culture that makes sense of the world and the individual's place in it. Research on the effects of September 11 on group identities might try to link different measures of group identification with different behaviors after September 11: giving blood or money, community volunteer work, revising a will, changing travel plans, spending more time with family. The distinctions between patriotism and nationalism, and between constructive and blind patriotism, as cited above, are steps in this direction.

Group dynamics research has shown that shared threat is a particularly potent source of group cohesion; similarly, as discussed above, the threat represented by the September 11 attacks seems to have raised U.S. patriotism and national identification. Research also shows that high cohesion leads to accepting group norms, respect for group leaders, and pressure on deviates (Duckitt, 1989). Similarly, U.S. response to the September 11 attacks seems to have included new respect for group norms (less crime, more politeness), new respect for group leaders (President Bush, Mayor Giuliani), and new willingness to sanction deviates (hostility toward those who sympathize with Arabs and Muslims; see Knowlton, 2002).

Conclusion

In the first part of this paper, group dynamics theory was the perspective brought to bear in understanding the power of cause and comrades in moving normal people to terrorism. In particular I suggested that the power of a group to elicit sacrifice depends upon its terror-management value, which is another way of talking about the social reality value of the group.

Group dynamics research and the psychology of cohesion also provide a useful starting point for theorizing about the origins and consequences of group identification, including many aspects of public reaction to terrorism. Terrorism is a threat to all who identify with the group targeted, and at least the initial result of an attack is always increased identification—increased cohesion—in the group attacked. The non-obvious quality of this idea is conveyed by the many unsuccessful attempts to use air power to demoralize an enemy by bombing its civilian population (Pape, 1996).

In sum, I have argued that both origins and effects of terrorist acts are anchored in group dynamics. Along the way I have tried to suggest how the response to terrorism can be more dangerous than the terrorists.

References

Ajzen, I., & Fishbein, M. (1980). *Understanding attitudes and predicting behavior.* New York: Prentice Hall.

Allport, G. W. (1954). *The nature of prejudice.* Cambridge, MA: Addison Wesley.

Barker, E. (1984). *The making of a Moonie: Choice or brainwashing.* London: Basil Blackwell.

Bearak, B. (2002, February 11). Afghan toll of civilians is lost in the fog of war. *International Herald Tribune*, pp. 1, 8.

Beck, A., & Katcher, A. (1996). *Between pets and people: The importance of animal companionship.* West Lafayette, IN: Purdue University Press.

Brewer, M. (2001). Ingroup identification and intergroup conflict: When does ingroup love become outgroup hate? In R. D. Ashmore, L. Jussim, & D. Wilder (Eds.), *Social identity, intergroup conflict, and conflict reduction* (pp. 17–41). New York: Oxford University Press.

Brown, R. (1986). *Social psychology, the second edition.* New York: Free Press.

Citrin, J., Wong, C., & Duff, B. (2001). The meaning of American national identity: Patterns of ethnic conflict and consensus. In R. D. Ashmore, L. Jussim, & D. Wilder (Eds.), *Social identity, intergroup conflict, and conflict reduction* (pp. 71–100). New York: Oxford University Press.

Duckitt, J. (1989). Authoritarianism and group identification: A new view of an old construct. *Political Psychology, 10,* 63–84.

Festinger, L. (1950). Informal social communication. *Psychological Review, 57,* 271–282.

Frank, R. L. (1988). *Passions within reason: The strategic role of the emotions.* New York: Norton.

Friedman, A. (2002a, February 5). Forum focuses on "wrath" born of poverty. *International Herald Tribune*, p. 11.

Friedman, T. (2002b, January 28). The pain behind Al Qaeda's Europe connection. *International Herald Tribune*, p. 6.

Fries, J. H. (2001, December 22). Complaints of anti-Arab bias crimes dip, but concerns linger. *New York Times*, p. B8.

Galanter, M. (1980). Psychological induction into the large group: Findings from a modern religious sect. *American Journal of Psychiatry, 137,* 1574–1579.

Gil-White, F. (2001). Are ethnic groups biological "species" to the human brain? *Current Anthropology, 42,* 515–554.

Higgs, R. (1987). *Crisis and leviathan: Critical episodes in the growth of American government.* New York: Oxford University Press.

Horowitz, D. L. (2001). *The deadly ethnic riot.* Berkeley: University of California Press.

Kinder, D. (1998). Opinion and action in the realm of politics. In D. T. Gilbert, S. Fiske, & G. Lindzey (Eds.), *The handbook of social psychology* (Vol. II, pp. 778–867). New York: McGraw-Hill.

Knowlton, B. (2001, December 20). How the world sees the United States and Sept. 11. *International Herald Tribune*, pp. 1, 6.

Knowlton, B. (2002, February 12). On U.S. campuses, intolerance grows. *International Herald Tribune*, pp. I, IV.

Kosterman, R., & Feshbach, S. (1989). Towards a measure of patriotic and nationalistic attitudes. *Political Psychology, 10*, 257–274.

Kurtz, H. (2002, February 2–3). America is "doomed," Bin Laden says on tape. *International Herald Tribune*, p. 5.

Lazarus, R. S. (1991). Cognition and motivation in emotion. *American Psychologist, 46*, 352–367.

Lelyveld, J. (2001, October 28). All suicide bombers are not alike. *New York Times Magazine*, pp. 48–53, 62, 78–79.

Makiya, K., & Mneimneh, H. (2002, January 17). Manual for a "raid." *New York Review of Books, XLIX*, pp. 18–21.

McCauley, C. (1991). Terrorism research and public policy: An overview. In C. McCauley (Ed.), *Terrorism research and public policy* (pp. 126–144). London: Frank Cass.

McCauley, C. (1998a). Group dynamics in Janis's theory of groupthink: Backward and forward. *Organizational Behavior and Human Decision Processes, 73*, 142–162.

McCauley, C. (1998b). When screen violence is not attractive. In J. Goldstein (Ed.), *Why we watch: The attractions of violent entertainment* (pp. 144–162). New York: Oxford University Press.

McCauley, C. (2001). The psychology of group identification and the power of ethnic nationalism. In D. Chirot & M. Seligman (Eds.), *Ethnopolitical warfare: Causes, consequences, and possible solutions* (pp. 343–362). Washington, DC: APA Books.

McCauley, C. (2003). Making sense of terrorism after 9/11. In R. S. Moser and C. E. Frantz (Eds.), *Shocking violence II: Violent disaster, war, and terrorism affecting our youth* (pp. 10–32). New York: Charles C. Thomas.

McCauley, C., Coleman, G., & DeFusco, P. (1978). Commuters' eye-contact with strangers in city and suburban train stations: Evidence of short-term adaptation to interpersonal overload in the city. *Environmental Psychology and Nonverbal Behavior, 2*, 215–255.

McCauley, C., Jussim, L., & Lee, Y.-T. (1995). Stereotype accuracy: Toward appreciating group differences. In Y.-T. Lee, L. J. Jussim, & C. R. McCauley (Eds.), *Stereotype accuracy: Toward appreciating group differences* (pp. 293–312). Washington, DC: APA Books.

McCauley, C., & Segal, M. (1987). Social psychology of terrorist groups. In C. Hendrick (Ed.), *Review of Personality and Social Psychology, Vol. 9* (pp. 231–256). Beverly Hills, CA: Sage.

Myers, D. G. (2001). Do we fear the right things? *American Psychological Society Observer, 14*, 3, 31.

Pape, R. A. (1996). *Bombing to win: Air power and coercion in war.* Ithaca: Cornell University Press.

Pfefferbaum, B., Flynn, B. W., Brandt, E. N., & Lensgraf, S. J. (1999). Organizing the mental health response to human-caused community disasters with reference to the Oklahoma City bombing. *Psychiatric Annals, 29,* 109–113.

Pyszczynski, T., Greenberg, J., & Solomon, S. (1997). Why do we need what we need? A terror management perspective on the roots of human social motivation. *Psychological Inquiry, 8,* 1–20.

Rettew, D. C., Billman, D., & Davis, R. A. (1993). Inaccurate perceptions of the amount others stereotype: Estimates about stereotypes of one's own group and other groups. *Basic and Applied Social Psychology, 14,* 121–142.

Rummel, R. J. (1996). *Death by government.* New Brunswick, NJ: Transaction Publishers.

Sabini, J. (1995). *Social psychology* (2nd ed.). New York: Norton.

Schatz, R. T., Staub, E., & Lavine, H. (1999). On the varieties of national attachment: Blind versus constructive patriotism. *Political Psychology, 20,* 151–174.

Sengupta, S. (2001, October 10). Sept. 11 attack narrows the racial divide. *New York Times,* p. B1.

Sidanius, J., & Petrocik, J. R. (2001). Communal and national identity in a multiethnic state: A comparison of three perspectives. In R. D. Ashmore, L. Jussim, & D. Wilder (Eds.), *Social identity, intergroup conflict, and conflict reduction* (pp. 101–129). New York: Oxford University Press.

Sprinzak, E. (1991). The process of delegitimization: Towards a linkage theory of political terrorism. In C. McCauley (Ed.), *Terrorism research and public policy* (pp. 50–68). London: Frank Cass.

Stouffer, S. A., Lumsdaine, A. A., Lumsdaine, M. H., et al. (1949). *The American soldier, volume 2: Combat and its aftermath.* Princeton, NJ: Princeton University Press.

Tversky, A., & Kahneman, D. (1971). Belief in the law of small numbers. *Psychological Bulletin, 2,* 105–110.

CHAPTER 3

Unresolved Trauma: Fuel for the Cycle of Violence and Terrorism

Timothy Gallimore

Trauma: A Psychic Wound

Trauma is an attack on the self. *Trauma* comes from the Greek word that means "to wound or to pierce." Traumatic events generally involve a threat of injury or death that causes the victim to feel intense fear, helplessness, loss of control, and impending annihilation. Trauma can occur following the experience or witnessing of military combat, natural disasters, terrorist incidents, serious accidents, or violent personal assaults such as rape. These events are outside the range of normal human experience. They cause physical or psychological injury that produces mental or emotional stress. In our universal search to derive meaning from our experiences, our psyche is sometimes wounded, pierced by our inability to mentally process the incongruous, unpleasant, unexpected, dramatic, and shocking events that come our way. The resulting psychological condition is trauma. Prolonged or repeated abuse can also cause trauma.

Humans react to traumatic events with the autonomic nervous system, or with basic reflexes. At the moment of the threatening experience, victims may freeze in terror, unable to escape the event; run away; or flee in panic to get away from the event. Or they may fight to stop or end the threat.

The emotional symptoms of trauma are sadness, depression, anxiety, fear, irritability, anger, despair, guilt, and self-doubt. Victims may develop phobias, sleep disorders, eating disorders, and conduct disorders. Trauma victims may also experience mental confusion and become emotionally impaired and socially dysfunctional.

Clinical research shows that about 30 percent of trauma victims develop a psychiatric illness called post-traumatic stress disorder (PTSD), which may last a lifetime. According to the National Center for PTSD, the traumatic events most often associated with PTSD in men are rape, combat exposure, childhood neglect, and childhood physical abuse. For women, the most common events are rape, sexual molestation, physical attack, being threatened with a weapon, and childhood physical abuse.

General knowledge about trauma came out of concern for soldiers who developed PTSD after being exposed to the shock of military combat. There is documentation of the illness in historical medical literature starting with the Civil War, where a PTSD-like disorder was known as Da Costa's Syndrome. There are descriptions of PTSD in the medical literature on combat veterans of World War II and on Holocaust survivors. However, careful research and documentation of PTSD began in earnest after the Vietnam War.

The research shows that about half of all American veterans who served in Vietnam have experienced PTSD. The estimated lifetime prevalence of PTSD among these veterans is 30.9 percent for men and 26.9 percent for women. An additional 22.5 percent of men and 21.2 percent of women have had partial PTSD at some point in their lives (Kulka et al., 1990). Research on Persian Gulf War veterans shows a PTSD rate ranging from 3 percent to 50 percent (Wolfe & Proctor, 1996). About 48 percent of soldiers in deployed units met criteria for PTSD, and they have a lifetime prevalence of 65 percent. According to one study, the psychological aftermath of war-zone participation in the gruesome task of handling human remains was profound (Sutker, Uddo, Brailey, Vasterling, & Errera, 1994).

People with PTSD develop hyperarousal or a persistent expectation of danger. They have an indelible imprint of the traumatic experience that can be triggered years later by traumatic reminders that cause them to have "flashbacks" in which they relive the traumatic event. They may also display a numbing response to the trauma and enter an altered state of consciousness in which they disassociate or detach themselves from reality as a defense against the traumatic experience.

According to Herman (1997), overwhelming trauma robs us of our power and autonomy. Trauma breaches the attachments of family, friendship, love, and community, undermining the belief systems that give meaning to human experiences and violating the victim's faith in a natural or divine order. More importantly, trauma destroys identity, shatters the construction of self, and robs the individual of the basic human need for safety.

The salient characteristic of traumatic events is that they cause helplessness and terror. "The terror, rage, and hatred of the traumatic moment live on in the dialectic of trauma" (Herman, 1997, p. 50). Trauma produces shame and guilt that are associated with being a victim of violence and abusiveness. We are all exposed to varying degrees of traumatic experiences, but not everyone becomes dysfunctional or traumatized because of those experiences. We learn to live with unhealed, deep emotional wounds as we go through our daily lives.

> We live in a society that is organized around unresolved traumatic experience.... [T]he effects of multigenerational trauma lie like an iceberg in our social awareness. All we see is the tip of the iceberg that is above the surface crime, community deterioration, family disintegration, and ecological degradation. What lies below the surface of our social consciousness is the basis of the problem—the ways in which unhealed trauma and loss have infiltrated and helped determine every one of our social institutions. (Bloom & Reichert, 1998, p. 9)

Violence is the primary cause of this unhealed trauma.

Violence: The Urge to Avenge

Violence is any relation, process, or condition by which an individual or a group violates the physical, social, and/or psychological integrity of another person or group. Violence seldom ends with the original violation of the victim. Violence is cyclical. Many injured individuals describe a need to avenge their hurt by retaliating against their assailants with even more violence than the victims experienced. This urge for revenge has been characterized as a basic human need. We seek revenge when we experience injustice and become outraged.

The act of avenging promotes trauma, as does the inability or powerlessness to avenge a perceived wrong or injury. Both victims and perpetrators of violence are exposed to trauma: "Traumatized people imagine that revenge will bring relief, even though the fantasy of revenge simply reverses the roles of perpetrator and victim, continuing to imprison the victim in horror, degradation, and the bounds of the perpetrator's violence" (Minow, 1998, p. 13).

In addition to direct or individual, personal violence, there exist also collective or group violence and structural violence. Collective violence is often related to group or ethnic identity. Most forms of terrorism involve collective violence, in which there is a targeted outsider, an enemy identified as the "other." In what is called the violence of differentiation, the enemy is dehumanized by myth and propaganda in order for perpetrators to justify injuring and/or killing members of the target group. In pursuit of their identity needs, groups have committed mass violence of ethnic cleansing and genocide (Staub, 1999).

The structural barriers are an important part of the cycle of violence. Robbed of meaningful social roles, status, respect, and identity in the broader society, some disenfranchised individuals turn to violence and terrorism. All societies and their institutions have degrees of structural violence that are endemic. They produce deprivation and frustration that may drive some people to commit violence in order to meet their needs (Burton, 1997).

Structural violence perhaps explains the generational dysfunction in the lifestyles of families and identity groups. The parent-child relationship is governed by societal norms. It is a relationship of unequal status and power, as is the relationship between groups in society. Parents abuse their children and powerful groups take advantage of weaker groups. Violent youth who are victims of domestic violence often victimize others in their quest for revenge. These young perpetrators of violence are also traumatized by the violent acts they commit and by witnessing the injury they inflict on others. The mimetic theory of violence explains this cycle of "paying back" for the violence one experiences.

Mimetic Structures of Violence

The mimetic theory comes from the work of Rene Girard (1977), who hypothesized that violence is generated through scapegoating and mimetic desire. The premise of mimetic desire is that people imitate the actions of others whom they admire. On first examination, it seems that victims of violence would hate, rather than admire, their assailants. However, the basic human need for power causes victims to desire the position of power that their victimizers occupy. Power and control become the objects of desire and victims identify in a positive way with that aspect of their aggressors. Victims become perpetrators in order to regain power. They model the behavior of their victimizers.

Studies show that adolescents who were abused or witnessed abuse are more likely to commit violent acts, including murder. A child who is abused imitates the violence that his family models for him. "It is accepted that violence is learned through modeling within the family" (Hardwick & Rowton-Lee, 1996, p. 265). In addition to the abuse that they suffer, children who witness unchallenged abuse at home or in the community learn that violence is normal and acceptable. "It further models aggression as a way of dealing with conflict and acting in interpersonal situations" (Staub, 1999, p. 187).

The mass media are additional significant structures of mimetic violence in American society. The bulk of media content serves primarily to model violence. Whether it is conflict-based news reporting or cultural/entertainment programming, the focus is on violence. Children absorb a steady diet of violent media content that encourages them to imitate violence and to develop a high tolerance for violence. Their heroes, role models, and objects of desire come largely from this content.

Collective violence also comes out of the rivalry between groups for desired objects—resources and power. "Thus, mimesis coupled with desire leads automatically to conflict" (Girard, 1977, p. 146) and conflict leads to violence. Possession of the desired object gives a sense of superiority, victory, revenge, honor, and/or vindication. When violence is introduced in a rivalry or conflict for an object of desire, violence is returned (imitated) but with increased intensity and severity. The violence becomes the focus of attention as it spirals out of control. "The mimetic attributes of violence are extraordinary—sometimes direct and positive, at other times indirect and negative. The more men strive to curb their violent impulses, the more these impulses seem to prosper. The very weapons used to combat violence are turned against their users. Violence is like a raging fire that feeds on the very objects intended to smother its flames" (Girard, 1977, p. 31).

The psychiatrist and author Frantz Fanon (1963, 1967) systematically examined this mimetic cycle of violence. Fanon was attempting to explain the violence that accompanied the liberation movement to end colonial rule in Africa and the Caribbean. He found that those freed from colonial masters began imitating their oppressors. They were expressing a mimetic desire for the object (power) possessed by the model, who was both admired and hated at the same time. The victim hates the oppressor or aggressor for the injury inflicted on him, but he admires the oppressor because of his position of power and control. By imitating the violence of the aggressor, the victim sheds his victimization and satisfies his urge for revenge—not by attacking his aggressor, but by victimizing those perceived to be less powerful and less desirable than himself. Often the new victim is a member of the oppressed group to which he also belongs.

Human Needs and Violence

The basic human needs have been identified as meaning, identity/belonging or connectedness, material well-being, stimulation/creativity, self-actualization, self-determination, and security/safety. These needs are assumed to be universally inherent in human beings. Theorists argue that individual personal identity, the separation of the self from others, is the most fundamental need of all humans. Among the basic needs, meaning/justice, agency/self-esteem, recognition, and dignity/respect are said to be nonnegotiable identity needs. Identity needs are objects of mimetic desire. People will engage in conflict and extreme violence to satisfy these basic needs. That violence often triggers trauma because violence robs victims of the basic human needs that make us emotionally stable and psychologically functional.

Fear produces a need for security. Anger produces a need for meaning, including for justice. Depression is the root of the need for self-esteem (Sites, 1990). Meaning is the most significant human need and it is that basic need that is deprived when a person is traumatized. He cannot make sense of his traumatic experiences because they are out of the range of normal, predictable experiences. Their incongruousness challenges the mind because the traumatic events do not fit in the schema developed over time for processing experiences. Psychological and emotional dysfunction develops as a result. The manifestations are debilitating stress, disassociation, depression, disengagement from normal social relations, and loss of a sense of safety and knowledge of self.

Violence can be prevented by satisfying the need for security and identity. Otherwise, conflicts will develop over satisfiers of those needs. The needs that are met or satisfied by violence include revenge, power, security/self-defense, and the social need of belonging. Trauma and the personal violation caused by violence rob individuals of their basic need for safety, dignity, trust, connectedness, justice, and self-worth. In order to recover or heal, victims must rid themselves of the shame, guilt, helplessness, and vulnerability they experience from the traumatic event.

Trauma invokes the basic human need or urge to avenge to restore autonomy, self-esteem, dignity, and identity. Victims of trauma and violence externalize their injury/hurt by exacting revenge against the victimizing perpetrator or the hated "other." In those cases, "Violence is idealized to enhance self-esteem and as a defensive response to an individual's (or group's) sense of entitlement to revenge" (Volkan, 1997, p. 162).

Unresolved childhood trauma is common in youth with violent behavior. Shame and humiliation destroy self-esteem and a healthy identity. Anger, rage, and violence are the original defenses against shame. "Men who assault their wives experience high levels of chronic anger, high levels of chronic trauma symptoms, a tendency to externalize the cause of their violence, and an admixture of shame and guilt about their violence" (Dutton, van Ginkel, & Starzomski, 1995, p. 211).

There is a strong relationship between shame and anger. It has been called the "shame-rage spiral" (Scheff, 1987). Shame disturbs self-identity, and negative identity promotes self-hatred and violence. Fear, hate, and rage are produced by trauma, and traumatized people have the fuel for starting and continuing violent conflict.

Identity Disorder and Violence

Needs are inextricably bound to identity and identity formation. When basic needs are not met, it leads to frustration and ultimately to violence. Those who experience trauma from abuse, violence, and acts of terror develop identity disorders, self-hatred, and fatalism, and they can become suicidal. From the psychodynamic viewpoint, all violence may be attributed to "psychotic parts of the personality" (Kernberg, 1998, p. 198). In fact, "most cases of severe violence emerge within the broad spectrum of severe personality disorders, and are seen typically in cases of the syndrome of malignant narcissism, the antisocial personality, severe, chronic self-mutilation and suicidal behavior, and severe paranoid personality disorders" (Kernberg, 1998, p. 198).

Identity crisis and identity disorder are risk factors for violent youth. Low self-esteem and self-hatred are critical elements in violent youth. Young people who are preoccupied with fantasies of death and violence can develop a "morbid identity" that enables them to kill (Hardwick et al., 1996). "Identity formation in very violent young people so far seems to have been given little specific attention. However, it is known in the abuse field that some survivors of abuse adopt a victim identity whereas others identify with the abuser and go on to be perpetrators of abuse and violence themselves" (Hardwick et al., 1996, p. 270).

People join groups in order to participate in violence or to experience violence vicariously through their membership. They also find a positive identity in the group to replace their damaged personal identity (Staub, 1999, p. 187). Terrorist groups may serve several functions, but at their core is violence. The Ku Klux Klan is an example of a terrorist group that serves the benign psychological and social needs of its casual members. However, it is part of the white supremacy movement, whose goal is "power and domination; its history, rhetoric, and analysis direct it into violence; its language draws to it people who will be capable of violence, along with many other people. Without periodically re-earning its reputation for violence, the movement would disappear. Violence is a key to understanding the multiple meanings of the movement for different kinds of members" (Ezekiel, 1995, p. xxix).

Malignant Narcissism

Identity or personality disorders motivate trauma victims and others to commit violence. Their violence is an expression of the hurt they experienced, usually in childhood. "Narcissistic personality organization develops as a defensive adaptation to childhood hurts and humiliations as well as deficiencies in self-esteem" (Volkan, 1997, p. 247).

The malignant narcissist hurts or kills others in order to feel good about himself. Aggression builds his self-esteem by making him feel powerful and dangerous. Malignant narcissism might explain the destructive behavior of gang-bangers who perpetrate much of the violence in American urban centers. These psychologically damaged individuals seek aggressive triumphs to verify their self-worth. In conditions of poverty and oppression, the currency of status and value is the degree of raw power that a person can wield. It is to the advantage of the emotionally insecure to be perceived as dangerous and threatening. The level of fear that one can evoke in this environment is directly translated into personal respect because there are few other accepted positive measures of success. Although the pattern of violence produces external public status and respect, it is born from a deep sense of personal deficiency and self-hatred.

Self-hate is converted into hatred of strangers. One's own deficiencies and inadequacies—the hated parts of one's self—are projected on the

stranger, the foreigner, and attacked in him. The hate is directed at someone who supposedly threatens the substance of the self. The enemy-other
is needed to stabilize one's self in a symbiosis of opponents. . . . It is an
entanglement in which the other experiences what is meant for oneself.
Unbearable conflicts, impulses which are defended against, destructive-
ness, and self-hate are projected onto the chosen enemy, who becomes the
target of hostility. (Streeck-Fischer, 1999, p. 261)

Terrorism: Targeted Violence

Terrorism is a violent act, or other acts that threaten human life,
and is meant to intimidate or coerce a government or segment of a
civilian population to further the political or social objectives of the
perpetrator. Those who organize formally or informally to plan and
carry out systematic targeted violence are terrorists. Terrorists use
bombings, shootings, kidnappings, hijackings, and other forms of violence primarily for political purposes. Their goal is to produce constant fear and the threat of injury or death in the target of their
violence. Terrorism causes stress because of the continual uncertainty and danger of attack. Over time, this stress can cause trauma
in the targets even if no attack is ever carried out.

The availability to and possession of guns by Americans contribute
to fear and an ongoing low level of terrorism in daily life. Random
acts of extreme violence terrorize residents and visitors in urban
areas because of the unpredictability of their occurrence. Workplace
violence and recent mass shootings add to this general fear of
coworkers. A number of highly publicized shootings has increased
fear of U.S. postal workers as a particular occupation group. "Going
postal" is now a commonly accepted term for describing workplace
shootings and a disproportionately violent response to a perceived
wrong.

American terrorists are often motivated primarily by racial animus.
To the extent that their terrorist actions are political, it is in advancing the idea that the races should not mix and that African Americans
should be sent back to Africa. An extension of this racist motive is
seen in acts of terror and ideological dogma against Catholics, Jews,
and immigrants. Among American terrorists are right-wing fringe
groups made up of white supremacists, white separatists, skinheads,
neo-Nazis, and advocates against gun control. Domestic terrorists
also include lone aggrieved individuals who are anti-government and
against state power. Gang members, wannabes, and misguided youth

infected with the racist poison of their peers and parents compose a third category of perpetrators of terrorism in the United States.

The Symbionese Liberation Army and the FALN (Fuerzas Armadas de Liberación Nacional [Armed Forces of National Liberation]) Puerto Rican separatist group were among the few domestic terrorist organizations with an obvious political motive. These left-wing organizations were active in the 1960s and 1970s but disappeared with the end of the social unrest and protests that characterized that era in American history. The Black Panther Party may also have been considered a terrorist organization with political grounding. However, the FBI weakened the organization when it arrested or killed many of the Black Panthers at the end of the 1960s.

Terrorist Leaders

Some of the most villainous leaders of modern times have been victims of personal trauma. Politicians such as Joseph Stalin, Adolf Hitler, and Slobodan Milosevic had traumatic childhood experiences that rendered them damaged goods despite their rise to power. Although it is difficult to apply clinical concepts to complex global sociopolitical phenomena, some researchers have argued that traumatized leaders have projected their unresolved trauma onto a hated "other" and galvanized popular support for their campaigns of terror, mass murder, and genocide (Gilligan, 1996; Kernberg, 1998; Staub, 1999; Volkan, 1997).

As a child, Stalin suffered abuse, serious injury, and disease that disfigured him physically and damaged his self-esteem. Stalin became an embittered, shame-filled person possessed by the thought of avenging the humiliation and injustices of his youth. One researcher argues that Stalin's infamous purges and wars were "a restaging of previous traumas" (Ihanus, 1999, p. 71). Stalin tried to boost his low self-esteem by projecting his rage onto enemies who vicariously carried "the burden of his self-hate and shame" (Ihanus, 1999, p. 75).

Adolf Hitler was abused, shamed, and humiliated by his father, who was described as "a clinical alcoholic who tyrannized his family" (Redlich, 1998, p. 8). Adolf stayed in his parents' bedroom until he was six or seven years old. He was subjected to "the common trauma of witnessing parental sexual intercourse in the shared bedroom" (Redlich, 1998, p. 14).

Hitler is infamous for advocating the superiority and purity of the Aryan race that was to make Germany great. However, records show that one of his grandfathers was of Jewish origin (Redlich, 1998, pp. 11–13). In light of his anti-Semitic ideology, Hitler's Jewish ancestry no doubt caused him emotional stress and affected his self-esteem. Researchers have concluded that the shame and humiliation he suffered at the hands of his father most likely caused Hitler's cruelty and quest for vengeance (Redlich, 1998, p. 14).

Others have argued that a national sense of shame and humiliation can also give rise to collective violence and group victimization. Hitler rose to power because he promised to undo the shame that Germans felt over previous military defeat. Hitler was able to galvanize national anger and shame of the symbolic defeat to perpetuate collective violence on the scale of genocide (Gilligan, 1996, pp. 66–69). Hitler said that shame, disgrace, and humiliation "should arouse the German people to a common sense of shame and a common hatred" of the Jews (Gilligan, 1996, p. 275).

Slobodan Milosevic, who also came from a dysfunctional family, used the shame of symbolic defeat to perpetrate mass violence. Milosevic is described by those who know him as an angry, aloof, and self-centered man who found solace from his personal hurts in the Serbian nationalistic crusade of ethnic cleansing that he conducted in the former Yugoslavia (Volkan, 1997, p. 67). Milosevic was successful in reviving the collective memory of his Serbian followers and using the chosen trauma of the group's historic defeat six hundred years earlier at the Battle of Kosovo as entitlement to avenge their loss. Like the Germans of Hitler's time, the Serbs were humiliated and powerless when Milosevic made his appeal to take vengeance by exterminating the other ethnic groups living among the Serbs in greater Yugoslavia.

We could also add Pol Pot of Cambodia and others to the list of narcissistic leaders who were responsible for the deaths and injury of untold millions. These are some of the more prominent international examples of traumatized individuals who orchestrated state-sponsored terrorism. On close examination, we find that the recent American terrorists also share this background of trauma and abuse that may have motivated them to kill and injure their fellow citizens. Hitler's racist ideology remains alive in the minds of recent American terrorists. It was especially influential with the two students who committed the mass murder at Columbine High School on April 20, 1999, the anniversary of Hitler's birth.

Trauma and the Terrorist Personality

The history of childhood victimization and trauma is not confined to the notorious political figures of our times. Based on interviews with terrorist leaders in Northern Ireland, political psychologist

Jeanne Knutson found that "all had been victims of terror themselves, all had experienced violations of their personal boundaries that damaged or destroyed their faith in personal safety" (Volkan, 1997, p. 160). These violations occurred in beatings or abandonment by parents, parental divorce, incest or other sexual abuse, and rejection by peer groups. The common element among all these terrorists was the experience of personal trauma during their formative years.

Based on my clinical hypothesis, the terrorist personality appears to develop from a painful and dysfunctional childhood in which the individual forms personality and identity disorders. The terrorist responds to his personal identity problems and attempts to strengthen his troubled internal sense of self by seeking power to hurt and by expressing entitlement to power. These psychologically damaged individuals seek power and sanction for their violent actions through membership in groups and organizations that give them a sense of shared identity in an attempt to replace their flawed personal identity.

Trauma tears apart a complex system of self-protection that normally functions in an integrated fashion (Herman, 1997). Trauma fragments the personality of its victims and drives them to the basic survival strategies of shock reflexes as a defense against the traumatic experience. The basic freeze, flight, or fight responses are limbic reflexes of a disassociative state that individuals enter in order to cope with traumatic experiences. The trauma victim may freeze in a state of numbness, flee from the threat in terror, or fight in a fit of rage in order to survive.

According to Pomeroy (1995), the "fragmented self" is exposed when trauma victims lose protection of the outer circles or boundaries of the self, leaving only the core shock reflexes of freeze, flight, and fight survival strategies. The antisocial or terrorist response to trauma originates from the shock reflex of rage. "If you don't have boundaries and you aren't able to fight, but you do have rage, then you become a terrorist" (Pomeroy, 1995, p. 97). People who have been traumatized are more likely to use violence to solve conflict and relieve stress. Theorists believe that trauma victims resort to violence because they have lost their sense of self. In turning to violence and terrorism, victims seek a substitute identity and a substitute sense of power.

The practice of bullying (teasing, taunting, threatening, and hurting a weaker person) appears to be a significant trigger for retaliatory violence and acts of terrorism. It has been recognized that "victims of abuse, including bullying, can become perpetrators who themselves often feel as though they are primarily victims" (Hardwick et al., 1996, p. 267). "Bullying contributes to the evolution of perpetrators into even more aggressive people" (Staub, 1999, p. 190). Many of the terrorists analyzed in this study were victims of bullying.

Those who experience trauma usually go through a stage of blaming themselves for allowing the traumatic event that happened to them. They also project their anger at the external perceived cause of their trauma. This struggle between the hated guilty self and the culpable assailant sets up the conditions for violence—violence against the self to end their emotional suffering or violence against others on whom they have projected their trauma. At the extremes, the trauma victim either commits suicide or homicide. Terrorists seek to kill the victimized aspects of themselves and the victimizing aspects of those they identify as aggressors or the cause of their suffering.

"Those who become terrorist leaders or their lieutenants have a psychological need to 'kill' the victimized aspects of themselves and the victimizing aspects of their aggressors that they have externalized and projected onto innocent others" (Volkan, 1997, p. 162). Streeck-Fischer (1999) also described this cycle of violence that arises out of self-hatred. Self-hate is changed to hatred for the victimizing "other." In this cycle, the rage from previous trauma is transformed into hatred. There develops a tension "between a hateful self and a threatening, hateful and hated object that needs to be controlled, to be made to suffer, to be destroyed" (Kernberg, 1998, p. 203).

Trauma victims sometimes join groups to rid themselves of their victimization and to repair their damaged self-image. They often are attracted to violent organizations like the Ku Klux Klan or the neo-Nazis because of their need to identify with a figure of power and success. Hitler and his Third Reich appeal to these individuals who see in them a powerful conqueror of Europe obliterating the hated enemy. Fascism appeals to feelings of powerlessness. Hitler rose to power by addressing a national sense of defeat, humiliation, isolation, and powerlessness of the Germans. Although their members seek power and safety in these organizations, "Fear is at the center of these groups, fear and a sense of isolation. Belonging to the group affords comradeship within struggle. The mythical 'white race' is the larger family for which these spiritual orphans long" (Ezekiel, 1995, p. xxv).

Some members of the white supremacist organizations develop the terrorist personality. These members form underground cells and become a "Klan within the Klan." The added secrecy and conspiracy of their cells satisfy the psychological needs of these individuals. Often the overriding need is to commit violent acts of revenge. The individual who acts is the real engine of the organization. He is the terrorist. "He believes the ideology literally, word for word—there is an Enemy, the Enemy is Evil. He believes that ideology because he wants it: He wants the grounds for radical action. He must have radical action. Violence is the language in which he can speak his message; his spirit needs the comradeship of the tight terrorist cell" (Ezekiel, 1995, p. xxxi).

American Terrorists

I will now examine four instances of terrorism in America. They involve white supremacist organizations, a mentally ill individual, a right-wing political zealot, and young men who carried out mass shootings in their schools. Analysis of these terrorists shows some common themes in their childhood experiences. The common element among all these terrorists is unresolved trauma. They reported being filled with shame, humiliation, rage, and hatred. These are all elements in the mimetic cycle of violence as described earlier in this chapter.

Many of these victimized individuals sought membership and acceptance in terrorist groups to compensate for their identity disorders and low self-esteem. The racist ideology that the terrorist white supremacist groups espouse offers a venue for traumatized individuals to seek revenge for the abuse and bullying that they experienced. These similarities support my clinical hypothesis that unresolved trauma motivates victims to repeat the cycle of violence by becoming perpetrators in an attempt to avenge their victimization.

The KKK: Defending the U.S.A.

The Ku Klux Klan is the oldest and most persistent American terrorist organization. The Klan was, at one time, a state-sanctioned, if not state-sponsored, terrorist organization. In the 1920s, the Klan was the official law enforcement agency in many states, including Indiana. In most Southern states, Klan membership was the unofficial ticket to power and status. Those in political office and in the police ranks were Klan members or Klan supporters representing the Jim Crow segregation that was the legal order of the day.

The original Ku Klux Klan was organized at Pulaski, Tennessee, in May 1866 by ex-Confederate elements that wanted to maintain white supremacy in Southern communities after the Civil War. The Klan feared that outraged former black slaves would cause an insurrection. Dressed in flowing white sheets, their faces covered with white masks, and with skulls at their saddle horns, Klan members posed as spirits of the Confederate dead returned from the battlefields. Although the Klan was often able to achieve its aims by terror alone, it also used whippings and lynchings against blacks and political opponents.

> These lynchings were meant to terrorize the black population and keep it quiescent and under white control. Many of the victims were burned alive, chained to iron stakes that had been driven into the ground; others were hanged. The lucky ones were shot soon after the burning or the hanging began; there are many accounts, however, of desperate men crawling from the flames and being pushed back in. The newspaper accounts are grueling, the cruelty astonishing. Bodies were slashed; fingers were cut off. Often the victim's testicles or penis were cut off. (Ezekiel, 1995, p. 311)

In 1915, the Klan added to its white supremacy an intense nativism, anti-Catholicism, and anti-Semitism. It furnished an outlet for the militant patriotism aroused by World War I and it stressed fundamentalism in religion. Civil rights activities in the South during the 1960s helped to strengthen the Klan. The Klan had a resurgence of popular support in the early 1990s that culminated in the candidacy of Klansman David Duke for elected office in Louisiana.

The continued existence of the Klan and other white supremacist organizations demonstrates the deep roots that racism has in American culture. There are still three or four main Klan groups operating in the United States. There are about 30 neo-Nazi groups and more than a hundred active skinhead organizations. Together they were responsible for hundreds of assaults and 108 murders between 1990 and 1993, according to figures from various organizations that monitor these terrorist hate groups.

The Klan has slowly been merging with the other white supremacist organizations. What binds them together is the Christian Identity theology. This doctrine was imported from Europe. It posits that the Aryan peoples of Northern Europe—whites only—are the true chosen children of God, the lost tribes of Israel. This racist ideology teaches that only whites are human and the dark races or "mud people" resulted from whites mating with animals. Jews are seen as the evil spawn of Eve mating with the Serpent, or Satan. Christian Identity adherents argue that God has called his chosen people to North America so they can fulfill God's plan for them to dominate the earth, rule over the dark races, and fight to the death to eliminate the Jews.

While the motives for joining white supremacist groups may be many, researchers who have studied and interviewed members of the Klan, neo-Nazis, and skinheads have found that the white racist movement allows members to feel like victims who have been unjustly victimized. They want, and need, to belong to a group so that they can feel better about themselves and have the sense that they are part of a group that is acting for the greater good of the victimized group.

For several years, Raphael Ezekiel studied a neo-Nazi group in Detroit. He found that the group was made up of young urban whites who feared blacks because they bullied them in school and on the city streets. They faced violence and fighting to survive or defend their honor when teased or bullied in their racially divided city. The youngsters sought refuge in the terrorist group from the structural violence of urban poverty. Their lives were characterized by personal loss and trauma. All of them suffered the loss of a parent through separation, divorce, or death. They came from dysfunctional families in which they experienced violence from alcoholic and abusive parents. Every member of the group had experienced the trauma of childhood diseases or of being born with physical deficiencies.

The fundamental reason for joining the supremacist group was terror. "These were people who at a deep level felt terror that they were about to be extinguished. They felt that their lives might disappear at any moment. They felt that they might be blown away by the next wind" (Ezekiel, 1995, p. 156). Through membership in the group, they tried to find power over the perceived oppressor or threat to their survival. They were also seeking meaningful relationships and a sense of belonging to find their identity and build self-esteem.

The Unabomber: A Lone Ranger

Theodore Kaczynski represents the lone individuals who become terrorists because they are emotionally unstable. Kaczynski was a brilliant mathematician who graduated from Harvard University. He was on the faculty at the University of California–Berkeley before mental illness drove him to a hermit's existence in a small cabin in the wilderness of Montana. There he wrote his manifesto, stating his goal to destroy the existing form of society. He claimed to be fighting against those who were corrupting America with technology. Between 1978 and 1995, Kaczynski conducted a campaign of terror by sending 16 mail bombs to businesspeople and academics in seven different states. Nicknamed the Unabomber, he eluded police for 17 years, until his brother turned him in for a reward offered by the FBI. Kaczynski's bombs killed 3 people and injured 23 others. He is now serving four consecutive life sentences plus 30 years in federal prison.

Sally Johnson, chief psychiatrist and associate warden of health services at the Federal Correctional Institution in Butner, North Carolina, wrote a forensic report of Kaczynski's mental condition. He was diagnosed with paranoid schizophrenia. Johnson made her evaluation after interviewing Kaczynski, his family, and people who knew him. She also analyzed psychological tests and studied the Unabomber's journals, which document more than 40 years of his life. The Ninth Circuit Court of Appeals in San Francisco ruled that the psychiatric report should be made public in order to provide a better understanding of the Unabomber's motivations. The events of his life discussed below were taken from that psychiatric report (Johnson 1998).

Kaczynski's life of trauma apparently started very early. As a result of an allergic reaction, he was hospitalized for several days when he was approximately nine months old. Kaczynski's mother reported that the hospitalization was a significant and traumatic event for her son because he experienced a separation from her. She described him as having changed after the hospitalization. He became withdrawn, less responsive, and more fearful of separation from her after that point. Kaczynski said that he was abused during childhood. He described the abuse as severe verbal psychological abuse. Kaczynski constantly sought an apology from his parents for emotionally abusing him.

Kaczynski identified two events in his life as being highly significant and triggering episodes of depression. The first was when he skipped directly from the fifth grade to the seventh. He said he did not fit in with the older children and that he endured considerable hostility, verbal abuse, and teasing from them. He said that, "By the time I left high school, I was definitely regarded as a freak by a large segment of the student body" (Johnson, 1998).

Kaczynski said that during high school and college, he would often become terribly angry and because he could not express that anger or hatred openly, he would indulge in fantasies of revenge. However, he was afraid to act on his fantasies, and described himself as having frustrated resentment toward school, parents, and the student body. During his college years, he also had fantasies of living a primitive life and envisioned himself as "an agitator, rousing mobs to frenzies of revolutionary violence" (Johnson, 1998).

The second pivotal incident came when he was 25 and a graduate student at the University of Michigan. Kaczynski sought psychiatric help after experiencing several weeks of intense and persistent sexual excitement involving fantasies of being a female. He decided to undergo sex change surgery that required a psychiatric referral. He set up an appointment with a psychiatrist at the university health center. While in the waiting room, he became anxious and humiliated over the prospect of talking to the psychiatrist about his problem. When the doctor arrived, Kaczynski did not discuss his real concerns, but rather claimed he was feeling some depression and anxiety over the possibility that he would be drafted into the military. Kaczynski describes leaving the office and feeling rage, shame, and humiliation over this attempt to seek evaluation.

Kaczynski said,

> As I walked away from the building afterwards, I felt disgusted about what my uncontrolled sexual cravings had almost led me to do and I felt—humiliated, and I violently hated the psychiatrist. Just then there came a major turning point in my life. . . . I thought I wanted to kill that psychiatrist because the future looked utterly empty to me. I felt I wouldn't care if I died. And so I said to myself why not really kill the psychiatrist and anyone else whom I hate. What is important is not the words that ran through my mind but the way I felt about them. What was entirely new was the fact that I really felt I could kill someone. My very hopelessness had liberated me because I no longer cared about death. I no longer cared about consequences and I said to myself that I really could break out of my rut in life and do things that were daring, irresponsible or criminal. (Johnson, 1998)

Kaczynski described the source of his hatred as social rejection and the "fact that organized society frustrates my very powerful urge for physical freedom and personal autonomy." He also described experiencing anger from other sources and then turning his hatred toward organized society.

McVeigh: The Neo-Nazi Patriot

Timothy McVeigh, the Oklahoma City bomber, committed the greatest act of terrorism ever perpetrated against Americans by an American. On April 19, 1995, McVeigh killed 168 people and injured 642 others when he blew up the Murrah Federal Building with a truck bomb. He had suffered war trauma during military service in the Persian Gulf. He was a victim of bullying and humiliation in his childhood. McVeigh also carried psychological scars from his parents' three separations and their eventual divorce.

McVeigh was on a crusade against the U.S. government, which he saw as a bully and a threat to the right-wing values he espoused. McVeigh contended that his terrorist act was in revenge for the government's killing of his right-wing compatriots at Waco and at Ruby Ridge. He maintained that he was a political martyr and said his death sentence was nothing more than state-assisted suicide. While on death row, McVeigh called himself a patriot who was fighting for the greater good against a bullying government. In defiance, he said he would invoke the text of the poem "Invictus" as a final statement before his execution. The poem talks of going "beyond this place of wrath and tears." He got his final wish on June 11, 2001, in an execution chamber at the federal prison in Terre Haute, Indiana.

In his fit of wrath and revenge, McVeigh chose April 19 for his attack, to coincide with the anniversary of the government's assault on the Branch Davidian compound in Waco, Texas, on April 19, 1993. McVeigh and his accomplices were associated with a right-wing militia group and were probably aware that the first shot of the Revolutionary War was fired on April 19, 1775, at the Battle of Lexington. A major issue in that war was the right to bear arms. McVeigh's attack was also coincidentally close to Hitler's birthday—April 20. Despite the racist political ideology that surrounded McVeigh's crusade, it was the boost to self-esteem that he found in the right to own and use weapons that led him on his path to being a patriot.

McVeigh's first encounter with a bully came on the Little League baseball field. The bully punched McVeigh and he fled to the family car to weep. He was humiliated and embarrassed in front of his team. The incident further injured his pride because he was not very athletic and he already felt a failure in the eyes of his father, who was an accomplished softball player. "But that humiliation on the Little League field—at the hands of a bully—was something he would remember forever. Over time, he would develop a seething hatred of bullies—or any person, institution or even nation that seemed to be picking on the weak" (Michel & Herbeck, 2001, p. 20).

Young McVeigh was close to his grandfather, who taught him how to handle guns, and the boy used his skills with firearms to build his self-esteem. McVeigh developed a fascination with guns and, when he got older, he built a shooting range in his backyard to hone his skills as a marksman. He became part of the gun culture and read gun magazines such as *Soldier of Fortune*. McVeigh saw an advertisement in the magazine that prompted him to buy *The Turner Diaries*. The book tells the story of a gun enthusiast who reacted to laws restricting firearms by making a truck bomb and destroying the FBI headquarters in Washington, D.C. The novel also promotes Hitler's racist ideology advocating the killing of blacks and Jews, whom Hitler considered inherently evil. McVeigh said he liked the book because of its support for the rights of gun owners and not because of its racist content (Michel et al., 2001, p. 39).

McVeigh soon tired of his life centered on shooting expensive guns. He joined the Army in May 1988. It was his experience as a soldier in the Persian Gulf War that traumatized McVeigh and so enraged him against injustice that he decided to take revenge on the U.S. government by bombing the federal building in Oklahoma City.

McVeigh rose through the ranks to become an Army sergeant. He was awarded the Bronze Star and the coveted Combat Infantry Badge. One of McVeigh's experiences while fighting in Iraq was to use a Bradley armored vehicle to bulldoze Iraqi soldiers and bury them alive in their trenches. Some accounts allege that McVeigh had to scrape the body parts of enemy soldiers off the tracks of his tank. A soldier who fought with McVeigh said their unit made ready for battle by chanting, "Blood makes the grass grow. Kill! Kill! Kill!"

After his discharge from the Army in 1992, McVeigh went to a Veteran's Administration hospital in Florida because he was horrified by memories of the Iraqi soldiers he had killed in the Gulf War. The staff turned him away because he sought counseling under an assumed name (Michel & et al., 2001, p. 288).

In an interview with CBS Television, McVeigh placed emphasis on his experiences as a soldier. He said the war disillusioned him and deepened his anger against the government. He apparently hoped that the bombing of the federal facility would precipitate a civil war and ultimately the overthrow of the government by rightist militia forces. In the interview, McVeigh said his anger against the federal government was deepened by the killing of right-wing activist Randy Weaver's wife and son by federal agents at Ruby Ridge, Idaho, in 1992 and by the killing of some 80 members of the Branch Davidian religious sect in Waco.

Based on what is known about mimetic violence and the revenge motive, we could conclude that the Oklahoma City bombing was a result of untreated war trauma. When he attacked the Murrah Federal

Building, McVeigh carried out a traumatic reenactment of the violence he experienced during the Gulf War.

The Columbine Massacre

On April 20, 1999, Dylan Klebold and Eric Harris shot to death 11 students and a teacher and wounded 24 other students at Columbine High School in Littleton, Colorado. They then killed themselves. The two 18-year-old gunmen were filled with hatred and rage. They planted pipe bombs and other explosives in the school in an attempt to destroy the building. Their homemade arsenal included 48 carbon dioxide bombs, 27 pipe bombs, 11 propane containers, 7 incendiary devices with more than 40 gallons of flammable liquid, hand grenades, and 2 duffel bag bombs with 20-pound liquefied petroleum tanks.

There has been some debate about the motives of the Columbine terrorists. However, police investigators concluded that Klebold and Harris planned the shooting as a suicide mission driven by their indiscriminate hate and their intention to wipe out most of their classmates and teachers. There is ample evidence that Harris and Klebold were bullied, ostracized, and alienated by their schoolmates.

Like Timothy McVeigh, the teenage gunmen also considered their attack on Columbine High School to be a "military operation" against a bully. War and the military fascinated both Klebold and Harris. The Columbine terrorists were preoccupied with violence. Harris kept a journal in which he raged against everyone, including minorities and whites. It even included ranting against racism. His diary opens with the telling phrase, "I hate the fucking world." Harris maintained a Web site that was replete with violent content. Two years before the attack, Klebold wrote in his journal that he would go on a "killing spree." Their class writing assignments focused on killing and on mass murderer Jeffrey Dahmer. The two also made a video for a class project in which they dramatized the shooting that they eventually carried out.

Harris apparently shared the anti-gun-control sentiments that McVeigh held. Harris wrote angry and profanity-filled comments in his journal criticizing the passage of the Brady Bill, which requires background checks and a waiting period before the purchase of a weapon. Harris was concerned that he would not be able to obtain a gun because of the law. He said he wanted the weapon for "personal protection." According to him, "It's not like I'm some psycho who would go on a shooting spree" (Dedman, 2000).

The Columbine killers also had racial and genocidal motives, as evidenced by the content of their diaries and their fascination with vengeful and hate-driven Nazi ideology. Harris's journal contained statements praising Hitler's "final solution." Their schoolmates said Klebold and Harris belonged to a group called the "Trench Coat Mafia." They worshipped Hitler and addressed each other in German. The two also wore swastikas and armbands proclaiming, "I hate people." Their classmates reported that the two played war games with cards and the winner gave the "Heil Hitler" salute.

In seeking to attract attention, terrorists carefully choose the date and place of their attack. Klebold and Harris chose April 20, Hitler's birthday, to carry out the Columbine massacre. They had originally planned the attack for April 19, the anniversary of the Oklahoma City bombing. They said in their writings that they intended to "top the body count" of McVeigh's bombing in their attack at the school.

Other School Shooters

Most of the other recent perpetrators of shootings in American schools also lacked the political motive or agenda typical of terrorists. These young people, almost exclusively males, experienced trauma and were driven by the desire for revenge against peers who bullied or humiliated them. Nine school shootings have occurred since the Columbine shooting. Another dozen were foiled when concerned students reported the planned attacks to police and school officials. There is evidence that aggrieved students may be mimicking the actions of the Columbine shooters. The trend has educators, parents, and students worried that the next terrorist attack may occur at their school.

Charles Andrew Williams is typical of these abused and enraged school shooters. "His schoolmates bullied him. His mother rarely saw him. His father neglected him. Even his friends taunted him—and may well have goaded him into his shooting rampage" (McCarthy, 2001, p. 24). When Williams told classmates at Santana High School that he was going to "pull a Columbine," they did not believe he would shoot his peers. "Two of his friends called him a 'pussy' and dared him to do it" (McCarthy, 2001, p. 24). He did it a few days later on March 5, 2001, when he killed 2 students and wounded 13 others at the school in Santee, California.

The U.S. Secret Service published a report on school violence based on information about 41 shooters, ages 11 to 21, who were involved in 37 school shooting incidents between 1974 and 2000. Data for the study was collected from journals and interviews with friends of the shooters and from the adolescents who were incarcerated (U.S. Secret Service, 2000, p. 2). The patterns and themes that emerged from the study mirror those present in the Columbine shooting and the other cases of terrorism discussed in this chapter.

Fantasy thoughts about revenge were a common motive mentioned, along with despair, hate, and rage. The students who turned on their peers had lost their hope and faith in people. Some wrote of desperation associated with aggressive acts. Kip Kinkel of Springfield, Oregon, wrote, "Hate drives me . . . I am so full of rage . . . Everyone is against me . . . As soon as my hope is gone, people die" (Dedman, 2000). On May 21, 1998, a day after he murdered his parents, Kinkel killed 2 students and wounded 26 others.

The Secret Service study found that two thirds of the attackers had been bullied and tormented by other children. The students who used guns at school did not just snap and kill on impulse. More than three-fourths planned their attack in advance after airing grievances at school. More than half described revenge as a motive for their attack. The shooters were obsessed with violence and their self-esteem and identity became invested in getting even.

More than half of the shooters experienced extreme depression and anxiety. Three-fourths had an important loss in relationships, a humiliating failure, or a loss of status with their peers before the shooting. They did not have the coping skills to deal with loss, shame, and embarrassment. Three-fourths of the students had mentioned suicide or made suicidal gestures. Half threatened to kill themselves before the attacks and six killed themselves during the attack.

Time magazine published a comprehensive study of school shooters in its May 28, 2001, issue. A team of journalists analyzed the lives of 12 school shooters "who had terrified their classmates and periodically traumatized the nation since 1997" (Roche, 2001, p. 34). They were all males who committed their crimes when they were between 11 and 18 years old.

The team of journalists interviewed some of the shooters, along with psychologists and law enforcement officials who evaluated them. They concluded that "almost all the shooters were expressing rage, either against a particular person for a particular affront or, more often, against a whole cohort of bullying classmates" (Roche, 2001, p. 34). One of the shooters told a psychiatrist that he felt going to prison would be better than continuing to endure bullying at school.

Evan Ramsey was bullied, demeaned, teased, taunted, and assaulted by his peers at Bethel Regional High School in Bethel, Alaska. On February 19, 1997, 16-year-old Ramsey took a shotgun to school and killed the principal and one student and wounded two others.

Ramsey was fueled by anger and the urge to avenge years of humiliation at the hands of his schoolmates. He admitted that he shot his schoolmates because he was "sick of being picked on in school."

The *Time* report quotes Park Dietz, a forensic psychiatrist who has interviewed numerous school shooters. Dietz said the shooters tend to have in common "some degree of depression, considerable anger, access to weapons that they aren't ready to have, and a role model salient in their memory" (Roche, 2001, p. 38). Dietz told a *Time* reporter that, so far, the role models for the shooters have "always been a mass murderer who has been given ample coverage in your magazine" (Roche, 2001, p. 38).

The journalists said that if the shooters were not suffering overtly from mental illness before their crimes, many of them clearly are now. Eight of the 12 convicted terrorists that *Time* interviewed have had some sort of mental disorder diagnosed since their crimes. These include depression, personality disorders, and schizophrenia. Most are plagued by nightmares and insomnia. For some, guilt and remorse about their crimes have added to their emotional problems. For all, the severed family relationships, isolation, and boredom of prison life are taking their toll.

Psychologists say that these young terrorists are likely to be suicidal for much of their lives and will suffer repeated flashbacks characteristic of the trauma that they inflicted on their victims who survived the attack or witnessed the killing of their peers. The cycle of violence and trauma is clearly seen in the trauma that these perpetrators are now experiencing in prison. If they were not traumatized before their crimes, they certainly were traumatized as a consequence of their crimes.

Conclusion: Violence, Trauma, and Terrorism

The American terrorists analyzed provide some support for the clinical hypothesis that unresolved trauma may play a significant role in the cycle of violence being carried out by terrorists. Abuse and childhood trauma are common to the terrorists analyzed for this study. Violence produces trauma. Trauma produces rage. Rage produces hatred. Hatred produces antisocial, violent, terrorist behavior. Victims create other victims. It is an unquenchable circle of fire that fuels itself.

By examining the personality of the perpetrator, we find evidence that unresolved personal trauma produces narcissistic and paranoid leaders who use historical group trauma, or chosen trauma, to move the masses to murder. Individuals who were victimized perpetuate the cycle of violence by seeking revenge for their psychological injuries. Rage over perceived injustice and the desire for revenge were the primary motives for the American terrorists examined in this study.

Youth who are going through identity formation are more susceptible to mimetic desire and mimetic violence. They imitate the violent actions of their abusive families, peers, and role models who influence and shape their identity. They also return (avenge) the violence they experienced in order to assert power and control over perceived weaker victims than themselves. Most of the young school shooters were victims of peer bullying. They imitated violence as a solution to their self-esteem and identity problems and as a satisfier of their basic needs.

Trauma, identity disorder, and low self-esteem lead to self-hatred. Violence is then directed against the hated self. Once the self is robbed of worth and value, numbing, disassociation, hopelessness, and fatalism set in. This leads to violence against the self (suicide) and violence against the "other" (homicide) who is also judged to be of no significance or worth. In one sense, perpetrators of violence kill themselves first and then they kill others. Their violence against others is an expression of their self-hatred and unresolved trauma.

References

Bloom, S., & Reichert, M. (1998). *Bearing witness violence and collective responsibility.* New York: Haworth Press.

Burton, J. (1997). *Violence explained: The sources of conflict, violence and crime and their prevention.* Manchester, England: Manchester University Press.

Dedman, B. (2000, October 15). School shooters: Secret Service findings. *Chicago Sun-Times.* Retrieved March 1, 2001, from http://www.suntimes.com/shoot/find15.html.

Dutton, D., van Ginkel, C., & Starzomski, A. (1995). The role of shame and guilt in the intergenerational transmission of abusiveness. *Violence and Victims, 10,* 121–131.

Ezekiel, R. S. (1995). *The racist mind portraits of American neo-Nazis and Klansmen.* New York: Viking Penguin.

Fanon, F. (1963). *The wretched of the earth* (C. Farrington, Trans.). New York: Grove Press. (Original work published 1961.)

Fanon, F. (1967). *Black skin white masks* (C. Markmann, Trans.). New York: Grove Press. (Original work published 1952.)

Gilligan, J. (1996). *Violence: Our deadly epidemic and its causes.* New York: G. P. Putnam's Sons.

Girard, R. (1977). *Violence and the sacred* (P. Gregory, Trans.). Baltimore: Johns Hopkins University Press. (Original work published 1972.)

Hardwick, P., & Rowton-Lee, M. (1996). Adolescent homicide: Towards assessment of risk. *Journal of Adolescence, 19,* 263–276.

Herman, J. (1997). *Trauma and recovery.* New York: Basic Books.

Ihanus, J. (1999). Water, birth and Stalin's thirst for power: Psychohistorical roots of terror. *The Journal of Psychohistory, 27,* 67–84.

Johnson, S. (1998, January 16). *Forensic evaluation of Theodore John Kaczynski.* Docket number CR S-96–256 GEB. San Francisco: Ninth Circuit Court of Appeals.

Kernberg, O. (1998). Aggression, hatred, and social violence. *Canadian Journal of Psychoanalysis, 6,* 191–206.

Kulka, R. A., Schlenger, W. E., Fairbank, J. A., Hough, R. L., Jordan, B. K., Marmar, C. R., & Weiss, D. S. (1990). *Trauma and the Vietnam War generation: Report of findings from the National Vietnam Veterans Readjustment Study.* New York: Brunner/Mazel.

McCarthy, T. (2001, March 19). Warning. *Time, 157,* 24–28.

Michel, L., & Herbeck, D. (2001). *American terrorist Timothy McVeigh and the Oklahoma City bombing.* New York: HarperCollins.

Minow, M. (1998). *Between vengeance and forgiveness: Facing history after genocide and mass violence.* Boston: Beacon Press.

Pomeroy, W. (1995). A working model for trauma: The relationship between trauma and violence. *Pre- and Perinatal Psychology Journal, 10,* 89–101.

Redlich, F. (1998). *Hitler: Diagnosis of a destructive prophet.* New York: Oxford University Press.

Roche, T. (2001, May 28). Voices from the cell. *Time, 157,* 32–38.

Scheff, T. J. (1987). The shame-rage spiral. A case study of an interminable quarrel. In H. B. Lewis (Ed.), *The role of shame in symptom formation* (pp. 109–140). Hillsdale, NJ: Erlbaum.

Sites, P. (1990). Needs as analogues of emotions. In J. Burton (Ed.), *Conflict: Human needs theory* (pp. 7–33). New York: St. Martin's Press.

Staub, E. (1999). The roots of evil: Social conditions, culture, personality, and basic human needs. *Personality and Social Psychology Review, 3,* 179–192.

Streeck-Fischer, A. (1999). Xenophobia and violence by adolescent skinheads. In *Trauma and adolescence* (pp. 251–269). Madison, CT: International University Press.

Sutker, P., Uddo, M. M., Brailey, K., Vasterling, J., & Errera, P. (1994). Psychopathology in war-zone deployed and nondeployed Operation Desert Storm troops assigned graves registration duties. *Journal of Abnormal Psychology, 103,* 383–390.

U.S. Secret Service (2000, October). *An interim report on the prevention of targeted violence in schools.* Washington: U.S. Secret Service National Threat Assessment Center.

Volkan, V. (1997). *Bloodlines from ethnic pride to ethnic terrorism.* New York: Farrar, Straus and Giroux.

Wolfe, J., & Proctor, S. (1996). The Persian Gulf War: New findings on traumatic exposure and stress. *PTSD Research Quarterly, 7,* 1–7.

CHAPTER 4

Us & Them: Reducing the Risk of Terrorism

Stephen D. Fabick

We must live together as brothers, or perish together as fools.
—*Martin Luther King, Jr.*

As the world gets smaller—with CNN, the Internet, and transportation advances—different cultural groups have more contact with each other. With this comes the opportunity for greater understanding, but also greater conflict. Our enhanced technology requires an enhanced psychology. Our world no longer has the luxury of easy answers such as blind tribal loyalty, ingroup aggrandizement, and outgroup dismissal and disdain.

In a more interdependent world, collaboration trumps competition in the long run, even for the powerful. Wise leaders of powerful groups realize the transitory nature of such a power imbalance. And in a world in which terrorism is the seductive equalizer,[1] the powerful have no other choice ultimately. The asymmetrical warfare of terrorism requires a reassessment of the ways to deal with such threats. Transformative thinking is needed in a world where survival depends more on cooperation than on competition.

Such thinking starts on a personal level with the appreciation that the disenfranchised poor are no less important than others. And it continues with the realization that countries with the highest disparity in wealth have the greatest incidence of stress, violence, and crime (Albee, 2000). Such transformative vision then extends to the powerful fully understanding the sense of threat that others can feel is posed by their greater power, and the privileged having sensitivity to the envy fostered by their bounty and appreciation of the resentment kindled by their higher status. Teddy Roosevelt recognized that those wielding a big stick must speak softly.

It has been argued that people in the majority may be no more prejudiced than people in the minority. But the disenfranchised cannot be oppressive or racist, since such structural violence rests not just on prejudice but also on power. So, because the powerful have more impact socially, economically, militarily, and psychologically, so too do they have greater responsibility to exercise intergroup care and judgment.

Americans don't have to look elsewhere to see the effects of oppression. The original purpose of slavery in America was to maintain an economic advantage for the labor-intensive industries of the South. Unlike slaves in some societies in which prisoners of war were enslaved, American slaves were dehumanized. The residue of this evil is apparent. Though black men constitute less than 6 percent of the general U.S. population, they account for 48 percent of the state prison population (Haney & Zimbardo, 1998). And gross economic disparity continues unabated between blacks and whites in America. Though the majority of whites today are not personally responsible for this problem—that is, they are not racist—they benefit from their "white privilege" and thus are primarily responsible for fixing the problem (McIntosh, 1988). And because of their greater power, whites are more able to effect such change. This burden of American power, a form of modern-day *noblesse oblige*, extends to international relations.

As Benjamin Barber points out in *Jihad vs. McWorld* (1996), many Muslims fear the encroachment of Western culture, i.e., a cultural genocide. Westerners don't need to apologize for everything about themselves, but need to be sensitive to the fears of Muslims. And the West may learn something from its adversaries that can't be learned from its allies. The history of the loss of advantage by a dominant group suggests that for every loss there is a gain. As men in the West have lost some competitive edge at the office, they have gained in their enhanced role in parenting. What can the West learn?

Westerners' greatest "ism" is not racism or nationalism, but materialism. Conversations center on consumption. Western men tend to discuss the acquisition of wealth, e.g., their investments and jobs, and Western women their consumption, e.g., shopping, restaurants, and vacations. The poor in the West shoot each other for jewelry and expensive athletic shoes. Perhaps what the West stands to gain the most from an attunement and responsiveness to the Muslim world is a personal and spiritual renewal. A sense of such an awakening was manifest in New York after the 2001 World Trade Center attack. Martin Luther King, Jr., saw the connection between materialism and racism (Wallis, 1994, p. 136):

> We must rapidly . . . shift from a "thing"-oriented society to a "person"-oriented society. When machines and computers, profit motives and property rights are considered more important than people, the giant triplets of racism, materialism and militarism are incapable of being conquered.

Relevance

Are psychological theory, research, and practice relevant in the "War Against Terrorism"? We have seen that multinational military intervention has a place, as does the "dirty business" of intelligence gathering. Certainly, diplomacy plays an essential role in countering the risk of terrorism. But what about psychology? Some track II diplomacy (working with midlevel leaders from large groups in protracted conflicts) relies directly upon psychological research and skills (Rouhana & Kelman, 1994; Lederach, 1995). Reich (1998, p. 279) concludes that psychological research has an important role in the understanding of terrorism:

> Most important for psychological researchers is the need to remember that terrorism is a complicated, diverse, and multidetermined phenomenon that resists simple definition, undermines all efforts at objectivity, forces upon all researchers moral riddles of confounding complexity, and is as challenging to our intellectual efforts to understand it as it is to our collective efforts to control it. It is an example and product of human interaction gone awry and is worth studying and understanding it in the human terms that befit it: as conflict, struggle, passion, drama, myth, history, reality, and, not least, psychology.

However, in applying social science to the understanding of terrorism, we must be cautious, since terrorism is essentially a political phenomenon. We cannot easily extrapolate what is known about violent people in general to terrorists. Kellen (cited in Reich, 1998, p. 49) states,

> Most violent people are not terrorists. What characterizes terrorists is the political, or pseudopolitical, component of their motivations, which

ordinary violent people lack. Terrorists . . . have the comparatively rare personality combination of the intellectual (albeit usually not brilliant ones) and the physically violent person in the extreme.

Furthermore, psychologists should not pathologize terrorists' personalities. Hoffman (1998, p. 158) stated, "Contrary to both popular belief and media depiction, most terrorism is neither crazed nor capricious." Terrorists don't voluntarily seek out psychological assessment or treatment. Even when social scientists have access to them after they have been captured, examination of the development of their radicalization is, by definition, post hoc. It is therefore processed through the filter of selective memory and self-justification, as well as intentional omission and deliberate distortion due to judicial contingencies and promotion of the particular political agenda of the terrorist. But they do seek media attention and converts. So terrorists' thinking has been examined in their writings and pronouncements. Overall, researchers (Jager, Schmidtchen, & Sullwold, 1981) who have studied terrorist personalities have concluded that there is no terrorist personality per se. That is, the type of person drawn to and radicalized into a terrorist subculture is unique to the particular political and social context. A terrorist is further socialized and radicalized once within the terrorist group. Moreover, the more insular the group from mainstream society, the greater the likelihood of its members' developing idiosyncratic thinking over time.

Researchers have identified some personality patterns, however. For example, left-wing terrorists are typically more educated, more middle class, and less indiscriminately violent than right-wing terrorists. Religious terrorists tend to be more violent than secular terrorists given the formers' tendency to see the targeted group as infidels. "Holy terrorists" justify more extreme forms of violence by seeing it as retribution for the nonbelievers' immorality, i.e., a "divine duty" (Hoffman, 1995).

Paraphrasing several authors, Reich (1998, p. 27) shows that terrorists have been described as action-oriented, aggressive, stimulus-hungry, and excitement-seeking. Particularly striking is their reliance upon the defenses of externalization and splitting. They exhibit a suspension of rational and empathic thinking in a compartmentalized way about their cause and about the humanity of target outgroup individuals. And though there is some support for psychological motivations such as abusive and neglectful relationships with parents playing some role in vengeance toward authority figures (Jager et al., 1981), there are no control group studies. And, as previously mentioned, each situation needs to be examined given the multiplicity of variables across societies in which terrorism has manifested. Overall, cultural and political factors may weigh more heavily in the development of a terrorist than individual personality.

Given the commonly reported tendency of terrorists to externalize blame to the target group, to split good and bad into "us" and "them" respectively, to justify their actions, and to dehumanize "them," it makes sense to draw upon the body of research that has addressed such intergroup tendencies, i.e., studies of prejudice and intergroup conflict. Since terrorism is one of the most extreme manifestations of prejudice and conflict that minority group members can perpetrate, it is reasonable to apply such research in our efforts to delineate new paradigms for the research. It also stands to reason that applied programs in intergroup and conflict reduction are relevant in the nascent psychosocial field of terrorism risk reduction.

There is a wealth of research and applied programs in the related areas of conflict resolution (Deutsch & Coleman, 2000) and prejudice reduction (Oskamp, 2000). Much work in social psychology has been done on why individuals identify with a certain group—their reference group—and counteridentify with another (Tajfel & Turner, 1979; Turner, 1985). Such work is relevant to understanding issues of terrorist development and recruitment as well as the support that such individuals receive socially, economically, and politically within their communities.

Research has clarified the conditions under which intergroup prejudice (Oskamp, 2000) and conflict (Fisher & Keashly, 1991) escalate, and aspects of this should apply to the intensification of terrorist threat. Even some work on the identification of types of individuals who are prone to bifurcation of good in their own racial or ethnic group and bad in targeted outgroups (Duckitt, 1992) may help our understanding of people drawn to terrorist action. Such identification might be useful in terms of discriminative profiling for security purposes. Most importantly, the work done in the areas of prejudice reduction and conflict resolution should help inform program development in terrorism risk reduction. As Crenshaw (cited in Hoffman, 1998, p. 247) wrote, "It is difficult to understand terrorism without psychological theory, because explaining terrorism must begin with analyzing the intentions of the terrorist actor and the emotional reactions of audiences."

Focus

This chapter will review the role of social identity (Tajfel, 1981), intergroup contact (Allport, 1954), competition (Sherif et al., 1988), individual psychodynamics (Volkan, 1988), power (Sidanius & Pratto, 1999), and social cognition (Bandura, 1998) in prejudice and conflict, and, by extension, terrorism. Then a program developed to moderate group prejudice and conflict—Us & Them: Moderating Group Conflict—will be described in detail.

Theory

Social identity theories assume that group members have a basic need for a positive social identity and that conflict between groups arises from the inevitable comparisons between them. Group identity consists of a variety of dimensions, such as religion, geography, and class. Minorities have trouble achieving favorable social comparisons—and therefore positive feelings about themselves—because of their typically inferior social and economic status.

Tajfel (1981) identifies three ways in which minority group members handle such a problem. If the social system is seen as legitimate and stable, and there are no clear ways to alter the system, such as in a feudal, slavery, or caste system, they acquiesce. In such societies, minority group members usually have internalized the majority group's justification for their lower status to some degree. This lowered self-regard helps maintain the status quo. If the status quo is perceived as illegitimate or unstable by the minority group, the system will be threatened. It is at this stage that states may turn to oppression and terror to preserve their faltering hold on power.

Social, political, and economic changes lead to minority group members' challenging the assumptions of their society about their inferior status. Education, industrialization, urbanization, democratization, capitalism, and mass communication foster comparisons based upon individual merit, not group membership. Such changes sow the seeds of group conflict as the aspirations of the disenfranchised rise. If the majority–minority status is seen as unstable—i.e., the intergroup walls are more permeable—most minority group members will try to assimilate into the majority.

Taylor and McKirnan (1984) suggest that the majority tends to accept highly qualified members of the minority because such assimilation contributes to the stability of the society. Other minority members may be pacified with the expectation that they will move up too if they try hard enough. However, if the system is perceived as not only unstable but also illegitimate, minority group members will move to change their inferior status. Some highly qualified members of the minority are not accepted by the majority or choose not to try. Additionally, some less well-qualified minority members believe that assimilation will not be possible. Then the highly qualified, non-assimilated minority group members begin to raise the consciousness of their group. Self-hate is replaced by pride. They may redefine their group's identity—for example, "Black is beautiful." The minority leaders ascribe responsibility for their lower social status to discrimination and oppression by the majority, not to minority inadequacy. Such consciousness-raising is followed by collective action. The minority begins to struggle against what it now sees as social injustice. The emergence of a charismatic leader is common. Such charismatic leaders may be regressive, like bin Laden, while others are transformative, like Gandhi.

Regardless, the initial response of the majority group is to portray the divisions between their groups as illegitimate or obsolete. But if such attempts fail, the conflict continues, and possibly escalates. If it escalates, the majority may resort to violence and suppression, or it may decide to negotiate to create a mutually acceptable situation. An implication of this research is that to reduce the risk of terrorism, powerful democracies need to be seen not only as militarily and politically strong, but also as legitimate.

One of the most researched theories of intergroup conflict and prejudice is the "contact hypothesis" (Allport, 1954). That research shows that a lessening of intergroup conflict and prejudice occurs under the following conditions: equal status between the groups in the situation; common goals; personal contact (the opportunity to get to know outgroup members as individuals); and support for such contact by each group's authority figures. Such conditions optimize the opportunity for interdependence and development of empathy. The contact hypothesis, and its more recent additions, has been supported by many studies (Pettigrew, 1998).

Intergroup contact under the wrong conditions deleteriously affects relationships. The size of the minority in comparison to the majority, the density of the minority population in a certain area, and the opportunities for superficial (and potentially, competitive) contact between the groups are variables that increase conflict. These factors can increase the sense of threat experienced by the majority. Forbes (1997), a political scientist, emphasized the negative influence of contact between groups when their larger communities are not supportive of such contact, are in conflict, and are disproportionate in size. So he simply extended the scope of the contact hypothesis research to larger constituencies.

A variant of the contact hypothesis is the "realistic group conflict theory" of Sherif (1966). This postulates that intergroup hostility arises from real or perceived competition caused by conflicting goals. The conflict is fueled by the zero-sum nature of the competition. That is, the desired resources are finite, or at least viewed as such; so members of each group believe that gains achieved by members of the outgroup will result in fewer resources for themselves.

Also, Sherif and Sherif (1953) noted that one's *reference group* and one's *membership group* may be different. For example, an individual may belong to a minority group but aspire to and identify with the majority group. Such individuals are typically seen by their membership group as social climbers, disloyal, and mistrusted.

Vamik Volkan (1988) has been the most important psychologist in the formulation of the psychoanalytic approach to intergroup conflict. He described the following stages of the development of self and other images from infancy. First, infants begin to differentiate themselves from the outside world and other people. Simultaneously, they begin forming rudimentary images of themselves and others. They cannot connect both pleasure and pain with the same person (for example, their mothers sometimes feeding them and other times not responding). So they form images of others that are either all good or all bad. Normally, infants begin to meld these opposing images of others and themselves in the second year. However, some images remain unintegrated or primitive, i.e., all bad or good. Later, some of those unintegrated images of self and caretakers are idealized as all good, or devalued as all bad. Then children project those idealized or disparaged images onto certain people. This is done to preserve a sense of internal goodness, safety, and power in the self, one's family, and one's group.

Volkan uses the term *suitable targets of externalization* (STEs) to describe people and objects that are the reservoirs of such images. STEs are culturally determined and include symbols, cuisine, attire, religious icons, and also individuals and groups of people. People experienced as friends, allies, and heroes are positive STEs; enemies are negative STEs.

Volkan and Itzkowitz (1994) describe each member of a group as having an individual identity that is like a garment protecting the individual from threats. But each person in an ethnic, religious, or national group also has a group identity that is like a large tent. Group members aren't preoccupied with the group identification unless they experience it as no longer protecting them. At such times, shoring up the "tent" takes precedence over individual identity needs.

The group identity tent is woven with shared rituals, symbols, leaders, and myths. *Chosen glories*, mythologized and idealized collective achievements and victories, are important in defining "us" versus "them." Even more powerful are *chosen traumas*, which are mythologized losses, injustices, and humiliations suffered by the group. Finally, *borders*, both physical and psychological, clarify the distinction between ingroup and others (Volkan, 1992).

Minorities are common STEs for the psychic discards of the dominant group. So minority group members may be discriminated against because of a mixture of real attributes, but also projected negative qualities of the majority. Unfortunately, more vulnerable minority group members may absorb such characteristics, leading to lowered self-regard.

Another psychoanalytic perspective is offered by Perlman (2002), who spoke of terrorism as a pathogenic response to suffering that is not redressed, a perversion of the search for justice that has been thwarted, and a securing of the need for equality and freedom at any cost. The infliction of humiliation, powerlessness, and terror onto the powerful is experienced as expiation and victory by terrorists. By making the powerful helpless, equality is achieved. But a preferable solution is to achieve equality the other way, by empowering the helpless. "The intifada seemed to turn Palestinians from victims to masters of their fate" (Andoni, 1997). For many, especially men, the feeling of impotence is often intolerable. They would rather be bad. In a personal communication of 2002, Perlman cited a study of suicide bombers by Ann Marie Oliver and Paul Steinberg of the Center for Middle Eastern Studies at Harvard. They describe such suicide missions as a preemptive strike. Rather than let the enemy kill them, they kill themselves to deprive the enemy and attain control over the inevitable. Volkan has described suicide bombers as "preferring to die physically rather than psychologically."

Bertrand Russell (1938) wrote, "The fundamental concept in social science is power, in the same sense in which energy is the fundamental concept in physics." The asymmetry of power between groups can foster subjugation and oppression. But reprisals by the repressed are not uncommon, terrorism among them. A prolonged sense of powerlessness can have dire consequences (Sashkin, 1984) and result in irrationality and violence (Kanter, 1977).

Social dominance theory (Sidanius et al., 1999) focuses on how group-based hierarchies in society determine disproportionate access to power, wealth, and status, whereas subordinate groups suffer greater disenfranchisement, poverty, discrimination, and imprisonment. Social hierarchies are structured by age and gender generally. Depending on the society, other dimensions for such stratification include: race, ethnicity, caste, clan, religion, class, nation, and many others factors important in a given society.

Coleman (2000) clarifies that power does not have to be a negative factor in group relations. He sees problems stemming from misconceptions about power, such as the concept that there is only a fixed amount of power between groups, that power only flows in one direction (usually from the more powerful to the less), and that power means "power over" not "power with."

However, as demonstrated in the classic Stanford Prison study (Haney, Banks, & Zimbardo, 1973), power can easily corrupt. As religion has been labeled the opiate of the masses, so, too, could power be seen as the "opiate of the elite." Kipnis (1976) described how those having power acquire a "taste for power," an inflated esteem and a devaluing of the less powerful. Fiske (1993) and Mindell (1995) described the insensitivity to the less powerful that is fostered by the possession of power.

Social learning theorist Albert Bandura and others have addressed the perceptual and cognitive distortions that foster violence, including terrorism. He wrote (Bandura, 1998, p. 163),

> From a psychological standpoint, third-party violence directed at innocent people is a much more horrific undertaking than political violence in which particular political figures are targeted. . . . to slaughter in cold blood innocent women and children in buses, in department stores, and in airports requires more powerful psychological machinations of moral disengagement.

Conscious justification of violence allows a person to commit acts normally outside his or her moral code. A psychologically healthy soldier may take pride in his ability to kill the enemy if he believes that he is fighting a just war. The terrorist may think that more people will suffer, especially his people, if he doesn't sacrifice the lives of innocents from the oppressive group. The unconscious mechanism of ingroup–outgroup bias (also known as the ultimate attribution error) facilitates such justifications. It refers to the tendency to imbue our own group members with greater value than the outgroup.

Another means of what Bandura calls the moral disengagement of the terrorist relies on euphemistic labeling. Terrorists describe themselves as "freedom fighters" and refer to "hostages" as "spies," while America sanitizes killing with terms like "collateral damage," "neutralizing," and "surgical strikes." This is another example of ingroup–outgroup labeling bias—our "dissemination of information" is the outgroup's "spreading propaganda," and our "disinformation" is their "lies."

Another example of this "us" versus "them" bias is the finding that people rate aggressive actions of the other as more violent than they rate the action when a member of their own group is the instigator (Duncan, 1976). Similarly, ingroup–outgroup bias leads to an overemphasis on personality as the explanation for ingroup members' virtuous behavior and an overemphasis on context as the explanation for reprehensible behavior by someone in the ingroup. The opposite attribution emphases are true in judging behavior of someone in the outgroup (Taylor & Jaggi, 1974). So terrorists can minimize their slayings as the only defensive weapon at their disposal against an oppressive, intractable regime. Counterterrorists can judge their retaliation as restrained compared with the carnage of the terrorists.

Another way one will relax self-sanction is through the displacement of responsibility. Milgram (Helm & Morelli, 1979) found that under certain conditions (e.g., anonymity between the student and the subject, gradual increases in the "voltage," and being directed to do so by an authority figure who would "take responsibility for the consequences"), 65 percent of students would administer enough shock to an experimental subject until the student believed the subject had passed out or died. A key ingredient facilitating that abandonment of normal moral restraint was the assumption of responsibility by the authoritative laboratory professor. Likewise, acts such as suicidal bombings and hostage taking normally proscribed by Islam receive endorsement through circuitous justifications by Shi'ite clerics (Kramer, 1998). Bandura (1998) points out that the most reliable terrorists are those who are bound by a sense of duty to their superiors while relinquishing personal responsibility for the suffering they inflict.

Dehumanization is another psychological tool in the suspension of self-monitoring. It's easier to kill a "Jap" or a "gook" than a person. "It requires conducive social conditions rather than monstrous people to produce heinous deeds" (Bandura, 1998, p. 182). Empathizing with the other is the opposite of dehumanization. If one of the terrorists piloting the hijacked planes on September 11 empathized with his potential victims and their loved ones, he could not have completed his mission. Likewise, terrorism is less likely to be an attractive option to a disenfranchised or oppressed people who feel the humanizing effect of support from the larger world.

The attribution of blame is "another expedient that can serve self-exonerative purposes; one's own violent conduct can then be viewed as compelled by forcible provocation" (Bandura, 1998, p. 184). The cycle of violence escalates as terrorists and governments each focus on the latest assault of the other without appreciating the provocative nature of their own violence.

The previously mentioned Milgram studies on obedience underscore the process of what Bandura terms "gradual moral disengagement." Terrorists get socialized into more and more extreme attitudes and modes of violence over time. Sprinzak (1998) writes about the radicalization of the Weathermen. Their opposition to particular social policies grew into increasing estrangement from the society and violent confrontations with police, and eventually they turned to terrorism in an effort to destroy the system.

One group's defense is often experienced by members of the enemy group as an assault. Mistrust and defensiveness lead to caution and control, which can evoke a defensive and hostile reaction, which is then viewed as proof of the initial view. Unchecked, such self-fulfilling prophecies (Merton, 1952) tend to spiral into greater levels of hostility and violence.

Us & Them: Moderating Group Conflict Program

Need. Within each of us, to some degree, lies the need to split good and bad, that is, to externalize unacceptable aspects of ourselves onto others. Likewise, within each group, there is some tendency to attribute disowned aspects of the group to other groups. Historically, this tendency has been adaptive; yet as our world shrinks due to technological advances, a new approach is required. As nuclear risk remains and terrorist threats grow, we need to adapt. The change in our technology demands a change in our psychology.

Description. The Us & Them program is designed to highlight the dynamics common to prejudice and conflict along many dimensions—for example, race, class, culture, nationality, religion, and ethnicity. Furthermore, education about these common dynamics in the workshop relies on a balance of teaching basic concepts, experiential learning through structured activities, and post-workshop dialogue and action.

"Us & Them" refers to the polarization of two or more groups. Such divisiveness is fueled by an exaggerated sense of one's own group as special and good. Accordingly, other groups are devalued and feared.

The universal tendency to identify with our group and counter-identify with other groups has to do with issues of identity, comfort, and survival. Group boundaries exist to give cohesiveness to groups and to exclude disavowed parts of group members. They tend to provide order and prevent fusion within a large, chaotic world. Group identity tends to confer some sense of belonging, goodness, and worth.

"Us & Them" thinking is magnified at times of an intergroup conflict of interests, such as intensified economic competition, religious conflict, or territorial dispute. And though we realize that prejudice and conflict have important historical, economic, and political causes, we focus on how such tensions are fueled psychologically—and how we can moderate them.

Participant Characteristics

Representation. The groups involved in the program should be representative of the major groups involved in the conflict in the region. Efforts need to be made to involve all such ethnic, religious, racial, or national groups. Uninvolved groups may be motivated to derail progress among the involved groups, especially if they feel uninvited in the first place.

Age. Although on several occasions the program has been modified for children (with a shorter duration, simplification of concepts and language, etc.), participants should be adolescents or adults. A children's program may be developed in the future.

Openness. Openness is another important participant characteristic. The majority of participants in past programs were already predisposed to peaceful conflict reduction. However, optimal program impact occurs with participants in the midrange of prejudice toward "them" in the particular conflict. The program is not likely to succeed with the most prejudiced members of the community. And obviously, terrorists and their active supporters cannot be reached by such programs.

Influence. Ideally, we try to involve community leaders. The involvement of such people has the greatest post-program impact on communities.

Conflict intensity. We usually envision the program being implemented before violent conflict. However, we appreciate the cyclical nature of conflict, as well as the need for interventions during intractable conflicts. So there is a role for the program after cessation of hostilities, since it may help prevent another round of active conflict. However, the more intense the conflict, the less likely it is that disputants will be willing and free to become involved. Doing so could run the risk of their larger constituencies' seeing them as weak or disloyal, and mistrusting or ostracizing them. Therefore, the best time for the program is when intergroup tension is at a moderate level. In terms of Fisher and Keashly's (1991) model of conflict escalation—discussion, polarization, segregation, and destruction—the program could be implemented in all but the fourth phase, though the endorsement of community leaders is essential in the segregation phase.

Us & Them Program Format

Phase One. The Us & Them: Moderating Group Conflict workshop is the first phase of the three-phase program. The workshop is designed to be experiential, so brief talks by the presenter(s) are followed by more lengthy participant exercises. Each didactic segment covers an aspect of Us & Them dynamics: "What do we mean by Us & Them?"; "Why does Us & Them thinking occur?"; "How does Us & Them thinking develop in children?"; "When does Us & Them thinking escalate?"; "Who is prone to exaggerated Us & Them thinking?"; "The problem with extreme Us & Them thinking"; and "Resolving extreme Us & Them thinking." Masters for overhead transparencies are provided for each segment of the sample talk.

The experiential activities are the core of the workshop. The exercises are sequenced to facilitate learning objectives in the following order: (1) self-awareness; (2) other-awareness; and (3) a bridge between the diverse groups participating in each workshop. Exercises are categorized by their learning objectives, i.e., self-awareness, other-awareness, creation of a bridge between groups, and in some cases, a combination of two of those objectives.

Phase Two. The second phase of the program occurs after the workshop. It entails formation of dialogue groups (based upon the Study Circles format). Groups have the following characteristics:

- They are composed of 8 to 12 people who meet regularly over a period of weeks or months to continue to engage in dialogue. The composition of the group is balanced along the dimension of interest, e.g., race, ethnicity, or religion.

- A dialogue is facilitated by a mutually respected person from each of the participant groups. The facilitators do not act as experts, but serve the group by keeping the discussion focused, helping the group to consider a variety of views, and asking difficult questions.

- The format of the dialogue can be based on the most relevant discussion guide from the Study Circles Institute.

- The group progresses from a session on personal experience (how does the issue affect me?) to sessions providing a broader perspective (what are others saying about the issue?) to a session on action (what can we do about the issue here?).

Phase Three. The next phase of the program, Joint Community Action, flows from the second. It involves a collaborative project developed and implemented by workshop participants from the diverse groups. Community action can be either a response to group conflicts or a coordinated effort to strengthen intergroup understanding before problems erupt. Projects could involve efforts to reduce neighborhood violence, joint social gatherings, collaborative political action, and so forth. Sample projects are described and relevant resources are provided in the Participant Booklet to facilitate the process.

Presenter's Manual and Participant Booklet. The Presenter's Manual includes relevant research and materials for workshop presentations, such as a sample talk, originals for overhead projector transparencies, many participant exercises, sample agendas for various lengths of workshops, ideas for opening and closing presentations, audiovisual resources, a bibliography, and a typeset brochure with space for the presenter's name and contact information.

The manual also includes the original copy of the Participant Booklet, which features basic workshop material, guidelines for forming dialogue groups after the workshop, ideas for joint community projects, and lists of resources, such as organizations, publications, and videos.

Group Process Considerations

Attention is paid to the dynamics necessary to optimize prejudice and conflict reduction as identified by the previously mentioned conflict hypothesis research. Dynamics include:

- Fostering the equality of participating group members by counterbalancing pre-workshop contact with group representatives; thoughtful seating arrangements in the workshop; balancing the number of participants from involved groups; striving for approximately equal status of participants; and using presenters who are not from participating groups. Presenters demonstrate respect for all participants, as well as for healthy diversity.

- Facilitating participants' common goals, e.g., the superordinate goal of the reduction of intergroup misunderstanding and tension; encouraging participants to engage in a collaborative process to achieve such outcome goals, e.g., introspection of their own attitudes, education about the other group members' experiences to enhance empathy with them, and exercises and follow-up activities designed to create greater connection with participants from the other group(s). Group interdependence is highlighted and valued.

- Establishing a forum for participants to get to know "them" as individuals through the exploration of common interests, experiences, and aspirations (recategorization and cross-categorization; socialization opportunities; and structured dialogue and exercises designed to increase participants' empathic understanding of "them").

- Gaining the endorsement of the participating groups' community leaders. In some communities, it is not advisable to implement the program until tensions decline. If resources permit, holding the program outside the region may provide the psychological space and security conducive to open participation.

Purpose

To help participants understand and moderate their intergroup prejudice and conflict.

Objectives
Knowledge

- Greater awareness of the origins of one's own images of "them," and a reduction in distorted perceptions of "them."

- Increased knowledge of the outgroup participants' history, beliefs, values, culture, perceptions of "us," experience of the conflict, and aspirations.
- Appreciation of the mutual influence between the groups (and the more powerful group's exertion of greater influence).
- Greater sensitivity in dominant group members of the benefits of privilege they have taken for granted and sensitivity to feelings of the disadvantaged group's members.
- Increased knowledge of why and how leaders and the media influence intergroup attitudes and conflict.
- Understanding the power of primary identification, but also the possibility of cross categorization with members of "them" on other dimensions.
- Increased awareness of collaborative processes and possibilities between participating groups.

Skills

- Greater introspection ability in order to more nondefensively and fully see one's own distorted images, stereotypes, and prejudging of "them."
- The ability to talk directly, openly, and constructively to "them" about one's views and feelings about "us," the conflict, and "them."
- The ability to accurately and empathically listen to "them" talk about their views and feelings toward their group, the conflict, and "us."
- The skill to speak up effectively when someone from either group expresses a demeaning or inaccurate representation of either group.
- Enhanced coalition-building skills with the participating groups.

Attitudes

- Realization that group pride does not rely on downward comparisons to other groups.
- Humanizing "them," manifested by greater empathy and respect for "them."
- Increased appreciation of intergroup diversity.
- Increased appreciation of intergroup interdependence.
- Movement toward forgiving "them."
- Ability to envision a more constructive common future.
- Understanding that peace requires conscious, courageous, ongoing action.

Actions

- Intentional and collaborative interaction with "them" during the program.
- Commitment to continue such cross-group interaction after the program.
- Willingness to encourage greater understanding of "them" within one's group.

Sponsoring Organization

Psychologists for Social Responsibility (PsySR) is a U.S.-based, nonprofit, international network of psychologists who draw upon the research, knowledge, and practice of psychology to promote durable peace at community, national, and international levels. With members in 47 states of the United States and 39 other countries, PsySR is building a cross-cultural network to facilitate communication about the complex and multidisciplinary problems of fostering cultures of peace.

The Us & Them: Moderating Group Conflict program—originally titled Us & Them: The Challenge of Diversity—was developed by members of the Michigan chapter of PsySR. The program was adopted by the national organization in 1994. Over the past decade, Us & Them programs have been conducted for a wide variety of groups. Programs have focused on problems ranging from international ethnic conflict to racial tension in Detroit.

Note

1. The term "terrorism" is used in this chapter to refer to violence usually committed by non-state entities, in contrast to "terror," which is used by those in power to maintain it.

References

Albee, G. W. (2000). Commentary on prevention and counseling psychology. *Counseling Psychologist, 28*, 845–853.

Allport, G. (1954). *The nature of prejudice.* Cambridge, MA: Addison-Wesley.

Andoni, L. (1997, Summer). Searching for answers to Gaza's suicide bombings. *Journal of Palestinian Studies, 36.*

Bandura, A. (1998). Mechanism of moral disengagement. In W. Reich (Ed.), *Origins of Terrorism: Psychologies, Ideologies, Theologies, States of Mind.* Washington, DC: Woodrow Wilson Center Press, 161–192.

Barber, B. (1996). *Jihad vs. McWorld: How globalism and tribalism are re-shaping the world.* New York: Ballantine Books.

Coleman, P. (2000). Power and conflict. In M. Deutsch & P. Coleman (Eds.), *The handbook of conflict resolution: Theory and practice* (pp. 108–130). San Francisco: Jossey-Bass.

Deutsch, M., & Coleman, P. (Eds.) (2000). *The handbook of conflict resolution: Theory and practice.* San Francisco: Jossey-Bass.

Duckitt, J. (1992). *The social psychology of prejudice.* New York: Praeger.

Duncan, B. (1976). Differential social perception and the attribution of intergroup violence: Testing the limits of stereotyping of blacks. *Journal of Personality and Social Psychology, 34,* 590–598.

Fisher, R., & Keashly, L. (1991). A contingency approach to third party intervention. In R. Fisher (Ed.), *The social psychology of intergroup and international conflict resolution.* New York: Springer-Verlag.

Fiske, S. (1993). Controlling other people: the impact of power on stereotyping. *American Psychologist, 48,* 621–628.

Forbes, H. (1997). *Ethnic conflict: Commerce, culture, and the contact hypothesis.* New Haven, CT: Yale University Press.

Haney, C., Banks, W., & Zimbardo, P. (1973). Interpersonal dynamics in a simulated prison. *International Journal of Criminology and Penology, 1,* 69–97.

Haney, C., & Zimbardo, P. (1998). The past and future of U.S. prison policy. *American Psychologist, 53,* 709–727.

Helm, C., & Morelli, M. (1979). Stanley Milgram and the obedience experiment: Authority, legitimacy, and human action. *Political Theory, 7,* 321–346.

Hoffman, B. (1995). Holy terror: The implications of terrorism motivated by a religious imperative. *Studies in Conflict and Terrorism, 18,* 4.

Hoffman, B. (1998). *Inside terrorism.* New York: Columbia University Press.

Jager, H., Schmidtchen, G., & Sullwold, L. (Eds.) (1981). *Analysen zum terrorismus 2: Lebenslaufanalysen.* Darmstadt, Germany: Deutscher Verlag.

Kanter, R. (1977). *Men and women of the corporation.* New York: Basic Books.

Kipnis, D. (1976). *The powerholders.* Chicago: University of Chicago Press.

Kramer, M. (1998). The moral logic of the Hizballah. In W. Reich (Ed.), *Origins of terrorism: Psychologies, ideologies, theologies, states of mind* (pp. 131–160). Washington, DC: Woodrow Wilson Center Press.

Lederach, J. (1995). *Preparing for peace: Conflict transformation across cultures.* Syracuse, NY: Syracuse University Press.

McIntosh, P. (1988). White privilege and male privilege: A personal account of coming to see correspondences through work in women's studies. Center for Research on Women Working Paper Series, No. 189. Wellesley, MA: Wellesley College.

Merton, R. (1952). *Social theory and social structure.* New York: Free Press.

Mindell, A. (1995). *Sitting in the fire: Large group transformation using conflict and diversity.* Portland, OR: Lao Tse Press.

Oskamp, S. (Ed.) (2000). *Reducing prejudice and discrimination.* Mahwah, NJ: Lawrence Erlbaum Associates.

Perlman, D. (2002, January 27). Presentation at American University's Center for Global Peace and the International Peace and Conflict Resolution Program, Washington, DC.

Pettigrew, T. (1998). Intergroup contact theory. *Annual Review of Psychology, 49,* 65–85.

Reich, W. (Ed.) (1998). *Origins of terrorism: Psychologies, ideologies, theologies, states of mind.* Washington, DC: Woodrow Wilson Center Press.

Rouhana, N., & Kelman, H. (1994). Promoting joint thinking in international conflicts: An Israeli-Palestinian continuing workshop. *Journal of Social Issues, 50,* 157–178.

Russell, B. (1938). *Power: A new social analysis.* New York: Norton.

Sashkin, M. (1984). Participative management is an ethical imperative. *Organizational Dynamics, 12,* 4–22.

Sherif, M. (1966). *In common predicament: Social psychology of intergroup conflict and cooperation.* Boston, MA: Houghton Mifflin.

Sherif, M., Harvey, O., White, B., Hood, W., Sherif, C., & Campbell, D. (1988). *The robbers' cave experiment: Intergroup conflict and cooperation.* Middletown, CT: Wesleyan University Press.

Sherif, M., & Sherif, C. (1953). *Groups in harmony and tension: An integration of studies of intergroup relations.* New York: Harper & Brothers.

Sidanius, J., & Pratto, F. (1999). *Social dominance: An intergroup theory of hierarchy and oppression.* New York: Cambridge University Press.

Sprinzak, T. (1998). The psychopolitical formation of extreme left terrorism in a democracy: The case of the weathermen. In W. Reich (Ed.), *Origins of terrorism: Psychologies, ideologies, theologies, states of mind* (pp. 65–85). Washington, DC: Woodrow Wilson Center Press.

Tajfel, H. (1981). *Human groups and social categories: Studies in social psychology.* Cambridge, England: Cambridge University Press.

Tajfel, H., & Turner, J. (1979). An integrative theory of intergroup conflict. In W. G. Austin & S. Worchel (Eds.), *The social psychology of intergroup relations* (pp. 33–48). Monterey, CA: Brooks/Cole.

Taylor, D., & Jaggi, V. (1974). Ethnocentrism and causal attribution in South Indian context. *Journal of Cross-Cultural Psychology, 5,* 162–171.

Taylor, D., & McKirnan, D. (1984). Theoretical contributions: A five stage model of intergroup relations. *British Journal of Social Psychology, 23,* 291–300.

Turner, J. (1985). Social categorization and the self-concept: A social cognitive theory of group behavior. In E. J. Lawler (Ed.), *Advances in group processes* (Vol. 2, pp. 77–122). Greenwich, CT: JAI Press.

Volkan, V. (1988). *The need to have enemies and allies: From clinical practice to international relationships.* Northvale, NJ: Jason Aronson.

Volkan, V. (1992). Ethnonationalistic rituals: An introduction. *Mind and Human Interaction, 4,* 3–19.

Volkan, V., & Itzkowitz, N. (1994). *Turks and Greeks: Neighbors in conflict.* Huntington, England: Eothen Press.

Wallis, J. (1994). *The soul of politics.* New York: New Press.

CHAPTER 5

Countering International Terrorism: Perspectives from International Psychology

John M. Davis

I believe in the power of love in interpersonal relations, but love directed toward the missile or the distant anonymous human being pushing the button would be useless. The alternative, therefore, once diplomacy and other steps short of violence fail to destroy or end the evil, is either submission to it or a reluctant use of force and violence to destroy it.

—*Max M. Kampelman (1991, p. 377)*

The focus of this chapter is on understanding and predicting the development of international terrorist activities through the perspective of international psychology. This chapter is written with full awareness that much information that would be helpful and relevant in countering terrorism is not accessible to the scholar. Both the terrorist organizations and the intelligence organizations responsible for countering terrorism depend heavily on secrecy for their effectiveness. So the scholar has to work without access to much important information. A further difficulty is that the scholarly work of developed societies, because it is public, is accessible to both the intelligence organizations and the terrorist organizations. In addition, in an open society, as opposed to a police state, the terrorist has access to targets and many resources that can be turned to destructive use. Because of these obstacles, the task of the researcher seems like a balancing act. This is the challenge that faces us today. It is not a new problem, even though the world in general has become aware of terrorism and terrorism is now a byword in the daily news. I believe that, in spite of the challenges, research into terrorist activity can substantially ameliorate this pressing problem.

The Danger of International Terrorism

How serious is the threat of international terrorism? Experts disagree. In a recent article on the future of terrorism, Johnson (2001) concluded that terrorism is on the decline. He based this conclusion on the small number of Americans who have died as a result of terrorism compared with the much larger numbers of deaths due to other causes.

Segal (1993) also downplayed the threat of international terrorism and characterized it as low-level warfare. He observed, "It is the terror in terrorism that almost makes it modern day political theatre on our television screens. But despite the 'good copy' the hijackings, shootings, and bombings provide, there is little evidence that all the sound and fury actually has forced great political change" (p. 119). He further commented that terrorists "usually resort to terror because they are too weak and the opposing state too strong to be challenged in more conventional guerilla warfare or via the ballot box. Thus, an upswing of terrorism is often a sign of stability rather than imminent collapse" (p. 119).

On the other hand, Laqueur (1999) pointed to a rising danger of terrorism. He attributed this increasing danger to the increasing availability of weapons of mass destruction combined with increasing numbers of fanatics (the latter he attributes to the prevalence of science fiction, religious cults, conspiracy theories, and apocalyptic beliefs, as well as areas of state-sponsored terrorism in geographic areas experiencing conflict). Narcotics and organized crime also contribute.

These works addressing the issue of whether terrorism is a decreasing or an increasing danger were all written prior to the attacks on September 11, 2001. The attacks on the World Trade Center in New York City and on the Pentagon in Washington, D.C., have changed the perspective, not only of Americans, but also of all people in developed countries. Earlier discussions centered on the small number of deaths in comparison to death caused by other factors. However, a simple "body count" to measure the seriousness of the damage from terrorism is far too narrow a criterion. I will argue that terrorism is a substantial problem for both developed and developing countries, and that the potential damage wreaked by terrorism is far broader and the danger much greater than some of the above authors have perceived. The costs of terrorism include not only the number of people killed and wounded but also the effects of fear on people's behaviors, thoughts, feelings—indeed, on their entire lifestyle. In addition, there are very serious economic costs. Bombing and destruction cause devastation of physical infrastructure, as well as Internet and other nonphysical disruption. Perhaps most important are the costs involving diminished freedom in society. Hostage taking, plane hijacking, assassination, killing of political or military personnel, and murder of civilians are becoming frequent occurrences and each restricts our freedom and/or costs lives.

The fact that terrorism is on the rise globally and is an increasing threat to all civilized countries means that now is the time for psychologists to pay more attention to it and to improve public understanding of the problem and its possible solutions. This chapter discusses the lessons that can be learned from social, cross-cultural, and international psychology for countering international terrorism. It includes issues of language and communication, as well as social identity and social influence. It embraces issues of majority/minority influence processes and group processes. In addition, the chapter draws on international psychology's knowledge of intercultural communication, including aggression and violence and interpersonal attraction/dislike. Finally, this chapter includes practical proposals derived from research and theory for reducing and countering the threat of international terrorism.

Problems of Defining International Terrorism

The definition of terrorism poses numerous challenges and has been discussed by many authors (Cooper, 2001; Hoffman, 1998; Laqueur, 1987; Pillar, 2001). There is much disagreement and there are many differing viewpoints. I will refer to several definitions and discuss the merits of each.

The earliest definition is that given by Laqueur (1987). He traced the term *terrorism* to the Jacobin period (late eighteenth century) when it had a positive connotation. The definition of terrorism in the 1798 supplement of the *Dictionnaire de l'Académie Francaise* stated simply: "système, régime de la terreur." Laqueur also provided historical examples of terrorist movements from a variety of cultures, including European, Middle Eastern, Christian, Indian, Chinese, and North American.

Pillar (2001) also addressed the difficulty raised by attempts to define the term and noted, in particular, the problem of indiscriminate use and application of the word *terrorism*. His discussion included a summary of the failure in the U.N. General Assembly to reach an internationally accepted definition. In his discussion of terrorism and U.S. foreign policy, he used primarily the definition quoted below from the U.S. Code and explicated the various elements of the definition. Pillar argued that the most salient aspect of terrorism is that it is a method rather than a set of causes or adversaries. Thus, in Pillar's words, "terrorism is a problem of what people (or groups or states) *do*, rather than who they are or what they are trying to achieve" (p. 18).

Reich (1998) carried this argument a step further. He stated that terms such as *hatred, revulsion*, and *revenge* best represent the feelings and motivations of many terrorists, and that precisely these words should be used in discussing the subject rather than milder terms, such as *anger* or *frustration*, that psychologists may be more comfortable with. Of necessity, the conditions that psychologists have been able to study scientifically in the laboratory are merely pale reflections of the more extreme emotions and behaviors involved in terrorism. Nevertheless, even the milder conditions that are ethically possible for laboratory study can inform theory and policy, and this section of Reich's chapter is especially useful in this regard. It is ripe with reasonable and heuristic suggestions for connections between the questions raised by terrorist activity and possible answers from psychological research. He suggested ways to conduct research on aggression, group dynamics, interpersonal relations, and social influence.

Simmons and Mitch (1985) are among the few empirical researchers who have reported work along the lines that Reich advocated. Their study examined the consequences of applying the label *terrorism* to an act of public aggression. They varied the descriptions of violent events along several dimensions and identified the characteristics that most influence the labeling of an event as a terrorist act.

Hoffman (1998) devoted an entire chapter to defining terrorism, and his final definition is the most useful one. He traced the term from its definition in the *Oxford English Dictionary*, through its use during the French Revolution, and discussed other European uses as well. He addressed some of the reasons why terrorism is so difficult to define and pointed out that even different departments and agencies of the U.S. government (for example, the U.S. Department of

State, the Federal Bureau of Investigation, and the U.S. Department of Defense) use different definitions for terrorism. He further noted that terrorism is often erroneously considered to be synonymous with guerrilla warfare or violent criminal behavior. He emphasized, however, that it is important to distinguish it from these other terms. In conclusion, he organized 22 definitional elements of terrorism (such as violence, force, threat, coercion, and publicity) into a table that could be helpful to psychologists seeking to develop an operational definition. He concluded that the most viable and commonly used definition is the one contained in Title 22 of the United States Code, Section 2656f(d): "Premeditated politically-motivated violence perpetrated against noncombatant targets by subnational groups or clandestine agents, usually intended to influence an audience" (p. 38).

As stated above, the term *terrorism* has been extensively defined and explored. For the subject of this chapter, all that remains is to broaden the definition to include an international application. This is easily done. According to the U.S. Department of State Report *Patterns of Global Terrorism 2000* (2001, p. vi), the term *international terrorism* means "terrorism involving citizens or the territory of more than one country."

Problems Faced by the Scholar in Researching Terrorism

In addition to the major challenges surrounding the research of terrorism, a number of more specific areas of concern have been described. Crenshaw (2000) identified and briefly commented on persistent problems faced by researchers of political terrorism. While she did not focus specifically on international terrorism, the problems she identified are still relevant. They involve definitions, collecting empirical data, building theory, and avoiding the attribution of pathology to terrorists. She argued that psychological explanations of terrorism must take multiple levels of analysis into account, linking the individual to the group and to society. She also argued that future research should look not only at the causes of terrorism, but also at the termination of terrorist campaigns, at government decision making, and at policy effectiveness. She discussed the possible use of psychological research on terrorism and the divide between the scholar and the policy maker or between the academic and the government. She cited George (1993) as an example of work that seeks to "bridge the gap" between academics and policy makers in the field of foreign affairs and agreed with George's suggestion that the task of academics is to diagnose problems rather than prescribe solutions. Crenshaw (2000) also interestingly commented that, as terrorism becomes less linked with communism and left-wing ideologies and as it increasingly also includes right-wing ideologies, scholars, at least in the United States, appear more willing to contribute their research and knowledge to the issue of terrorism. For a thorough discussion of the predominantly liberal bias of American psychologists, see Redding (2001).

Perhaps the most thorough and detailed discussion of the challenges faced by any scholar seeking to use a systematic and scientific approach to analyze and understand the phenomenon of terrorism is provided by Groebel (1989). Groebel pointed out that most of the data necessary for understanding international terrorism are either not available at all, or are available only in part. Moreover, the data that *can* be collected are often of uncertain reliability and validity. Groebel also provided a very useful framework (to be discussed in more detail later) for organizing and analyzing the data that are available.

International Psychology and Its Perspectives

International Psychology Defined

Holtzman (2000, 2001) has provided useful descriptions and discussions of international psychology. He defined the term as "various forms of organized psychology at the international level, including societies, congresses, journals, and other kinds of scientific and professional exchanges" (Holtzman, 2001, p. 781). He added that it can also refer to "the social psychology of international relations, or the comparative study of psychological processes across different nations and cultures, as in cross-cultural psychology" (p. 781).

The Development of Psychological Science around the World

Rosenzweig (1999) reported the preliminary results of a survey of the national psychological associations of 34 countries, conducted by the International Union of Psychological Science. The survey reported (among other things) the state of development and the level of resources available for psychological science. It also provided a useful summary both of the resources and of the growth and development of psychology in various nations of the world. Rosenzweig's findings showed that psychology is growing rapidly throughout the world, both in terms of the number of students and also in terms of the number of scientific researchers in the field. In addition, his report showed increasing pressure for the scientific work to demonstrate practical value within the cultures of the various nations.

Major Organizations of International Psychology

The growth of international psychology is reflected in the existence of four major organizations of international psychology that are described by Davis (2000a). The four organizations are the International Association of Applied Psychology (IAAP), the International Council of Psychologists (ICP), the International Association for Cross-Cultural Psychology (IACCP), and the International Union of Psychological Science (IUPsyS). Each of these organizations holds international conventions or congresses on a regular basis and issues a variety of publications. The membership of the first three associations is comprised of individual psychologists, while membership of the fourth consists of the national associations of psychology in various countries around the world. These four organizations have extensive networks of committees and task forces. They also support extensive communication among themselves, both formal and informal, and they cooperate on many projects. "Together the four associations represent psychologist members from more than 100 countries ranging from Albania to Zimbabwe" (Davis, 2000a, p. 37).

The International Association of Applied Psychology (IAAP)

IAAP was founded in 1920 in Geneva, Switzerland, and for many years held international conventions at irregular intervals in various countries of Europe. The first non-European meeting of IAAP was held in Montreal in 1974. Since 1974, congresses have been held at regular four-year intervals and have included non-European venues: Jerusalem in 1986; Kyoto in 1990; San Francisco in 1998; Singapore in 2002. IAAP publishes the journal *Applied Psychology: An International Review* (Davis, 2000a; Merenda, 1995).

International Council of Psychologists (ICP)

The ICP is an outgrowth of the National Council of Women Psychologists, founded in 1941 in the United States. For its first two decades, the membership of this organization consisted either exclusively or primarily of women. Until 1970, when it met in Tel Aviv, its meetings were held annually only in the United States. Its next non-U.S. meeting was held in 1976 in Paris. Currently, ICP schedules a meeting in a country outside the United States in alternate years (Davis, 2000a, 2000b; Merenda, 1995).

International Association for Cross-Cultural Psychology (IACCP)

The IACCP was founded in 1972 in Hong Kong. It has held its meetings mostly outside the United States. The first U.S.-held meeting was in Bellingham, Washington, in 1998. IACCP publishes the *Journal of Cross-Cultural Psychology*, which focuses on mainstream cross-cultural research and is available in most university libraries (Davis, 2000a).

International Union of Psychological Science (IUPsyS)

The IUPsyS was founded in 1951 in Stockholm. It has grown out of a series of international congresses of psychology that began in 1889 in Paris. These congresses convened at approximately four-year intervals in various cities of Europe through 1951, when IUPsyS was formed. At that time, the national associations of 20 countries became its charter members. By the time IUPsyS met in Stockholm in the year 2000 there were 64 national members. IUPsyS publishes the *International Journal of Psychology* (Davis, 2000a; Merenda, 1995; Rosenzweig, Holtzman, Sabourin, & Bélanger, 2000).

In summary, each of these four groups has contributed to the development of education and scientific knowledge in the various countries represented by their members. They have also made contributions toward increased understanding of human psychology. Much of the research presented at the meetings of these organizations has focused on comparisons across cultures. On both personal and professional levels, they have promoted international communication and understanding. Finally, through the contributions summarized above, they represent an important potential resource for countering the problems that foster international terrorism.

Perspectives from International Psychology

The reason the four organizations can be so effective is that they deal with different but complementary perspectives. The IAAP maintains a primary focus on advancing the application of scientific knowledge internationally in the various fields of applied psychology. The work of IAAP is organized into 13 divisions. Of particular importance to understanding and countering international terrorism are the divisions of psychology and law, political psychology, and psychology and national development (Davis, 2000a; Merenda, 1995; Pawlik & d'Ydewalle, 1996).

Promoting psychologist-to-psychologist networks around the world is the main focus of ICP. With the development of these networks, ICP aims to promote international understanding, cooperation across national boundaries, and goodwill among people of different cultures (Davis, 2000a, 2000b; Merenda, 1995; Pawlik et al., 1996).

The IACCP facilitates and conducts cross-cultural experimental research around the world (Davis, 2000a; Pawlik et al., 1996).

Connecting national psychologies and building scientific infrastructure worldwide is the ambitious aim of IUPsyS. An important function is the encouragement and support of educational and scientific resources in underdeveloped countries. The IUPsyS is also the most encompassing organization of international psychology. Because it works with national psychological associations of member countries rather than with individual psychologists, it is able to influence hundreds of thousands of individual psychologists worldwide (Davis, 2000a; Merenda, 1995; Pawlik et al., 1996).

These four major international organizations coordinate many of their initiatives through a network of liaisons, joint projects, and coordinated calendars for their various congresses, conventions, and meetings. Each of these organizations also has liaisons with many smaller, more specialized associations in psychology.

Causes of Terrorism: Applicable Psychological Theory and Research

Psychological Causes of International Terrorism

Personality of Terrorists

Traditional cross-sectional descriptions of personality are of little value for understanding terrorism unless these descriptions can be unified with the findings and theories of experimental psychology. As Eysenck (1997) has noted, descriptive and correlational approaches lack information about the causal nexus of behavior. More useful are

longitudinal studies of hostile, aggressive, antisocial patterns of behavior such as those reviewed by Caprara (1996) and Rutter (1997).
Even longitudinal approaches to the study of the aggressive personality may be less useful than the recognition that schemas of "enemy,
evil, revenge, hate" probably predict aggressive behavior best. What
is the most reliable cause of aggression? Attack is, or threat, or the
perception of threat.

Brown (1944) recognized that it was not just the personality of
Hitler but the psychologically threatened condition of the entire
German society that explained German behavior during World
War II. Brown wrote:

> Ever since 1933 I have listened to all of Hitler's broadcast speeches, as
> well as those of Goering, Goebbels, and other leading Nazi, and—es-
> pecially since the outbreak of war—to the German broadcasts for
> German listeners, because they throw important light on the special
> psychological problem of German mentality. It is the duty of anyone
> who is trained in psychology to study these revelations as fully as
> possible, with a view to the future. The problem is really a medico-
> psychological one. Germany is a sick nation, and we need to understand
> how she has reached the state in which she now is if we are to form a
> reliable opinion as to the best way of treating her later on. If we treat
> her in the wrong way later on it will be more than an international
> calamity, it will be a world crime. (pp. 49–50)

Thus, Brown stated quite clearly that psychologists have a duty to
study such threats.

A particularly useful resource on the motivation and personality of
the individual who becomes a terrorist is the book edited by Reich
(1998), *Origins of Terrorism: Psychologies, Ideologies, Theologies, States
of Mind.* Particularly useful are the two lead chapters by Crenshaw
(1998) and Post (1998). Crenshaw analyzed the actions and motivations of terrorists with the assumption that they are the result of logical thinking and strategic choice in pursuit of a rational goal. Post
examined the actions and motives of terrorists with the assumption
that they are, instead, driven by psychological forces. Other valuable
chapters are those by Bandura (1998), Kellen (1998), Kramer (1998),
and Rapoport (1998). Bandura argued that psychological processes of
moral disengagement are involved in terrorist behavior and thought.
Kellen provided a detailed analysis of terrorism in West Germany.
Kramer examined the moral logic of Hezbollah, and Rapoport examined the religious terrorism of Islam.

Aggression and Human Nature

While many areas of psychological research are useful to an understanding of psychological terrorism, research and theory on human aggression bear the most obvious and directly relevant relationship. For that reason, I will review the work on aggression first.

The psychological literature contains numerous definitions of aggression. Most of these are similar to that offered by Baron and Richardson (1994). They defined aggression as "any form of behavior directed toward the goal of harming or injuring another living being who is motivated to avoid such treatment" (p. 5).

Psychologists have searched for at least a century for answers to the question of the extent to which human aggression is due to innate factors and the extent to which it is due to the influence of the social environment. Early psychologists favored a biological view. For example, James (1936, 1987) considered human violence to be a powerful instinct that was a natural result of the struggle for survival. Another early psychologist, McDougall (1908), also considered aggression to be a basic human instinct. Freud (1963) concurred; he considered aggression to be a basic component of human motivation and anger to be activated by objects of hate. This biological view was further strengthened by the discoveries of brain mechanisms involved in aggressive behavior (Cannon, 1925).

The research supporting the view that human aggression has biological aspects continues to this day. However, most psychologists—and social psychologists in particular—now see the causes of human aggression as complex: biological processes contribute to aggression in combination with aversive stimuli from the environment. Stimuli arising from conflict with others is seen as a particularly potent cause. Much of the work in social psychology has focused on the cultural/environmental conditions and the psychological processes combining all these factors—that is, those involving frustration, poor impulse control, the cultural and individual construal of negative emotions, and social and group norms that support violence. Thus, the view of today's social psychologists is that the causes of aggression are much more complex than previously thought. They include the individual's genetic endowment, past learning and experience, and also the individual's assessment of aspects of the situation that punish (inhibit) or reward (promote) aggression.

Geen (1998) has organized the current social psychological research on aggression and antisocial behavior into five psychological processes. These processes are instigation (usually in the context of interpersonal conflict and involving cognitive processes), social and learning history of the individual (which determines the likelihood that aggressive behavior will be enacted in situations of conflict), skills in processing interpersonal information and tendencies to attribute hostile intent to others, social and cultural variables (norms, beliefs, expectations) regarding the appropriateness of aggression in conflict situations, and personality variables that moderate aggressive behavior patterns.

These five processes can be best understood by incorporating them into the framework of social learning theory, which also provides a structure for understanding the influences that contribute to the development of enduring patterns of individual aggression. Social learning theory emphasizes the role of observation and imitation in the acquisition of responses and behavior patterns, and it emphasizes reinforcement and punishment as the primary influences on the performance and maintenance of these behaviors. The normal child in many societies has frequent opportunities to observe many aggressive behaviors. These opportunities occur in real-life situations at school, in the community, and at home, as well as in the fantasy world provided by the media. Thus, from a very early age humans learn, at least in rudimentary form, how to enact many aggressive behaviors. Fortunately, the vast majority of children and adults never perform the aggressive acts that have been demonstrated to them countless times. Most children and adults never shoot a gun at another person, or stab another with a knife or other sharp object, or seek to harm another with explosives, even though these aggressive acts have been modeled over and over in the media. A few individuals, however, because of real or imagined patterns of reinforcement for past aggressive behavior, do carry out aggressive acts. Thus, social learning theory makes an important distinction between the learning of aggression (acquired through observation) and the performance of aggression (influenced by reinforcement and punishment).

These principles have been well supported. Research has shown that most people learn how to perform many aggressive acts but only a few perceive that the reinforcement contingencies make it worth their effort to perform these acts. For example, Bandura (1986) reviewed studies that showed the influence of aggressive models on learning and also showed the effects of expected rewards and punishments on aggressive performance. Thus an individual who has used aggression many times to achieve valuable goals expects that future aggression will be similarly rewarded. The validity of this analysis has been supported by the research of Perry, Perry, and Rasmussen (1986) and by Boldizar, Perry, and Perry (1989). Furthermore, social learning theory also proposes that all individuals develop and refine mental frameworks (scripts/schemas) that serve as internal standards to guide their behaviors. In addition, people learn and refine mental representations of social norms regarding which actions are appropriate responses to interpersonal conflicts. Thus, as Huesmann (1988) has shown, individuals who persistently show aggressive behavior are those who have used aggression successfully in the past, have participated in many aggressive situations, and continue to add to and perpetuate their aggressive behavior patterns.

While much psychological research on aggression contains the implicit assumption that all aggressive behavior is undesirable and should be controlled or eliminated, a few researchers regard aggression as a normal part of much social interaction rather than as a deviant element. Such researchers include Da Gloria (1984), Da Gloria and DeRidder (1977), Felson and Tedeschi (1993), Mummendey and Mummendey (1983), and Tedeschi and Nesler (1993). All have investigated social groups, subcultures, and cultures in which aggression and violence are considered appropriate and desirable as a means of reaching a goal. Obvious examples come from sports and law enforcement. However, even in these situations where high levels of aggression are considered appropriate and desirable, powerful rules or social norms generally exist. When these rules and social norms are violated (for example, police brutality), the aggressive behavior is generally perceived as reprehensible.

The Melding of Aggression and Political Ideology

Just as norms regarding appropriate and inappropriate aggression have developed to regulate many types of interpersonal aggression, norms have also developed to regulate types of intergroup aggression. Cultures and social groups have various norms regarding the appropriate use of aggression in intergroup conflict and hostility. When a member of one group transgresses against a member of another group, the victim or aggrieved individual or group engages in a process of attribution regarding the cause. Was it an accident or an intentionally hostile act indicating evil traits and malicious intent? Whether overt aggression will follow is influenced by several factors, including the nature of the original transgression, the outcome of the attribution process, and the degree of preexisting negative attitudes toward the out-group (DeRidder, Schruijer, & Tripathi, 1992; Schruijer, 1992).

Many lessons learned from research on aggression can be applied to aspects of terrorism. A number of cross-cultural studies have examined factors related to levels of violence and aggression embedded in the social norms of various cultures and subcultures. Archer and Gartner (1984) compiled statistics from 110 nations for the period from 1960 to 1970 to create a comparative crime data file. These data indicate that nations typically exhibit levels of postwar violence that have increased relative to prewar levels.

Attack or perceived threat of attack is perhaps the most reliable cause of aggression (Buss, 1961). Terrorist aggression is probably no exception. Social psychological research on aggression has shown that attack, threat, and even perceived threat serve as the most reliable instigators of aggression. Moreover, when individuals respond to an attack of another person by harming the attacker, they do not label their own behavior as aggression but rather as justified behavior (Harvey & Enzle, 1978). In an interesting historical example, Brown (1944) recounted how Hitler brought the various parts of the German nation under his control by convincing them they were under attack. Even music and drama played a part: Wagner made the ancient epic of *Das Nibelungenlied* into a vehicle for rousing German national feeling and making the theme of terrible vengeance widely known and emotionally acceptable. The epic provided the theme that became the preoccupation of the Nazis and was expressed in Hitler's use of concentration camps, his development of secret cells (Gestapo), and his policy of "meeting terror with ten-fold terror" (Brown, 1944, p. 55). The theme was also apparent in Goebbels's use of propaganda containing the stark message that the German people were fighting for their lives and must fight or be annihilated.

The situation of Germany under Hitler is not unique, and cultures of violence wherever they are found provide the conditions that can breed terrorism. Individuals trapped in those cultures are especially susceptible to the allure of violence and they come to see it as the only solution. For example, Brown (1944) described Hitler's "idealism" as the individual sacrificing for the group. Brown went on to assert that the "will to power" was aligned in primitive societies with the struggle for existence and the survival of the fittest, but in later times was aligned with cooperation rather than competition. Closely related to cultures of violence are cultures of war. Brown referred to Nietzsche's glorification of war and the justification of violence as a solution; Nietzsche had argued that war is a great good and had glorified it in *Also Sprach Zarathustra*.

For political violence to occur, a theoretical justification must legitimize the destructive activities (Groebel, 1989). Insight into the ideology of terrorist movements can be gained from a study of the literature of the German revolutionaries of the 1960s and 1970s. Kellen (1998) and Markovits (2001) have discussed the ideologies from this period that provided foundations for revolutionary and terrorist thinking and actions. The revolutionaries of the 1960s believed that the Western powers (mostly the United States) were inherently evil. They pointed out that, after World War II, the Western powers had propped up the very individuals who were prominent Nazi figures under Hitler. The revolutionaries argued that many of the judges in Germany and many of the political leaders supported by the Marshall Plan had previously been Nazis and supporters of Hitler during the war. Therefore, both the establishment in Germany and its Western supporters were corrupt. Arguments of a similar nature have become familiar in the ideologies of many terrorist movements and they bear a striking similarity to those used today. Although they will have somewhat different ideological bases, there will be a number of similarities to the German ideologies and conceptualizations. For example, in current revolutionary arguments from the Middle East, very similar arguments are being made to justify the terrorists' actions. Terrorists point to the government of Saudi Arabia and argue that it is corrupt and would be unable to remain in power except for the support of the Western governments. They also argue that Israel unjustly occupies land and oppresses the Palestinians and can continue to do so only because of Western (primarily U.S.) support.

Group Dynamics and International Terrorism

The study of group dynamics in psychology makes it clear that groups exert strong and subtle powers on the behaviors, thoughts, and emotions of individual group members. At the most basic level, groups provide categories of in-group versus out-group, us versus them, friend versus foe. Group pressure can exert a powerful influence on one's behavior and decision making, and even on one's perception of reality. A series of classic studies by Asch (1951, 1955) showed that people would erroneously perceive a simple visual diagram when subjected to subtle group pressure. A substantial minority of those individuals even denied that they had been influenced by the group and that their objectively incorrect answers were wrong. Bond and Smith (1996) have provided a more recent review of the cross-cultural results of the type of group conformity research pioneered by Asch.

Interpersonal Attraction and International Terrorism

The work on attraction, both at the individual level and at the group level, provides a useful framework for understanding many of the psychological dimensions of international terrorism. The attraction of individuals to groups; the dynamics within the groups; and the establishment of dislike, repulsion, and hate toward individuals and groups perceived as the enemy can all be better understood through the lens of interpersonal attraction research and theory. This theory also provides a useful framework for understanding the determinants as well as the consequences of attraction and repulsion, love and hate, and perceptions of friend and enemy. Moreover, while primarily concerned with elucidating the determinants of the positive and negative sentiments that individuals hold toward other individuals (Berscheid, 1985, 1998; Byrne, 1971; Davis & Lamberth, 1974; Gonzales, Davis, Loney, LuKens, & Junghans, 1983), this framework is useful at multiple levels. For example, it has been expanded to include the attraction and repulsion that individuals feel toward various groups (Davis, 1984).

Familiarity is an important determinant of attraction (Berscheid, 1985, 1998; Byrne, 1971). It is widely recognized that, in contrast to familiar people who are perceived as safe and friendly, unfamiliar people are often perceived as potentially dangerous. As demonstrated by Hartley (1946), people report dislike for and negative evaluations of national groups that are completely unfamiliar. When familiarity with a stimulus is varied through repeated exposure, attraction to that stimulus increases as a function of the number of exposures (Zajonc, 1968). This "mere exposure" effect has been found under a variety of conditions. For reviews, see Bornstein (1989) and Harrison (1977).

Another important determinant of attraction is reciprocity. Individuals are attracted to others who like them or evaluate them positively, and they dislike others who dislike them or evaluate them negatively. Attraction theorists conceptualize expressions of liking and esteem from another person as a powerful reward that is likely to be reciprocated; moreover, expressions of dislike or disapproval from another person is a powerful punishment that is also almost certain to be reciprocated. Positive evaluations and expressions of liking and/or respect from another person result in the expectation that

that person is a potential source of help and support. To an even greater degree, negative evaluations and expressions of dislike from another lead to the expectation that that person is a potential source of threat and harm (Berscheid, 1985, 1998; Byrne, 1971).

Similarity of attitudes, values, and beliefs comprises another powerful determinant of interpersonal attraction. Lamberth, Gouaux, and Davis (1972) demonstrated that similar attitude statements possess the rewarding properties of traditional reinforcers in an operant conditioning experiment. Thus, individuals who express similar attitudes provide pleasant experiences and are likely to be approached and perceived in positive ways. Byrne and Nelson (1965) combined data from a number of similarity-attraction experiments in order to examine the functional relationship between attitude similarity and attraction. The relationship can be expressed by the function $y = 5.44x + 6.62$. In other words, the level of attraction (y) that one individual reports for another person increases in a linear pattern as the proportion of similar attitudes (x) increases. In an experiment using this formula to make predictions of interpersonal attraction, Gonzales et al. (1983) found that people recognize the general effects of attitude similarity and dissimilarity on attraction but consistently underestimate the magnitude of these effects. Particularly noteworthy was the degree to which they underestimated how much a stranger would dislike them in the case of dissimilar attitudes. Disagreement in the form of dissimilar attitude statements also induces negative arousal that can adversely influence learning (Davis et al., 1974).

While most of the research on interpersonal attraction has focused on the determinants of one individual's attraction to another individual, Davis (1984) extended this approach in order to examine an individual's attraction to a group. He found that individuals are attracted to some groups and repelled by others as a function of similarity of attitudes, beliefs, and values. The factors that determine an individual's attraction to one group and avoidance of another are important precursors to understanding the gradual process by which individuals become attracted to, and in some cases members of, terrorist groups.

Countering International Terrorism

The preceding sections provide a theoretical and empirical foundation for understanding the psychology of terrorism and the importance of international psychology. I believe there are four principal ways in which international psychology can effectively contribute to the long-term effort to counter international terrorism. These are as follows: training more psychologists worldwide, sharing information worldwide, further utilizing the resources of the major international organizations in psychology, and educating the general public.

Train More Psychologists Worldwide

An important gap in psychological knowledge relevant to international terrorism is the lack of information, understanding, and skill in dealing with individuals of diverse cultures. While physicians, economists, and certain other professionals can apply their expertise internationally with fair success because they are dealing with circumscribed domains, the psychologist must be capable of accurately defining and investigating the multiple determinants of human behavior—a much more varied domain. Because so many determinants are embedded in language and in the cultural meanings and symbols that motivate and shape behaviors of individuals, thorough familiarity with and deep understanding of the relevant culture are essential. For many important cultures, such familiarity and understanding are lacking in the psychological literature.

In many cultures there is not an adequate body of professionals who are both culturally familiar and trained in psychology. In many other cultures there are individuals with both intimate knowledge of the culture and training in psychology, but the barriers of language and of publication processes prevent their contributions from being widely disseminated. For example, the work of an Italian psychologist who publishes only in Italian will be unavailable to most of the community of international psychology. Similarly, within the community of English-speaking psychologists, no one is available to provide a thorough understanding of Afghanistan or the Sudan or Lebanon or even the Palestinian West Bank of Israel.

Increase Psychological Research and Information-Sharing Worldwide

In addition to the need for training professional psychologists, there is a need for sharing information. Currently few psychological databases regarding terrorism are available in English, the language of the majority of present-day psychologists. Perhaps the most comprehensive database is one compiled by the German Ministry of the Interior that is available only in German (BMI, 1981–1984). Groebel

(1989) provided a cogent summary in English of the findings from these data. These data are a valuable resource on terrorism and should be translated into other languages for wider accessibility.

Language differences are the greatest barrier to worldwide sharing of information. The need for translation is a pressing one in today's world. However, a number of practical obstacles must be acknowledged. There are 191 nation-states in the world today and most are ethnically and linguistically heterogeneous. There are an estimated 2,000 to 5,000 distinct ethnic-linguistic groups (National Intelligence Council, 2000). Perhaps a viable solution to the problem of translation would be to begin translation efforts with the world's 10 foremost languages: Mandarin, English, Spanish, Arabic, Bengali, Hindi, Portuguese, Russian, Japanese, and German (listed in order of number of native speakers). Approximately 900 million individuals speak Mandarin as their native language; only 100 million speak German. While only 380 million people speak English as their mother tongue, approximately 1.6 billion people (almost one-third of the world's population) use English in some form on a daily basis. Thus, the world's published material is primarily available in English, and the U.S. media export English-language culture worldwide. Over 80 percent of Internet communication is in English, although an estimated 44 percent of Internet users have another first language (Fishman, 1998–1999). Thus, English is clearly the dominant repository for scientific data at present; nevertheless, increased translation to and from the other major world languages is needed.

Further Utilize the International Organizations of Psychology

Currently, one of the chief contributions of the international organizations of psychology is translation. For example, IUPsyS has sponsored the development and publication of several trilingual dictionaries of psychological terms. Such translation will continue to be an important part of the work of the international associations of psychology.

An additional important contribution that international psychological organizations are uniquely prepared to offer is capacity building for national psychological organizations that lag behind. Capacity building involves aiding and facilitating the development of education and training for psychologists, the establishment of psychological laboratories and clinics, the promotion of support for research funding, and the development of other essential infrastructure (Adair, 1995). A number of reference works in international psychology describe the status of psychological education and training, opportunities for scientific research, and the professional recognition of psychologists in various countries throughout the world (Gilgen & Gilgen, 1987; Ross, Alexander, & Basowitz, 1966; Sexton & Hogan, 1992; Sexton & Misiak, 1976).

In their programs for capacity building, the international associations in psychology periodically assess and report the level of development of national psychologies. In countries where psychology is nonexistent or not well developed, there is a high probability that other elements of modern infrastructure are poorly developed as well and that conditions are therefore ripe for fostering terrorism. Afghanistan can be taken as an example. In a guide to international opportunities for advanced training and research in psychology, Ross et al. (1966) included a chapter on psychology in Afghanistan (Ajmal, 1966). That chapter was authored by a psychologist from Pakistan and reported only on a single university, Kabul University, which had no department of psychology. Only a few courses in psychology were offered and these by the faculty of education to prepare students for administrative positions. Three subsequent similar reference works over the next three decades (Gilgen et al., 1987; Sexton et al., 1992; Sexton et al., 1976) had nothing to report on psychology in Afghanistan. For a personal and informative account of the plight of Afghan refugees fleeing the Soviet-Afghan war, see Dadfar (1994).

In addition to their roles in assessing development and providing translation services, the international psychology associations are also uniquely positioned to promote cross-cultural communication and international understanding. The IUPsyS, for example, accomplishes this role by publishing articles in both English and French in the *International Journal of Psychology*. In a typical article, the psychological ethics codes of 24 countries were compared (Leach & Harbin, 1997). Also, IUPsyS, in cooperation with IAAP and IACCP, sponsors the biennial Advanced Research Training Seminars (ARTS) to train young psychologists from developing countries in research skills. All four of the major international associations in psychology promote cross-cultural and cross-national research and cooperation. These initiatives range from small-scale, cross-cultural projects involving researchers and participants from two nations to large-scale projects involving dozens and sometimes scores of researchers, as many countries, and tens of thousands of participants.

Educate the Public

The above measures, while undoubtedly helpful, will be of little value without the support of the average citizens of many nations. Terrorists are adept at infiltrating open societies and are careful to disguise their intentions. Thus, the danger they pose can be countered only with the vigilance of alert citizens. These citizens must have accurate and reliable information about terrorism and also must have avenues for action when the need arises. Thus, the role of psychology in educating the general public becomes of prime importance in combating international terrorism. With increased alertness, initiative, and vigilance, ordinary people can find ways to maintain the privacy and other norms of an open society while still countering the dangers of terrorism. President George W. Bush's urgings that citizens be vigilant acknowledge the important role that average citizens must play in order to address the problem of terrorism. The alert flight attendants who in December 2001 detected a passenger with explosives in his shoes before he could destroy the plane and its passengers are a good example of citizen vigilance.

The situation in Germany under Hitler provides useful lessons. After World War I, Germany was devastated and the German people demoralized. Hitler put people to work and, in the early years, gave many hope and increased self-esteem. Tragically, this change was accomplished by the production of war materials and at the expense of "scapegoats"—Jews, Gypsies, and other groups. When individuals suffer chronic threats to their self-concept, as did the Germans after defeat in World War I, they may seek to restore self-esteem by comparing themselves with and derogating other individuals. (For a discussion of downward social comparison, see Osborne, 1996.) What can be learned? Wherever there are pockets of people who are suffering, there is potential for violence and terrorism. Much of the problem can be addressed by providing hope and opportunities for productive work. Of course, the hope must be realistic and the work must fit the skills of the people and be focused on positive values. Here education and educated people play a central role. The Afghan professionals living in Western countries and now returning to Afghanistan to help rebuild their country and bring it into the twenty-first century provide an excellent example.

Other broad and useful suggestions for countering the threat of international terrorism by ameliorating the cultural conditions that foster terrorism are reported by Reeves (1999). He recommended that "intelligence agencies must start working to separate hardcore terrorists from members of their gang and from their recruiting pool" (p.

264). He stated that, to accomplish this goal, legitimate grievances of the terrorists must be taken seriously and responded to constructively whenever possible. Moreover, there must be "a concerted international effort to create greater harmony between the West and the East" (p. 265). These things will not happen without broad support from the citizens of both Western and Eastern societies.

In particular, university personnel have an important role to play in this international effort to create greater harmony. In fact, universities must lead in the effort to pay attention to (rather than ignore) both the dangers and the suffering inherent in expressions of anger and hate. In Western countries, revolutionary groups may at times be found living and working at or near universities. University environments offer opportunities for easy and anonymous communication via the Internet. In addition, they offer resources for obtaining extensive information on many subjects that the terrorist may wish to learn about, access to inexpensive living arrangements, ostensible reasons for being in a country, access to libraries, and relative anonymity. Also, university and college campuses are locations where widely diverse ideologies are discussed and advocated. Such diversity of opinion is not only accepted but encouraged on campuses, and advocates of extreme ideologies often find a receptive audience there.

On university campuses one is also likely to find speakers and events that offer opportunities to express a variety of ideas. While some of these speakers and events may generate responses of antagonism or hate, it is in the best interests of citizens and governments in both Western and Eastern countries to support and encourage the expression of diverse opinions and ideologies. This atmosphere can be especially useful at universities in countries where terrorism may be brewing. It will encourage greater latitude of ideas, but may also serve to allow for unobtrusive measurement of the level of antagonism or hate and to identify individuals who are attracted to terrorist ideologies. Such persons are most likely to be in a cultural and social climate where many people agree with them and where they feel safe. This preference for being with others who share similar attitudes, beliefs, and values suggests the possibility of using a variety of unobtrusive techniques to detect the presence of individuals drawn to terrorist ideologies. One such technique for detecting the presence of individuals hostile to a particular ideology involves placing symbols of that ideology in public places and measuring the degree to which they are defaced or removed. For example, printed flyers or posters that announce speakers on Western-oriented topics could be

placed on walls or bulletin boards around universities and other public places. The extent to which these posters and flyers are defaced or
removed will indicate the extent to which they have aroused hostility.
In locations where substantial defacement or removal of the symbols
occurs, they can be replaced and the area put under more careful surveillance in order to observe and identify the responsible individuals.
While such unobtrusive measures may be limited in their usefulness,
they nevertheless provide simple and inexpensive methods for monitoring the level of hostility to particular ideas and groups. Webb,
Campbell, Schwartz, and Sechrest (1966) have provided a wealth of
guidance and further ideas for developing and using unobtrusive
measures in a variety of contexts.

While citizens, psychologists, and various government agencies
can each play their part, it is only by working together at the community, state, national, and international levels that we will successfully counter the danger of international terrorism. Netanyahu
(2001) recently presented a series of recommendations for fighting
international terrorism. He has served as a soldier in an elite anti-
terrorist unit of the Israeli army and also as prime minister of Israel.
He was invited to address the U.S. Congress nine days after the
September 11 terrorist attacks. His recommendations are:

1. Impose sanctions on suppliers of nuclear technology to terrorist
   states (p. 132).

2. Impose diplomatic, economic, and military sanctions on the terrorist states themselves (p. 134).

3. Neutralize terrorist enclaves (p. 136).

4. Freeze financial assets in the West of terrorist regimes and organizations (p. 137).

5. Share intelligence (p. 138).

6. Revise legislation to enable greater surveillance and action against
   organizations inciting to violence, subject to periodic renewal (p.
   139).

7. Actively pursue terrorists (p. 143).

8. Do not release jailed terrorists (p. 144).

9. Train special forces to fight terrorism (p. 144).

10. Educate the public (p. 146).

While Netanyahu presented these recommendations to a broad audience and while in most instances such actions remain the purview of
governments, he has nevertheless provided a useful array of actions

that address the problem of international terrorism. The recommendation that is most relevant to psychologists of any nation is the final one, that of educating the public. That recommendation is echoed by the goals of this chapter: to point out the value of applying the scientific knowledge and resources of international psychology to the effort to counter international terrorism, and to educate society in general about these matters.

Note

A grant from Psi Chi, the National Honor Society in Psychology, provided support for some of the research cited in this chapter. I thank Carol J. Davis and Randall E. Osborne for helpful comments on earlier versions of this chapter and Brigitte Vittrup for help in locating some of the references.

References

Adair, J. G. (1995). The research environment in developing countries: Contributions to the national development of the discipline. *International Journal of Psychology, 30,* 643–662.

Ajmal, M. (1966). Afghanistan. In S. Ross, I. E. Alexander, & H. Basowitz (Eds.), *International opportunities for advanced training and research in psychology* (pp. 4–5). Washington, DC: American Psychological Association.

Archer, D., & Gartner, R. (1984). *Violence and crime in cross-national perspective.* New Haven, CT: Yale University Press.

Asch, S. E. (1951). Effects of group pressure upon the modification and distortion of judgement. In H. Guetzkow (Ed.), *Groups, leadership, and men: Research in human relations* (pp. 177–190). Oxford, UK: Carnegie Press.

Asch, S. E. (1955). Opinions and social pressure. *Scientific American, 193,* 31–35.

Bandura, A. (1986). *Social foundations of thought and action: A social cognitive theory.* Englewood Cliffs, NJ: Prentice-Hall.

Bandura, A. (1998). Mechanisms of moral disengagement. In W. Reich (Ed.), *Origins of terrorism: Psychologies, ideologies, theologies, states of mind* (pp. 161–191). Washington, DC: Woodrow Wilson Center Press.

Baron, R. A., & Richardson, D. (1994). *Human aggression.* New York: Plenum.

Berscheid, E. (1985). Interpersonal attraction. In G. Lindzey & E. Aronson (Eds.), *Handbook of social psychology* (3rd ed., pp. 413–484). New York: Random House.

Berscheid, E. (1998). Attraction and close relationships. In D. T. Gilbert, S. T. Fiske, & G. Lindzey (Eds.), *Handbook of social psychology* (4th ed., pp. 193–281). Boston: McGraw-Hill.

BMI (Bundesministerium des Innern) (Ed.) (1981–1984). *Analysen zum Terrorismus* (Vol. 1–4/2). Opladen, Germany: Westdeutscher Verlag.

Boldizar, J. P., Perry, D. G., & Perry, L. (1989). Outcome, values and aggression. *Child Development, 60,* 571–579.

Bond, R., & Smith, P. B. (1996). Culture and conformity: A meta-analysis of studies using Asch's line judgement task. *Psychological Bulletin, 119,* 111–137.

Bornstein, R. F. (1989). Exposure and affect: Overview and meta-analysis of research, 1968–1987. *Psychological Bulletin, 106,* 265–289.

Brown, W. (1944). The psychology of modern Germany. *British Journal of Psychology, 34,* 43–59.

Buss, A. H. (1961). *The psychology of aggression.* New York: Wiley.

Byrne, D. (1971). *The attraction paradigm.* New York: Academic Press.

Byrne, D., & Nelson, D. (1965). Attraction as a linear function of proportion of positive reinforcements. *Journal of Personality and Social Psychology, 1,* 659–663.

Cannon, W. B. (1925). *Bodily changes in pain, fear, hunger, and rage.* New York: Appleton-Century-Crofts.

Caprara, G. V. (1996). Structures and processes in personality psychology. *European Psychologist, 1,* 14–26.

Cooper, H. H. A. (2001). Terrorism: The problem of definition revisited. *American Behavioral Scientist, 44,* 881–893.

Crenshaw, M. (1998). The logic of terrorism: Terrorist behavior as a product of strategic choice. In W. Reich (Ed.), *Origins of terrorism: Psychologies, ideologies, theologies, states of mind* (pp. 7–24). Washington, DC: Woodrow Wilson Center Press.

Crenshaw, M. (2000). The psychology of terrorism: An agenda for the 21st century. *Political Psychology, 21,* 405–420.

Da Gloria, J. (1984). Frustration, aggression, and the sense of justice. In A. Mummendey (Ed.), *Social psychology of aggression: From individual behavior to social interaction* (pp. 127–141). New York: Springer.

Da Gloria, J., & DeRidder, R. (1977). Aggression in dyadic interaction. *European Journal of Social Psychology, 7,* 189–219.

Dadfar, A. (1994). The Afghans: Bearing the scars of a forgotten war. In A. J. Marsella, T. Bornemann, S. Ekblad, & J. Orley (Eds.), *Amidst peril and pain: The mental health and well-being of the world's refugees* (pp. 125–139). Washington, DC: American Psychological Association.

Davis, J. M. (1984). Attraction to a group as a function of attitude similarity and geographic distance. *Social Behavior and Personality, 12,* 1–6.

Davis, J. M. (2000a, Spring). Four international organizations in psychology: An overview. *Eye on Psi Chi, 33*–37.

Davis, J. M. (2000b). International Council of Psychologists. In A. E. Kazdin (Ed.), *Encyclopedia of psychology* (Vol. 4, pp. 341–343). Washington, DC/New York: American Psychological Association/Oxford University Press.

Davis, J. M., & Lamberth, J. (1974). Affective arousal and energization properties of positive and negative stimuli. *Journal of Experimental Psychology, 103,* 196–200.

DeRidder, R., Schruijer, S. G. L., & Tripathi, R. C. (1992). Norm violation as a precipitating factor of negative intergroup relations. In R. DeRidder & R. C. Tripathi (Eds.), *Norm violation and intergroup relations* (pp. 3–37). Oxford: Oxford University Press.

Eysenck, H. J. (1997). Personality and experimental psychology: The unification of psychology and the possibility of a paradigm. *Journal of Personality and Social Psychology, 73,* 1224–1237.

Felson, R. B., & Tedeschi, J. T. (Eds.) (1993). *Aggression and violence: Social interactionist perspectives* (pp. 13–45). Washington, DC: American Psychological Association.

Fishman, J. A. (1998–1999). The new linguistic order. *Foreign Policy, 113,* 26–40.

Freud, S. (1963). Instincts and their vicissitudes. In P. Rieff (Ed.), *Freud: General psychological theory* (pp. 83–103). New York: Collier. (Originally published 1915.)

Geen, R. G. (1998). Aggression and antisocial behavior. In D. T. Gilbert, S. T. Fiske, & G. Lindzey (Eds.), *The handbook of social psychology* (4th ed., Vol. 4, pp. 317–356). Boston: McGraw-Hill.

George, A. (1993). *Bridging the gap: Theory and practice of foreign policy.* Washington, DC: U.S. Institute of Peace.

Gilgen, A. R., & Gilgen, C. K. (Eds.) (1987). *International handbook of psychology.* New York: Greenwood Press.

Gonzales, M., Davis, J. M., Loney, G., LuKens, C., & Junghans, C. (1983). Interactional approach to interpersonal attraction. *Journal of Personality and Social Psychology, 44,* 1192–1197.

Groebel, J. (1989). The problems and challenges of research on terrorism. In J. Groebel & J. H. Goldstein (Eds.), *Terrorism: Psychological perspectives* (pp. 15–38). Seville, Spain: Publicaciones de la Universidad de Sevilla.

Harrison, A. A. (1977). Mere exposure. *Advances in Experimental Social Psychology, 10,* 39–83.

Hartley, E. L. (1946). *Problems in prejudice.* New York: King's Crown Press.

Harvey, M. D., & Enzle, M. E. (1978). Effects of retaliation latency and provocation level on judged blameworthiness for retaliatory aggression. *Personality and Social Psychology Bulletin, 4,* 579–582.

Hoffman, B. (1998). *Inside terrorism.* New York: Columbia University Press.

Holtzman, W. H. (2000). International psychology. In A. E. Kazdin (Ed.), *Encyclopedia of psychology* (Vol. 4, pp. 343–345). Washington, DC: American Psychological Association/Oxford University Press.

Holtzman, W. H. (2001). International psychology. In W. E. Craighead & C. D. Nemeroff (Eds.), *The Corsini encyclopedia of psychology and behavioral science* (3rd ed., Vol. 2, pp. 781–783). New York: John Wiley & Sons.

Huesmann, L. R. (1988). An information processing model for the development of aggression. *Aggressive Behavior, 14,* 13–24.

James, W. (1936). *The varieties of religious experience.* New York: Modern Library. (Originally published 1902.)

James, W. (1987). The moral equivalent of war. In *William James: Writings, 1902–1910* (pp. 1281–1293). New York: Library of America. (Originally published 1910.)

Johnson, L. C. (2001). The future of terrorism. *American Behavioral Scientist, 44,* 894–913.

Kampelman, M. M. (1991). *Entering new worlds: The memoirs of a private man in public life.* New York: HarperCollins.

Kellen, K. (1998). Ideology and rebellion: Terrorism in West Germany. In W. Reich (Ed.), *Origins of terrorism: Psychologies, ideologies, theologies, states of mind* (pp. 43–58). Washington, DC: Woodrow Wilson Center Press.

Kramer, M. (1998). The moral logic of Hizballah. In W. Reich (Ed.), *Origins of terrorism: Psychologies, ideologies, theologies, states of mind* (pp. 131–157). Washington, DC: Woodrow Wilson Center Press.

Lamberth, J., Gouaux, C., & Davis, J. (1972). Agreeing attitudinal statements as positive reinforcers in instrumental conditioning. *Psychonomic Science, 29,* 247–249.

Laqueur, W. (1987). *The age of terrorism.* Boston: Little, Brown.

Laqueur, W. (1999). *The new terrorism: Fanaticism and the arms of mass destruction.* New York: Oxford University Press.

Leach, M. M., & Harbin, J. J. (1997). Psychological ethics codes: A comparison of twenty-four countries. *International Journal of Psychology, 32,* 181–192.

Markovits, A. S. (2001). The minister and the terrorist. *Foreign Affairs, 80,* 132–146.

McDougall, W. (1908). *An introduction to social psychology.* London: Methuen.

Merenda, P. F. (1995). International movements in psychology: The major international associations of psychology. *World Psychology, 1,* 27–48.

Mummendey, A., & Mummendey, H. D. (1983). Aggressive behavior of soccer players as social interaction. In J. H. Goldstein (Ed.), *Sports violence* (pp. 111–128). New York: Springer.

National Intelligence Council (2000). *Global trends 2015: A dialogue about the future with nongovernment experts.* Retrieved November 4, 2001, from http://www.cia.gov/cia/publications/globaltrends2015/index.html.

Netanyahu, B. (2001). *Fighting terrorism: How democracies can defeat the international terrorist network.* New York: Farrar, Straus and Giroux.

Osborne, R. E. (1996). *Self: An eclectic approach.* Boston: Allyn and Bacon.

Pawlik, K., & d'Ydewalle, G. (1996). Psychology and the global commons: Perspectives of international psychology. *American Psychologist, 51,* 488–495.

Perry, D. G., Perry, L. C., & Rasmussen, P. (1986). Cognitive social mediators of aggression. *Child Development, 57,* 700–711.

Pillar, P. R. (2001). *Terrorism and U.S. foreign policy.* Washington, DC: Brookings Institution Press.

Post, J. M. (1998). Terrorist psycho-logic: Terrorist behavior as a product of psychological forces. In W. Reich (Ed.), *Origins of terrorism: Psychologies, ideologies, theologies, states of mind* (pp. 25–40). Washington, DC: Woodrow Wilson Center Press.

Rapoport, D.C. (1998). Sacred terror: A contemporary example from Islam. In W. Reich (Ed.), *Origins of terrorism: Psychologies, ideologies, theologies, states of mind* (pp. 102–130). Washington, DC: Woodrow Wilson Center Press.

Redding, R. E. (2001). Sociopolitical diversity in psychology: The case for pluralism. *American Psychologist, 56,* 205–215.

Reeves, S. (1999). *The new jackals: Ramzi Yousef, Osama bin Laden and the future of terrorism.* Boston: Northeastern University Press.

Reich, W. (1998). Understanding terrorist behavior: The limits and opportunities of psychological inquiry. In W. Reich (Ed.), *Origins of terrorism: Psychologies, ideologies, theologies, states of mind* (pp. 261–279). Washington, DC: Woodrow Wilson Center Press.

Rosenzweig, M. R. (1999). Continuity and change in the development of psychology around the world. *American Psychologist, 54,* 252–259.

Rosenzweig, M. R., Holtzman, W. H., Sabourin, M., & Bélanger, D. (2000). *History of the International Union of Psychological Science (IUPsyS).* Philadelphia: Taylor and Francis.

Ross, S., Alexander, I. E., & Basowitz, H. (Eds.) (1966). *International opportunities for advanced training and research in psychology.* Washington, DC: American Psychological Association.

Rutter, M. J. (1997). Nature-nurture integration: The example of antisocial behavior. *American Psychologist, 52,* 390–398.

Schruijer, S. G. L. (1992). On what happens when Dutchmen and Turks violate each other's norms: A perfect match of mutual expectations? In R. DeRidder & R. C. Tripathi (Eds.), *Norm violation and intergroup relations* (pp. 51–69). Oxford, England: Oxford University Press.

Segal, G. (1993). *The world affairs companion: The essential one-volume guide to global issues.* New York: Simon & Schuster.

Sexton, V. S., & Hogan, J. D. (Eds.) (1992). *International psychology: Views from around the world.* Lincoln: University of Nebraska Press.

Sexton, V. S., & Misiak, H. (Eds.) (1976). *Psychology around the world.* Monterey, CA: Brooks/Cole.

Simmons, C. H., & Mitch, J. R. (1985). Labeling public aggression: When is it terrorism? *The Journal of Social Psychology, 125,* 245–251.

Tedeschi, J. T., & Nesler, M. S. (1993). Grievances: Development and reactions. In R. B. Felsen & J. T. Tedeschi (Eds.), *Aggression and violence: Social interactionist perspectives* (pp. 13–45). Washington, DC: American Psychological Association.

U.S. Department of State (2001). *Patterns of global terrorism 2000* (U.S. Department of State Publication 10822). Washington, DC.

Webb, E. J., Campbell, D. T., Schwartz, R. D., & Sechrest, L. (1966). *Unobtrusive measures: Nonreactive research in the social sciences.* Chicago: Rand McNally.

Zajonc, R. B. (1968). Attitudinal effects of mere exposure. *Journal of Personality and Social Psychology Monograph Supplement, 9*, 1–27.

CHAPTER 6

HONING A TOOL AGAINST TERRORISM: MAKING UNITED NATIONS PEACE OPERATIONS MORE RAPID AND EFFECTIVE

Henry Breed

Half a year after the World Trade Center fell, the secretary-general of the United Nations, Kofi Annan, reflected in an interview on "the world's failure over a decade to act on warning signs in Afghanistan, [as it was] battered by political, economic, and natural disasters." He went on to outline "a clear, if complicated, trail from the absence of engagement with Afghanistan in the 1990s to the creation of a terrorist haven there to the attacks on the World Trade Center" (Crossette, 2002).

In making and linking these points, he gave voice and focus to what many had come to sense: that the attacks and the forces behind them had not arisen in a vacuum and that they could not be addressed in one. Yet agreeing on precisely what forces had shaped that moment, and in what manner and measure, would prove to be an elusive and explosive pursuit. And, since progress in addressing a problem is predicated on progress in understanding its causes and currents, deciding how best to respond would prove even tougher.

Many forces were put forward as factors in the terrorist attacks, the situation in Afghanistan, or both. Many organizations leapt into the breach to address them. Many new options were examined, and many existing activities and programs were reinvigorated or reinforced.[1] Of the latter, the United Nations alone had already created and galvanized its membership behind more than a dozen different counterterrorism conventions and instituted specific programs to

forward the goals they contained. It had also already set up specific
programs and offices to address political, humanitarian, social, and
developmental challenges confronting Afghanistan, albeit on a scale
constrained by the contributions received from United Nations member states and by competing crises elsewhere. Other multilateral organizations, governments, and nongovernmental organizations
(NGOs) had undertaken similar initiatives of their own, frequently
facing similar constraints.

Yet there was one option that, though often examined, was not employed in this context: a United Nations peace operation.

The coalition operation that went into Afghanistan had many of
the characteristics and components that its United Nations equiva-
lents had had, might have, or could have. Further, only shortly before
the attacks occurred, the United Nations Panel on Peace Operations
had been convened and had concluded a significant set of recommendations on ways in which these operations needed to be amended and
adjusted so that they might better respond to the challenges ahead.
Additionally, in the wake of the attacks, the man who had chaired that
panel and guided that process, Lakhdar Brahimi, was appointed by
the secretary-general as his special representative for Afghanistan. In
that capacity, he turned to and implemented many of the conclusions
and recommendations that the panel had put forward, in both the political process and the peace operation that evolved there. In short,
there were many links, but there was no bond.

Yet, even though no specific United Nations peace operation was
deployed in this context, there was clearly a great deal of cross-
fertilization, mutual benefit, and growth. One of the main means by
which this chapter will examine the links (both present and possible)
between this context, on one hand, and United Nations peace operations, on the other, is precisely by identifying both the relevant recommendations, readjustments, and realignments that emerged from
the panel's report and the ways that they are being applied (in
Afghanistan and situations like it) or might be applied. The point of
doing so is not to reflect on the road not taken, but—much more importantly—to identify the ways in which these recommendations and
operations might best be put to use in addressing the evolving challenges before us, to assess the synergies they have to offer in and to
a rapidly changing context, and occasionally even to anticipate the
ways that the lessons learned in applying the recommendations
might be applied to the recommendations in turn.

But what precisely is (or could be) the link between the context in question here (in which terrorism has greatly changed both the challenges before us and our perception of them) and peace operations (the means employed by the United Nations to address those challenges on the ground)? What light can that link shed on our understanding of the psychological origins and aspects of that context in general and terrorism more specifically? How can it illuminate the ways in which we choose to address them? What specific measures will need to be taken? By whom? What are some of the most promising and productive means of pursuing the goals that emerge? And what are some of the weaknesses or worries associated with them? How, in the final analysis, can a clearer understanding of the psychological aspects of this dynamic better undergird our actions and directions?

By looking first at the overall context and then at the evolution of peace operations as a response to it, it is these questions that this chapter explores.

Context

What is the overall context from which the challenges now before us emerged?

A decade ago, Jacques Attali (1991), president of the European Bank for Reconstruction and Development, wrote *Millennium*, a book in which he sketched the profile of the challenges that he believed would confront us now, at the threshold of a new thousand years. In the wake of September 11, 2001, it has become hauntingly prescient. In *Millennium*, Attali explained that

[l]ike all past civilizations, which sought to endure by establishing an order to ward off the threat of nature and other men, the coming new order will be based on its ability to manage violence. Unlike previous orders, however, which first ruled by religion, and then by military force, the new order will manage violence largely by economic power. Of course, religion and military might will continue to persist, especially in the peripheral developing countries. . . . [But] the central organizing principle of the future will be economic.

. . . [C]onflict is more likely now that the Cold War has ended and the market has triumphed. For it is precisely because so much of the world now shares the same desire for a prosperous order based on choice that conflict will arise. . . . For inequality will cleave the new world order as surely as the Berlin Wall once divided east from west.

[There will be ...] economic refugees and migrants on an unprecedented scale.... If the North remains passive and indifferent to their plight, and especially if Eastern Europe is brought into the orbit of prosperity through the full force of Western generosity while the South is neglected, the peoples of the periphery will inevitably enter into revolt and, one day, war.

But there is an even more ominous and less visible threat on the horizon. It has to do with the very warp and woof of the new world order and its liberal ideology of consumerism and pluralism. The essence of both democracy and the market is choice. Both offer the citizen-consumer the right to adopt or reject options, whether candidates or commodities, politics or products.... This capacity to change ... is the principal feature of the culture of choice on which the consumerist consensus rests. It informs both our political system and our economic order. Both are rooted in pluralism, and what might be called (perhaps awkwardly) the principle of reversibility. We have come to believe that nothing is (or should be) forever. Everything can be exchanged or discarded. Such a principle, however convenient in the short term, cannot anchor a civilization. Indeed, it undermines the chief imperative of all previous civilizations: to endure.

... The social vertigo induced by the principle of reversibility, which sanctifies the short term and makes a cult of immediacy, is already provoking reaction. The broad revival of religious fundamentalism ... the fanatic rejection of industrial life ..., the nostalgia for hierarchical social structures and tradition, raise the spectre that the democratic values and market principles inherent in the culture of choice will be constantly attacked, perhaps even overturned. (pp. 2–18)

Attali's explanations are searing, and their implications are frightening. Is the culture of "reversibility" a monster that we have ourselves created, at least in part? Is the "social vertigo" that Attali anticipates the equal and opposite—and perhaps inevitable—reaction to it? Were those who felled the World Trade Center targeting the "culture of choice"?

Attali's analysis brilliantly anticipates the context in question here, but it does not (and could not) anticipate the attack itself. Yet, if the world is to attempt successfully to address its new situation, some attempt to understand both that event and its perpetrators' motives must be made. "The religious fundamentalism, ... fanatic rejection of industrial life, ... and nostalgia for hierarchical social structures and tradition" that Attali mentions cannot but bring to mind the World Trade Center bombers, as does another prescient and perceptive reference.

In a speech he gave on terrorism in Jerusalem nearly 30 years ago, U.S. senator Henry Jackson recalled the words that George Bernard Shaw had given Joan of Arc (in his *Saint Joan*) when she was informed that she was to be burned at the stake:

> If I go through the fire, . . . I shall go through it to their hearts for ever and ever. (Safire, 1992, p. 534)

One cannot help but wonder whether, from however perverse a perspective, the terrorists who destroyed the World Trade Center saw themselves and their "fundamental" mission in the same light. If they did so, they did so with some reason. In very different ways, they did reach every human heart, even if—in the great vast majority of them—they inspired horror, fear, and outrage. In doing so, they reminded the world of a truth that the philosopher Miguel de Unamuno had uttered nearly a century before: "Martyrs create faith; faith does not create martyrs" (de Unamuno, 1913). The impact of their messianic mission, however, was none the less for that.

From both a multilateral and psychological perspective, nonetheless, it is important to try to garner some sense of what motivated these individuals—and what they hoped to achieve. What kind of faith were they propounding? What following were they hoping to generate?

To each of these questions, illuminating responses can be found in *The Law of Love and Violence*, a work that Leo Tolstoy wrote at the end of his long life, with the shadow of both World War I and the Russian Revolution bearing down on him, along with that of his own end. It is the political, philosophical, and psychological testament of someone whose sense of the currents of civilization was uniquely tuned. In it, expressing concern about the misuses of faith, such as those that resulted in the terrorist attacks, he avers that

> one can neither weigh nor measure the evil that false religion has caused and is still causing. Religion is the establishment of the relation that exists between man, God, and the universe, and the definition of man's mission that results from it. How miserable our lives would be if this relation and this definition were false. (Tolstoy, 1948, p. 29)

In addition to indicating the falseness of this base, he also considers the structures and strictures constructed from it, and the actions that result. He explains that

> perceiving the constant increase of their misfortunes, [men] employ the only means of salvation that, according to their conception of life, they consider rational: the oppression of part by the rest.

> Certainly, it is possible [for such men] to push a man forcibly in the
> direction that he refuses to take. . . . But how shall one understand the
> reasoning by which violence is a means of inviting men to do every-
> thing we wish them to do?
>
> Constraint always consists in forcing others, by threats of suffering
> or death, to do what they refuse to do. That is why they act against
> their own wishes as long as they consider themselves weaker than their
> oppressors. From the moment that they feel themselves stronger, they
> will not only cease to obey, but, irritated by the struggle and by all that
> they have suffered, they will first gain their liberty, and then in their
> turn they will impose their will upon those who disagree with them. So
> it should be evident that the struggle between oppressors and op-
> pressed, far from constituting a means of social organization, leads to
> disorder and . . . disagreement. (pp. 15–18)

The pattern Tolstoy describes and the particular kind of "groupthink" that it profiles seem almost tailored to fit both terrorists or
terrorist groups (such as al-Qaeda) and those who come within their
grasp. The vital difference, in the context in question, is that, with
luck, the tools that we are honing against precisely that cycle of con-
straint—in which repressor replaces repressor and violence begets
violence—might stand a better chance of breaking it. To improve
their odds, however, understanding both the psychology of the situation and of those caught in it will be crucial. So will be understanding the means at our disposal to address that situation and assist
those individuals and groups.

Alongside the line that stretches from Attali's understanding of
causes and currents to Tolstoy's understanding of their results and
ramifications, another line—describing and proscribing the ways in
which the world responds and can respond—needs also to be drawn.
In drawing it, the first and foremost question that needs to be asked
is: How can the international community support efforts—by and in
Afghanistan and countries like it—to emerge from the terror and violence that have subsumed them?

How Can We Respond?

When speaking of terrorism in Jerusalem 30 years ago, Senator
Jackson asked "What can be done?" and answered with five suggestions:

- We must "acknowledge that international terrorism is a 'collective
  problem'."

- We "must work against . . . efforts to define away terrorism. The idea that one person's terrorist is another's 'freedom fighter' cannot be sanctioned."

- "We must turn the publicity instrument against the terrorists, and we must expose . . . state support of terrorist groups whenever we identify it. . . . When an act of terrorism occurs, [we] should unite in sponsoring resolutions in the United Nations condemning the act. Where we have evidence of support for the terrorists by some other state, this support should be censured in the strongest terms.

- We "must work together to apply sanctions against countries which provide sanctuary to international terrorists."

- "Within each of our own countries, we must organize to combat terrorism in ways consistent with our democratic principles and with the strong support of our citizens." (Safire, 1992, pp. 537–539)

Thirty years ago, at a point in time when it could be rightly claimed that "terrorism is not a new phenomenon; what is new is the international nature of terrorism" (Safire, 1992), this list might have been seen as complete as well as concrete. In the midst of the Cold War and the multilateral limitations it entailed, restricting the United Nations's role to one of sanction and censure might have been perceived as reasonable. Today, neither of those is the case.

In the context in question here, in the shadow of the challenges it portends, as the secretary-general noted at the time,

> the United Nations is uniquely positioned to advance this effort. It provides the forum necessary for building a universal coalition and can ensure global legitimacy for the long-term response to terrorism. United Nations conventions already provide a legal framework for many of the steps that must be taken to eradicate terrorism—including the extradition and prosecution of offenders and the suppression of money laundering. (Annan, 2001)

The United Nations is also advancing this effort, in Afghanistan and in other conflict areas, by engaging actively in the political aspects of resolution, in humanitarian assistance, and in peacekeeping—as it has done throughout its existence.

During the Cold War, many of these efforts focused on addressing the impact of conflicts between countries. In the decade that followed it, peace operations within and without the United Nations broadened to embrace a broader spectrum of activity. Former Secretary-General Boutros Boutros Ghali's "Agenda for Peace" defined a continuum encompassing four areas of action—preventive diplomacy and deployment, peacemaking, peacekeeping, and post-conflict peace-building (United Nations, 2000c, para. 10). In places such as Cambodia, Guatemala, and El Salvador, all of these elements came into play at one moment or another; or even simultaneously. Peacekeeping in particular emerged from its Cold War functions of truce observation and burgeoned into a complex means of addressing multidimensional conflicts with numerous needs. Great optimism was felt, and great strides were taken. In the short space of five years, however, and again particularly in peacekeeping, many of these efforts had badly faltered. Somalia, Bosnia, Rwanda, and Burundi are but the best known and most painfully recalled of these.

Realizing that extensive reform was needed in both what the organization did and how it did it, the secretary-general convened a Panel on Peace Operations on March 7, 2000, to look into the problems existing and the solutions that could be found to them, to

> undertake a thorough review of United Nations peace and security activities, and to present a clear set of specific, concrete, and practical recommendations to assist the United Nations in conducting such activities better in the future. (United Nations, 1998, covering letter)

In its report (which subsequently became known as the Brahimi Report, after the chair of the panel), the Panel on Peace Operations did not focus on when or why to deploy an operation, though some both inside and outside the United Nations feel that it should have. It did not try to prescribe or proscribe specific conditions under which the organization must act or should. Realistically, it knew that decisions of this kind were and would be taken by member states, and on a case-by-case basis rather than under fiat.

What, then, were the parameters that the panel did define? And how did it deal with its subject within them?

First of all, the panel addressed the concern that, too often, in areas precisely like Afghanistan, "United Nations operations did not deploy into post-conflict situations but tried to create them" (United Nations, 1998, p. ix). In many of these situations, the prerequisites of peace—or of peace operations—were often not present. Though some of the operations thus created were able to surmount that impediment, a consensus developed that deployment in and under such conditions needed seriously to be reconsidered. Difficulties encountered reminded us that

> there are lessons that must be learned if we are to expect the peoples of the world to place their faith in the United Nations. There are occa-

sions when Member States cannot achieve consensus on a particular response to active military conflicts, or do not have the will to pursue
what many might consider to be an appropriate course of action. The
first of the general lessons is that when peacekeeping operations are
used as a substitute for such political consensus they are likely to fail.
There is a role for peacekeeping—a proud role in a world still riven by
conflict; but . . . if the necessary resources are not provided—and the
necessary political, military, and moral judgements are not made—the
job simply cannot be done. (United Nations, 2000e, para. 498)[2]

Essentially, while peace operations could be used to address conflicts,
they "should not be used as a substitute for addressing the root causes
of conflict" (United Nations, 1998, para. 49). To use one of the few
psychological terms to emerge from the multilateral lexicon, what
they require most is "political will."

With that point established, the other principal consideration to
which the panel turned was the vital need for more rapid and effective deployment. Experience had taught that rapid reaction and arrival alone were useless without the mandate, means, and direction
required to make presence effective. Yet it had also shown that a
clear direction and solid support would not stave off crisis if they
arrived too late. Rwanda, perhaps more than any other operation,
had borne agonizing witness to the inability of the international
community in general and the United Nations in particular to respond promptly or effectively to utmost need—and to the effects of
that inability.

Many authors have emphasized that the first stages of conflict, like
the first stages of dénouement, can be both the most fragile and the
most threatening. Looking back at the situation in Rwanda, Alan J.
Kuperman advanced the astounding assertion that, of the up to
800,000 people who perished in that country's five-month-long 1994
genocide, as many as 250,000 were slaughtered in the first two weeks
of it alone, at "the fastest genocide rate in history" (Kuperman, 2000,
p. 98). At that very moment, the United Nations Assistance Mission
in Rwanda (UNAMIR) was infamously reduced, first by unilateral
contingent withdrawal, then by a Security Council resolution, from a
strength of more than 2,000 to less than 270, and it would not be reinforced until the end of the year, well after the slaughter had ended.
Even in retrospect, a less-rapid, less-effective deployment than this
seems inconceivable. The low-water mark of United Nations peacekeeping operations had been reached. Above all, this was what needed
to be avoided or averted in the future. But how?

Against this grim history, the panel had to balance the realities, weaknesses, and impediments of the organization. It also, however, needed to take a long, hard look at each actor in the political process, whether an individual or an organizational unit, and it had to recommend ways in which the actions and interactions of those actors could be put to greatest service.

From a theoretical standpoint, based on game theory, Robert Axelrod offers a number of insights into how that progress might best be achieved:

> Mutual cooperation can be stable if the future is sufficiently important relative to the present. . . . When the future casts a large shadow, . . . it pays to cooperate . . . and . . . cooperation based on reciprocity is stable. . . . There are two basic ways of [enlarging the shadow of the future]: by making interactions more durable, and by making them more frequent.
>
> Hierarchy and organization [can be] especially effective at concentrating [such] interactions. . . . By binding people together in a long-term, multilevel [situation], organizations increase the number and importance of future interactions, and thereby [can] promote the emergence of cooperation among groups too large to interact individually. This in turn leads to the evolution of organizations for the handling of larger and more complex issues. (Axelrod, 1981, pp. 126–131)

It seems at many points that this is the perspective that the panel adopted, wittingly or not, in hammering out its assessments and recommendations. Moving from one actor to the next, we will see how that perspective is reflected.

The panel knew, for example, that the presence or absence, strength or weakness of any action taken by the United Nations was and is entirely dependent upon the political will manifested by (or through) its member states. It knew not only how thinly that lifeblood could trickle, but also how far through the labyrinth of structure and administration it had to course.

One of the ways in which member states had long been laboring to achieve an increasingly greater say in peace operations was through meetings of "troop contributors," both general and mission-specific.

Troop contributors meetings and briefings are convened to involve "prospective troop contributors [in] consultations at the earliest possible stage in order to provide them access to the information required to enable them to make an informed decision on participation" (United Nations, 1998, para. 53). A political committee within the

United Nations made up of member states has repeatedly underlined "the importance of consultations with troop-contributing countries," but has also pushed farther, volleying for "strengthening and formalizing the consultation process" and holding meetings *at the request of* troop-contributing countries, particularly when a new mandate is being considered." It has further suggested that countries that have committed personnel to a mission "should be invited to participate in meetings of the Security Council in which the Secretariat provides it with information on changes to the mission's mandate and concept of operations that have implications for the mission's use of force" (United Nations, 2000a, paras. 8–12, italics mine). Clearly, those countries that risk the lives of their young for peace deserve both the fullest knowledge of the situation available and the maximum protection that that knowledge can offer. If their interest and participation is to be sustained, it is essential. There is a balance to be considered, however. If the point were reached where the increasing involvement of troop contributors became a de facto broadening of the Security Council, the very rapidity and effectiveness that those troop contributors and others are seeking would be hampered, if not endangered. Yet a better balance must unquestionably be found; one that— whether through invitation to Security Council meetings on mandate formulation or some other means—gives possible troop contributors the comfort, confidence, reassurance, and input they require to be able to commit their contingents early and fully.

Two of the panel's recommendations do a great deal not only to maintain the fragile balance between these parties and others, but also to further effectiveness and rapidity. The first is that "the Security Council ... assure itself that [peace agreements involving the creation of peacekeeping operations meet] threshold conditions, such as consistency with international human rights standards and practicability of specified tasks and timelines." Recalling the international negotiations on Afghanistan that took place in Germany and their impact, one understands better both the need to insist upon these threshold conditions and the benefits to be gained by so doing. The second and more ingenious recommendation is that

> the Security Council should leave *in draft form* resolutions authorizing missions with sizeable troop levels until such time as the Secretary-General has firm commitments of troops and other critical mission support elements ... *from Member States.* (United Nations, 2000c, para. 64, italics mine)

This single brilliant stroke, if ever implemented, would alone address a host of problems that the panel and others have had to face: force strength, mandate, and security primary among them. For those very reasons, its future will be something to watch with concern—concern, however, and hope.

The other really hopeful sign as regards the Security Council is the growing trend of its deploying fact-finding missions to peace operations on the ground. The panel itself lamented (United Nations, 2000c) the way that the Secretariat felt increasingly constrained to refrain from telling "the Security Council what it needs to know, not what it wants to hear." That frustration was compounded by the realization of how little firsthand insight or experience those handling the mission from New York were gleaning from the ground. Those experiences convinced the panel of the utility—even the necessity—of fact-finding missions. Given the expenses that operations now entail, as the panel itself noted, such missions are wise investments entailing relatively minute expenditures, which can nonetheless be carefully accounted, audited, and defended. They should prove a "force multiplier" in every sense, and it is very encouraging that the council in particular is seeing their value and making use of them.

Concerning these missions, the panel argued that

> [o]n a political level, many of the local parties with whom peacekeepers and peacemakers are dealing on a daily basis may neither respect nor fear verbal condemnation by the Security Council. It is therefore incumbent that Council members and the membership at large breathe life into the words that they produce, as did the Security Council delegation that flew to Jakarta and Dili in the wake of the East Timor crisis last year, an example of effective Council *action* at its best: *res, non verba.* (United Nations, 2000c, para. 276)

This lesson, learned in East Timor, might, under other circumstances, have been learned or applied in Afghanistan. More important, the fruit it has borne will encourage those involved in addressing future challenges and crises to apply it to them. A number of such recent missions have also shown (and the panel has noted) that, just as there is benefit to be reaped from early missions to an operation by Secretariat staff and the Security Council, there is also benefit in ensuring that

> the entire leadership of a mission [is] assembled at Headquarters as early as possible in order to enable their participation in key aspects of

the mission planning process, for briefings on the situation in the mission area and to meet and work with their colleagues in mission leadership.... The Secretariat should routinely provide the mission leadership with strategic guidance and plans for anticipating and overcoming challenges to mandate implementation and, whenever possible, should formulate such guidance and plans together with the mission leadership. (United Nations, 2000c, para. 101)

Experience in Afghanistan and other recent crises have underlined that these steps are equally important in situations where, without the benefit of a United Nations peace operation, a special representative of the secretary-general (or the equivalent) has been assigned to address a crisis and guide a political or peace process.

The secretary-general, in his report on the implementation of the panel's recommendations (United Nations, 2000d, para. 64), made the analogous point that "those who will ultimately have to start up and run a mission on the ground should be involved in the planning of that mission."

One of the innovations recommended by the panel would help achieve precisely this. The panel advocates the participation of "advisor-observers" during peace negotiations to ensure that

tasks to be undertaken by the United Nations are operationally achievable ... and either contribute to addressing the sources of conflict or provide the space required for others to do so. Since competent advice to negotiators may depend on detailed knowledge of the situation on the ground, the Secretary-General should be pre-authorized to commit funds from the Peacekeeping Reserve Fund sufficient to conduct a preliminary site survey. (United Nations, 2000d, para. 58)

Clearly, the preliminary site surveys would form another and welcome strand in the net of deeper, earlier contacts with the field that include the missions by the Secretariat and Security Council that the panel also supports. Aside from assisting in determining such crucial issues as proposed mission strength and deployment, however, these site surveys would undoubtedly be of use precisely in assessing what support and material a mission would require, and how best it might receive it. Interestingly, in the case of Afghanistan, the advisor-observer function was not only present, it far exceeded in both range and rank anything anticipated by the language of the panel. Further, in a natural-enough division of labor (particularly given the coalition composition of the mission on the ground), the site survey work was actually undertaken by or through the contributing countries. From both of these initiatives, a greater ability to react rapidly and effectively resulted.

There is a vital and promising link to be made between the various points, possibilities, and options just covered. "Burnout" is always a risk of long involvement with one issue. And fresh perspectives can often be extremely useful. But the points that the panel and the secretary-general make above on early and extended participation are extremely important and promising. Too rarely has enough foresight been exercised to envisage the presence of a United Nations (or any other) peace operation early in a peace process. More rarely still has the United Nations become involved in or been brought in for the purpose of designing that presence in conjunction with and support of that peace process. And rarest of all have been the incidences where rapports and reputations on the ground have already been well established, where institutional memory is already broad and solid.

Other good and valuable recommendations on senior staffing emerge from the panel's report and those who react to it. The enhancement of "on-call" lists for special representatives of the secretary-general (SRSGs) and other senior staff will encourage rapidity and effectiveness, particularly if the panel's recommendation to broaden them to include senior officials in specific areas such as electoral assistance and human rights is fully followed. One United Nations political committee, in considering the smooth filling of these posts, recommended (United Nations, 2000a, para. 17) that "all mission leaders must be interviewed by the senior leadership, as a general rule, at United Nations Headquarters." If the mission is still nascent and New York is still its nexus, this clearly makes sense. Yet, in balancing effectiveness and rapidity, it needs to be remembered that the process of filling field posts is already notoriously cumbersome and slow. If these steps—admittedly good and necessary—are to be taken, where will the slack for them be found or created? And at what stage of implementation does it make more sense for senior officials (apart from the SRSG and deputy SRSG themselves) to be interviewed in the mission area? In considering questions of civilian personnel, the panel recommends that hiring authority be delegated to the field. The line between these two recommendations—the point at which ongoing contact with (and therefore an interview in) New York becomes essential—needs to be more fully and carefully drawn. But will that need to be decided on a mission-by-mission basis? And perhaps by the SRSG himself, whether in New York or once deployed?

Whether this decision is taken by the SRSG or someone else, the question of filling posts in the field is also tied, in a very practical way, to building local capacity and cooperation, as people locally hired are frequently local. This reality has in turn a profound psychological impact on the local population and their outlook on the mission. Often, in their own minds, local recruitment is used as a litmus test to gauge the (perceived) extent to which the international community is actually (and literally) working with them and investing in them. Their conclusions frequently determine (or at least affect) the degree of their cooperation and support.

The strengthening of the role of the SRSG is actually an area in which one of the panel's most cogent and promising recommendations emerges. Both the panel and the secretary-general recommend (United Nations, 2000c, para. 47a) that

> a small percentage of a mission's first-year budget should be made available to the representative or special representative of the Secretary-General leading the mission to fund quick-impact projects with the advice of the country team's resident coordinator.

Though they are unacknowledged, the proposal draws on lessons learned from two operations: The successes achieved by SRSG Aldo Ajello in Mozambique, in part through the use of precisely this kind of fund, and the frustration and failure encountered by the United Nations in Rwanda for lack of it or anything similar. Ajello's funds, it needs to be noted, were provided not by or through the United Nations, but rather by his own government, which took great interest in the Mozambican peace process. It was for this reason that the United Nations was unable to respond to similar requests in and from Rwanda: There has been, to this day, no United Nations fund from which to draw for such projects and expenses.

Small acts of support or good faith by Ajello—often rapid responses to slight requests of a logistical or material nature—proved invaluable in sustaining the parties, their good faith, and their participation in the peace process. Like local recruitment, these were sound, solid psychological investments. The United Nations Assistance Mission in Rwanda, in contrast, was never able to emerge from under the cloud of misgivings of both the parties, partly due to its inability to offer precisely this kind of gesture of good will and support.

During its tenure and beyond its departure, both Hutu and Tutsi lamented both the larger failure of the mission to achieve its mandate and its many smaller failures to provide the resources or support that would have aided the country in its reach toward recovery.

To imply that such initiatives were entirely absent is neither accurate nor fair. But as Shaharyar Khan, the SRSG in Rwanda, noted in a cable to New York shortly before the mission closed, they were taken "mainly through military and technical units, operating over and above their mandated tasks" (United Nations, 1996b, p. 1).

To prove this point, Khan then recounted a list of achievements that is both impressive and moving including rebuilding four bridges, repairing 13 roads and building 3 new ones, assisting in the reconstruction of Kigali Airport and the restoration of national telephone and radio networks, treating up to 1,600 patients in the mission's clinics and immunizing 62,000 (as well as training hospital staff and performing life-saving surgical operations on Rwandan citizens), transporting large quantities of food and up to a million refugees, and providing generators and engineering services (United Nations, 1996b, pp. 3–5). The end-of-mission report submitted by his force commander only a few days later closes with a similar synopsis. Both, however, acknowledge that the mission was still "looked upon with misgivings by both the ethnic parties" and conclude that "the peace as it exists can best be described as fragile" (United Nations, 1996a).

As one analyst explained,

The local population . . . is generally not able to comprehend the failure of their "trustees" to expend allocated funds promptly to deal with obvious and urgent needs and may grow resentful in the face of apparent indifference. . . . UN rules make it difficult for a mission to expend resources on anything other than the mission itself. This may not be problematic for most peace-support operations, but it would be helpful for an operation whose purpose is to facilitate the emergence of a new state, or at least to promote substantial autonomy, to permit the use of UN resources . . . by fledgling indigenous institutions. UN procurement rules should be revised to allow transitional administrators greater authority to buy goods and services directly. (Caplan, 2002, pp. 74–76)

These observations fully reinforce the need both for this kind of assistance and for a fund that would allow it to be provided more rapidly, effectively, fully, and freely. The end-of-mission report by the force commander, General Sivukumar, places such stock in just such an arrangement that he recommends that "a permanent advisor to the Agencies and NGOs [for coordinating this kind of quick-impact project] . . . would prove beneficial to the functioning" of the mission. Noting that part of the new focus of United Nations peace operations is "to create and strengthen political institutions and to broaden their base," the secretary-general's Millennium Report (United Nations, 2000b, paras. 221–222) argued that this kind of assistance is essential because "[p]eople will quickly become disillusioned with fledgling institutions, and even the peace process itself, if they can see no prospect for any material improvement in their condition." This is a risk that is still being run in Afghanistan and other conflict areas like it, where needs are identified, a small fraction of the aid needed to meet them is promised, and, even when promised, it tends to arrive too little and too late to meet many needs and expectations. The goals espoused—and the situations themselves—will continue to be placed in unnecessary peril as long as this continues. At a psychological level, the message transmitted by inaction is as strong as that transmitted by action; it is simply its equal and its opposite.

To help the SRSG address these challenges and situations, the role of the deputy SRSG (whether the local humanitarian coordinator or resident representative) was somewhat retailored as well. To signal the symbiosis required between the SRSG and the deputy, the Secretariat, and the United Nations's agencies and programs on the ground, the secretary-general emphasized in his reform proposal (United Nations, 1997, para. 119) that "in the field, the Special Representative . . . will have authority over all United Nations entities," but that the SRSG would receive senior-level support from the humanitarian coordinator or resident representative, recommending that that individual serve as deputy, as appropriate. Again, as Axelrod (1981) would note, the durability, frequency, and immediacy of interaction has been underscored. The net has again been strengthened and tightened. Greater, broader, and more sustained contact with the local population, leading to greater support and cooperation from them, is again the goal, the psychological and political purpose.

To achieve these aims, effective leadership is vital—across each and all of the areas discussed. Equally essential, however, is commensurate reform at the working level and on the ground. In recommending the creation of Integrated Mission Task Forces (IMTFs), the panel addresses the first of those needs.

Admitting that the task forces that had previously been convened to address specific situations or to guide the initial deployment of specific missions had functioned "more as sounding boards than executive bodies that . . . meet infrequently and . . . disperse once an op-

eration had begun to deploy" and acknowledging that "missions have
no single working-level focal point at headquarters that can address
all of their concerns quickly," the panel argued that the IMTFs
should constitute

> an entity that includes all of the backstopping people and expertise for
> the mission, drawn from an array of headquarters elements that mir-
> rors the functions of the mission itself. The notion of integrated, *one-
> stop support* for United Nations peace-and-security field activities
> should extend across the whole range of peace operations, with the
> size, substantive composition, meeting venue, and leadership matching
> the needs of the operation.... The supporting cast would remain sub-
> stantially the same during transitions [between phases and responsible
> departments].... [The IMTF's] size and composition would match
> the nature and the phase of the field activity being supported. *Task
> Force members should be formally seconded* to IMTF for [the period
> needed] by their home division, department, agency, or programme.
>
> ... An IMTF should be much more than a coordinating committee
> or task force of the type now set up at headquarters. It should be a tem-
> porary but coherent staff created for a specific purpose, able to be in-
> creased or decreased in size or composition in response to mission
> needs. Each Task Force member should be authorized to serve not only
> as a liaison between the Task Force and his or her home base, but as its
> *key working-level decision-maker* for the mission in question.
>
> IMTFs offer a flexible approach to dealing with time-critical, re-
> source-intensive, but ultimately temporary requirements to support
> mission planning, start-up, and initial sustainment. The concept bor-
> rows heavily from the notion of "matrix management" used extensively
> by large organizations that need to be able to assign the necessary tal-
> ent to specific projects without reorganizing themselves every time a
> project arises.
>
> IMTFs, with members seconded from throughout the United
> Nations system, as necessary, should be the standard vehicle for mis-
> sion-specific planning and support. (United Nations, 2000c, paras.
> 200–217, italics mine)

Clearly, in an organization where most officers bear responsibility
for more than one mission (and sometimes more than one area), this
innovation would entail substantial revisions and reforms. The definition of roles and timings alone will prove very sensitive. And it will
be important not to destabilize the current decision-making process
while the IMTFs are being put into place and into motion. Yet, regardless of those requirements (among others), there is undoubtedly
a great deal to be gained from having a hub that is indeed more uni-

fied, where all headquarters actors are in both immediate and frequent contact with each other, and where, perhaps most importantly, they are each and all empowered to be "key working-level decision-makers." Structurally, devolving that degree of authority to that extent would both simplify and expedite decision and action. The underlying assumption—or safeguard—would seem to be that the checks and balances now imposed sequentially by a vertical hierarchy could be adequately replaced by simultaneous lateral consultation within the context of the IMTF itself. To the extent that this proves true—and sufficient—the process, the organization, the mission, and the mission area will clearly gain a great deal from the change proposed.

Seconding the officers concerned, freeing and forcing them to focus solely on the mission in question and its needs, will also make line reactions and responses more rapid and effective, given that adequate ties and reporting to their "home bases" are assured. Further, involving those identified from the beginning, achieving the fullest and broadest representation possible, and ensuring smooth transitions between phases will maximize the retention of institutional memory and avoid the frustrating slippage so often encountered by the current system, most notably during handovers or reassignments.

These changes again recall Axelrod's perception on the psychological dynamic of such constructs, which "[b]y binding people together in a long-term, multilevel [situation], . . . increase the number and importance of future interactions, and thereby [can] promote the emergence of cooperation" (Axelrod, 1981, pp. 126, 131). Early indications from the United Nations missions in East Timor and other areas where IMTFs have been employed confirm that they have indeed brought progress toward the goals sought—and that they hold even greater potential for future operations.

The strength and success of the IMTF mechanism will also, of course, depend upon the support provided through it to elements and activities on the ground, and on their strength in turn. In three of those elements (military personnel, civilian police, and civilian personnel), the panel recommended changes that could help bring about that greater strength and success.

While all the actors and aspects examined thus far play crucial roles in achieving rapid and effective deployment, three elements actually *are* deployed, rapidly and effectively or not: military personnel, civilian police, and civilian personnel. Of these, military personnel are usually among the very first to arrive in the theater, and they are also usually at the core of efforts to plan and implement an operation's deployment. Their efforts, therefore, go to the heart of achieving the goals that the panel identified.

The inadequate provision of military personnel has been the bane of peacekeeping in the last decade, at times with disastrous results, and it has often seemed that the broader the mandates and needs of an operation have become, the wider the gap has gotten. There is a certain logic in this, of course, but there is also a certain irony.

The language of the panel's recommendation reflects this. Both moving and telling, it also demonstrates a sensitivity to the psychological needs and vulnerabilities of a population emerging from conflict that is rarely given voice in official documents:

> [T]he Panel believes that, until the Secretary-General is able to obtain solid commitment from Member States for the forces that he or she does believe necessary to carry out an operation, it should not go forward at all. To deploy a partial force incapable of solidifying a fragile peace would first raise and then dash the hopes of a population engulfed in conflict or recovering from war, and damage the credibility of the United Nations as a whole. (United Nations, 2000c, para. 61)

It is in this context and for these reasons that the panel believes that resolutions should be left in draft form, and it also points (United Nations, 2000c, para. 61) to ways in which it believes that such "commitment gaps" can be filled or diminished.

Among these, four are key. The formation of brigades (by member states or regional or other organizations) that can be quickly deployed has the advantage of units that are preformed and pretrained. But interoperability has yet to be achieved among them, and they still require parliamentary approval at the national level (which is not always speedily received) to be deployed.

On-call lists would be made up of up to a hundred officers of various specialties and nationalities, prequalified, pretrained, and deployable within seven days. "Interacting with the planners of the Integrated Mission Task Force" and assembled to coordinate the planning of the mission, the task of

> the "on-call team" would be to translate the broad strategic-level concepts of the mission . . . into concrete operational and tactical plans, and to undertake immediate coordination and liaison tasks in advance of the deployment of troop contingents, [. . . remaining] operational until replaced by deployed contingents. (United Nations, 2000c, para. 112)

In addition to these initiatives, the panel recommended the deployment of teams to assess the readiness of contingents before they deploy, and it also noted the need for "enabling forces, which include the provision of specialized units for movement control, communications, terminal or air-traffic control capability . . . [and] strategic lift assistance to troop contributors" (United Nations, 2000c, para. 84).

Parallel to these military measures, two important innovations were being propounded that relate specifically to the civilian police, as part of both

> a doctrinal shift . . . in how the Organization conceives of and utilizes civilian police in peace operations . . . [and] an adequately resourced team approach to upholding the rule of law and respect for human rights through judicial, penal, human rights and policing experts working together in a coordinated and collegial manner. (United Nations, 2000c, para. 40)

That coordinated and collegial collaboration would need to be accomplished at two levels: a new and independent rule-of-law unit that would report to the civilian police commissioner in the United Nations's Department of Peacekeeping Operations, and rule-of-law teams that would participate in IMTFs and other aspects of early mission deployment. In setting out resource requirements to implement the panel's recommendations to expand civilian police mandates and create rule-of-law teams, the secretary-general cautioned that

> [t]he ability of the United Nations civilian police to carry out their mandates is intrinsically linked to the ability of the local judicial and penal systems to carry out their responsibilities effectively. Yet, civilian police in peace operations are often deployed in areas where not only the local police, but also local judicial and penal institutions, have been severely weakened or have ceased to exist. In such areas, these institutions must be rapidly strengthened if United Nations civilian police are to succeed. (United Nations, 2000f, para. 5.99)

To extend Axelrod's concepts, for frequent and durable interaction to occur, for cooperation to thrive and for progress to be made, there must be parallel and analogous actors on each side. But yet, even in the absence of this, as the panel rightly noted

> United Nations civilian police monitors are not peacebuilders if they simply document or attempt to discourage . . . abusive or other unacceptable behaviour of local police officers—a traditional and somewhat narrow perspective of [their] capabilities. Today, missions may require civilian police to be tasked to *reform, train, and restructure local police forces according to international standards* for democratic policing and human rights, *as well as having the capacity to respond effectively to civil*

disorder and for self-defence. (United Nations, 2000c, para. 39, italics mine)

Again, as was the case with military personnel, the situation demands the strengthening of both mandate and means to achieve it. Again, in response to those demands, a forward bulwark is set that comprises elements both new and reinforced. In Afghanistan and the areas of conflict that follow it, success will continue to be measured by the extent to which that bulwark is reinforced, empowered, and defended, the extent to which these new structures have flesh put on their bones and are brought to life, the extent to which new links are made and strengthened.

As important to that success as the elements discussed thus far will be, another option—perhaps another challenge—has arisen alongside them that is both making different demands and offering new prospects: transitional administration.

If a line were drawn from traditional peacekeeping through the "wider peacekeeping" efforts undertaken in places like Cambodia and Mozambique, and withheld in Rwanda, then onward through the rule-of-law measures examined above, the next logical point on that line would be transitional administration.

In characterizing transitional administration operations, the panel notes (United Nations, 2000c, para. 77) that they

> face challenges and responsibilities that are unique among United Nations field operations. [They] must set and enforce the law, establish customs services and regulations, set and collect business and personal taxes, attract foreign investment, adjudicate property disputes and liabilities for war damage, reconstruct and operate all public utilities, create a banking system, run schools and pay teachers, . . . rebuild civil society and promote respect for human rights, in places where grievance is widespread and grudges run deep.

This is clearly the kind of work that the United Nations has taken on successfully in East Timor, and strongly similar to the body of work currently under way in Afghanistan. Yet there are misgivings about whether "the United Nations should be in this business at all" and whether such undertakings should be "considered an element of peace operations or managed by some other structure." The panel recognizes each of them (United Nations, 2000c, para. 78). At a very practical and immediate level, however, and partly in consideration of the kinds of crises now before us, the assumed response to each of these queries is positive.

Looking at the list of duties just detailed, one realizes immediately how vital to their success it is to have rapid access to and support from a broad range of civilian specialists. Given the breadth of demands represented, it is equally clear that collaboration with agencies, programs, and bodies outside the United Nations will also need to be strengthened. At the same time, the realization strikes that, incomplete as United Nations efforts have been to line up personnel for military and civilian police duties, they have been weaker yet in the civilian sector. One reason for this is that United Nations involvement in these activities has previously been primarily advisory; only recently has the organization actually been required to implement them. That, however, does not mitigate the need for rapid and effective response in these areas.

To ensure the greater presence, broader support, and quicker response that current and coming crises will require, the panel recommends that three options of interest in this context be examined and possibly implemented. Two of them—assigning "sectoral responsibility" to national contingents from individual member states and/or creating an international Civilian Standby Arrangements System (CSAS)—can be seen either as alternates or as complements. A third—the cementing of closer ties with a broader range of actors—would clearly be essential in any case.

Between the first two options offered, at least from my view, the promotion and solidification of the CSAS as proposed holds far more promise than the bloc assignment of entire national contingents to specific sectors of responsibility. Because specialized teams in given missions would need very specific expertise, both individually and collectively, the option of being able to draw prepared and preapproved *individuals* from an Internet-based roster and hire them in the field better ensures adequate coverage, both of disciplines and of mission needs. It allows a more tailored fit between the mission and the mission area. The roster proposed differs more in degree than kind from the more informal rosters now maintained, though it suggests greater range and rapidity. Nonetheless, the CSAS, if implemented as designed, would provide the mission and the organization greater fluidity, flexibility, and strength than the assemblage of national sectoral groups, large or small. It would result in a single woven fabric, not a patchwork quilt.

Additionally, better than national sectoral responsibility, CSAS would complement the effort to reach out to and involve nongovernmental organizations in a way that would assist the United Nations not only in the provision of personnel but also in the creation of broader understanding and political support, further strengthening the base of cooperation, as Axelrod suggested. This would be achieved in part by giving

> [t]he relevant members of the United Nations family . . . delegated authority and responsibility, for occupational groups within their respective expertise, to initiate partnerships and memoranda of under-standing with intergovernmental and non-governmental organiza-tions, for the provision of personnel to supplement mission start-up teams. (United Nations, 2000c, para. 144)

This possibility, however, brings Rwanda once again to mind. Hobbled by a lack of the kind of discretionary fund that had been used in Mozambique (and that the panel now recommends be used gener-ally), the mission nonetheless made constant efforts both to reach out to the agencies and nongovernmental organizations (NGOs) and to coordinate with them. The first of these were moderately successful; the latter met with more resistance. Why?

While it is important for agencies and NGOs to be acknowledged as players and provided a place at the table, it is equally important, from their view, that they be able to retain objective distance from the United Nations and its mission and remain free of association with them. The identity and the credibility of these organizations often rest both on the specificity of their mandate (human rights, famine relief) as it fits into the larger mosaic of international com-munity action and on the fact that they are precisely *nongovern-mental*. They are answerable solely to their donors and directors, not to the General Assembly or the Security Council. Thus, from their perspective, communication with the United Nations and its mission is clearly and mutually beneficial. Collaboration is possible and sometimes fruitful. But *coordination* of NGO efforts by the United Nations or under its auspices is an idea that, usually, has met with a lukewarm reception at best. As past crises have underlined and as present crises have reconfirmed, this option is thus not without limitations.

Yet, it is entirely possible, and imminently necessary, to make firmer and greater strides in creating broader understanding and po-litical support. It was in this context that the panel recalled (United Nations, 2000c, para. 269) that

> [t]he Secretary-General has consistently emphasized the need for the United Nations to reach out to civil society and to strengthen relations

with non-governmental organizations, academic institutions, and the media.

NGOs have already proven both vital and effective in this effort. As organizations not made up of member states, the criticisms that they could sometimes level at specific countries or situations often complemented positions or tacks taken by the United Nations.

Yet, however effective such NGO pronouncements might be in helping the United Nations highlight problems in a given area and in attempting to address them, it is ultimately the media that conveys, fails to convey, or decides not to convey these stories. The spark that ignites interest, creates debate, and generates movement toward action is theirs alone.

Despite this, public information activities and outreach are grossly undersupported—financially as well as politically, at the level of the United Nations, regional organizations (some of the U.S. coalitions being possible exceptions), member states, and mission areas. Though it is true that financing for public information remains a serious concern and an abiding frustration, the real problems facing the sector are deeper, more endemic. They touch on mode and method as well as means.

The panel, realizing this, identified a number of aspects and areas of public information that could benefit from reform including expanding and reinforcing communication within missions; identifying competent spokespeople; developing a peace operations extranet (POE) and co-managed Web sites to help spread the mission's message; strengthening public information approaches and activities in expanding sectors (such as human rights and civilian police), and developing local capacity.

Quite clearly and correctly, the panel argued (United Nations, 2000c, para. 147) that "[f]ield missions need competent spokespeople who are integrated into the senior management team and project its daily face to the world" to help achieve this. This recommendation (which is followed by a request that the Secretariat "increase its efforts to develop and retain a pool of such personnel"), however, raises another concern.

It is equally important (United Nations, 2000a, para. 31) that "consideration must be given to the promotion of local capacity" in public information. Creating such capacity is acknowledged to build an important bridge into the community, strengthen communication across it, and look toward the point at which information functions, like those of civilian police, will be assumed from within the theater.

Yet strengthening such capacity both in the public information sector and far beyond it will depend not only on the creation of cooperation within the community or within the mission itself. It will depend on a wider, broader, more vibrant, and proactive outreach by the organization and the international community at large, something that (particularly at critical moments) has often been sorely wanting.

Turning from the local back to the international, from a specific afflicted state to the sum of all member states, from capacity on the ground back to capacity across the globe, brings us full circle. It completes our consideration of the panel's recommendations and the role and relation of each party in and to them. It squares the entire net we have been examining here—the warp threads of rapidity, the woofs of effectiveness, and the contribution that each party makes (or can make) to tightening and strengthening the fabric.

Conclusion

Stepping back from that net for a moment, we can quickly see the greater strength and broader range that it will have, in Afghanistan, East Timor, or the areas that follow them, if the panel's recommendations are accepted and implemented. We can easily identify the strands that can strengthen the net, such as early visits to new mission areas by Security Council members; early United Nations presence in negotiations (possibly through "advisor-observers"); preliminary site surveys; early access by the secretary-general to $50 million to initiate deployment; early identification of possible troop contributors; early choice of mission leaders and rapid assembly of them at headquarters; preliminary missions to the area by the headquarters staff (both military and civilian) who will be handling an eventual operation; early and rapid constitution of an Integrated Mission Task Force (IMTF), and of preapproved military contingents and civilian staff (possibly as CSAS members), expedited and facilitated by enabling forces.

While these measures concentrate on early and rapid deployment, other strands of the net concentrate on increasing a mission's breadth and effectiveness, through strengthening its mandate and definition of self-defense; deploying rule-of-law teams; broadening civilian police activity; emphasizing human rights and building sustainable local capacity in this area; building local public information capacity, without forgetting to reach out within the mission itself; engaging the agencies and programs by involving either the humanitarian coordinator or the resident representative as the Deputy SRSG; collaborating more closely with NGOs; and reaching out more effectively both to the media and to the local population.

Each of these strands—both the warps that extend as early into an operation's life as possible and the woofs that stretch as broadly as feasible across disciplines and mission areas—will be essential if the improvements sought are to be reached and grasped.

What are some of the most promising and productive means identified by the panel to pursue these goals? And what are some of the weaknesses or worries associated with them? In what ways and for what reasons will they need to be watched?

Quick impact projects, considered for a decade, hold great promise. Yet they require the SRSG who chooses and oversees them to be fully informed and in command of the situation from the very moment of his or her arrival. At the far end of the year foreseen for them, additionally, some consequent strategy (whether it be local procurement, longer-term agency programs, or some other means) must then be ready to take over if their impact is to be realized fully. Because of the autonomy and delegation of authority they assume, their progress will need to be watched to see not only what support this initiative receives, but also what constraints and restraints are placed upon it.

IMTFs might indeed provide the more concise and consolidated headquarters support that missions require. Empowering line managers and desk officers could well result in more rapid reactions. But will this less vertical chain of command ensure the expertise required? And will the IMTFs actually receive, through full secondment of their members, the lifeblood, energy, and commitment that they will need to thrive? This initiative, encompassing the sensitive secondment issue in a Secretariat already overstretched, will be the bellwether of support within the house for the reforms set, and it should be watched carefully for that reason and indication.

Member states' commitment to reform will be tested more than anything else by whether they (in and through the Security Council) support and confirm the panel's recommendation that council resolutions authorizing missions remain in draft pending receipt of the support required to implement them. One of the oldest and deepest frustrations of the organization has been receiving mandates without means. Passing authorizing resolutions without providing the means they require has enabled member states to have their cake and eat it too—to avoid contributing to a mission and then lament the "failure" of the United Nations to acquit itself of the responsibilities they gave it. This is and has been a comfortable loophole to have. Will member states bear to see it closed, knowing that its closure will mean shouldering either responsibilities or costs? Their response on this issue will indicate their commitment to the reform for which they themselves have been calling.

The development, deployment, acceptance, and support of rule-of-law teams will prove a sure and sensitive indicator of the support (or lack of it) from the areas and countries where missions are deployed. Granted, peace operations are now created somewhat from a *menu à choix*, but as the continuum of international action moves through ethnic-conflict operations onward toward transitional administration, this element, the full and effective implementation of it, and the creation of the necessary local capacity to sustain it will all prove important indicators of the necessary longer-term view and commitment within the mission area itself.

Meeting the unique needs of public information, in rule-of-law and other emerging sectors, will test interest and commitment both within the organization and across a wider range. Regional organizations, member states, national broadcasting corporations, NGOs, and others, both within the mission area and beyond it, have shouldered some of the responsibilities in this area in the past. Will they be willing to take on the broader commitment now needed?

Finally, in Afghanistan and many other places like it, strengthening the range and reach of local capacity will test the willingness of the entire international community to redress, and not merely address, the crises that confront it. It will test commitment to the continuum that begins with the symptomatic response of a peacekeeping operation and moves through the curative work of reconstruction and sustainable, systemic development. Quick-impact projects, local procurement, auctioning and donating equipment no longer needed, and building local capacity from the ground up through the ministries, in one area and country after another, will show the international community's willingness or unwillingness not only to reform, but to reaffirm as well.

In convening and mandating the panel on United Nations Peace Operations, the secretary-general (United Nations, 2000a, covering letter) charged it to

undertake a thorough review of United Nations peace and security activities, and to present a clear set of specific, concrete, and practical recommendations to assist the United Nations in conducting such
activities better in the future.

It has acquitted itself of those responsibilities. The very real and
pregnant question now is: Will those to whom it has turned now acquit themselves of theirs?

Years ago, the Independent Task Force of the Council on Foreign
Relations commented (Soros, 1996) that

> some of the . . . challenges of recent years . . . have led to quick claims
> that the difficulty lay not in the problem but in the institution trying to
> deal with the problem.

As both experience and analysis have proven, that accusation—
while not entirely baseless—is inaccurate, incomplete, and unfair.
Other organizations have encountered similar obstacles and impediments. Coalitions, member states, and other entities have been confronted with similar challenges. Further, the United Nations is not a
monolith, but rather a body of various members and organs, each
with its own form and function, each with its own agendas and activities. The panel has made cogent, productive, and positive recommendations regarding each of them.

Reflecting on those recommendations, considering the causes and
currents that Attali described, remembering the results and ramifications that Tolstoy noted, and looking both at Afghanistan and beyond
it, the question that began this chapter returns anew: What can we do?

Remembering the linkage made by the secretary-general between
"the world's failure over a decade to act on warning signs in
Afghanistan" and the "clear, if complicated, trail from the absence of
engagement with Afghanistan in the 1990s to the creation of a terrorist haven there to the attacks on the World Trade Center" (Crossette,
2002), we now need to ask: Where does that trail lead from here?

In some ways, we are still too close to the point of the attack to see
where that trail will or might take us. Objective distance will come
only with time. Writing on diplomacy years ago, Henry Kissinger
(1994, p. 806) admitted that

> [w]henever the entities constituting the international system change
> their character, a period of turmoil inevitably follows.

In the interim, however, there are still important points to consider. Bertrand Russell once made an illuminating comment on the nature of "religious power" that links back to Tolstoy's point on false religion, noting that

> religious power is much less affected by defeat in war than secular power. . . . St. Augustine, in the *City of God*, which was inspired by the sack of Rome, explained that temporal power was not what was promised to the true believer, and was therefore not to be expected as the result of orthodoxy. (Russell, 1992, p. 247)

This ominous outlook recalls Osama bin Laden's comment when he was informed that he was wanted "dead or alive"—that if he were removed, that action would serve only to bring forward ten thousand more like him. Clearly, if left unaddressed, the kind of "social vertigo" that this comment reflects could spiral out of all scale. Terrorism could become an eternal threat and a perpetual problem. Can't that be avoided?

Attali offers one option:

> To avert this possibility, the market and democracy will have to be bound. . . . not by conservative values that preserve the past, but by conserving values that preserve the future. . . . In order to survive the triumph of our secular ideals, we need a new definition of the sacred. (Attali, 1991, p. 12)

The secretary-general (Annan, 2001) makes an analogous point:

> Terrorism threatens every society. As the world takes action against it, we have all been reminded of the need to address the conditions that permit the growth of such hatred and depravity. We must confront violence, bigotry, and hatred even more resolutely.

These two thoughts, between them, provide at least an initial indication of the direction we will need to take—and of the ways in which we will need to undergird the operations of the interim. They also underline the distance that we yet must travel to reach a deeper understanding of the events through which we are living, the responses we are making to them, and—perhaps more importantly—the psychology behind them.

Notes

Mr. Breed is writing in his personal capacity and the views he has expressed here are his own.

1. Collectively, all of these are well beyond the reach and remit of any single chapter. Individually, many of them could be very fruitfully examined in this context, and a number already have.

2. The passage is taken from the Report of the Secretary-General on the fall of Srebreniça.

References

Annan, K. (2001, September 21). Fighting terrorism on a global front. *New York Times*, p. A35.

Attali, J. (1991). *Millennium: Winners and losers in the coming world order* (pp. 2–18). New York: Random House.

Axelrod, R. (1981). *The evolution of cooperation.* New York: Basic Books.

Caplan, R. (2002). *A new trusteeship? The international administration of war-torn territories.* London: Oxford University Press (for the International Institute of Strategic Studies).

Crossette, B. (2002, March 7). Annan says terrorism's roots are broader than poverty. *New York Times*, p. A13.

de Unamuno, M. (1954). *The tragic sense of life.* New York: Dover. (Originally published 1913.)

Kissinger, H. (1994). *Diplomacy.* New York: Simon & Schuster.

Kuperman, A. J. (2000). Rwanda in retrospect. *Foreign Affairs, 79,* 94–119.

Russell, B. (1992). *Power.* New York: Routledge.

Safire, W. (1992). *Lend me your ears.* New York: W. W. Norton.

Soros, G. (1996). *American national interest and the United Nations: Statement and report of an independent task force* (p. 13). New York: Council on Foreign Relations.

Tolstoy, L. (1948). *The law of love and violence.* New York: Rudolph Field.

United Nations (1996a). End-of-mission report by Assistance Mission to Rwanda. April 19, 1996.

United Nations (1996b). UNAMIR Cable 1996/1771, "UNAMIR's Assistance to Rwanda." April 18, 1996.

United Nations (1997). Report of the secretary-general titled "Renewing the United Nations: A programme for reform." A/51/950.

United Nations (1998). Report of the Special Committee on Peacekeeping Operations. A/53/127.

United Nations (2000a). Comprehensive review of the whole question of peacekeeping operations in all their aspects. Report of the Special Committee on Peacekeeping Operations. (Extraordinary session to examine the recommendations of the Panel on United Nations Peace Operations.) A/C.4/55/6.

United Nations (2000b). Report of the Millennium Assembly of the United Nations ("We the peoples: The role of the United Nations in the twenty-first century. The Millennium Report"). A/54/2000.

United Nations (2000c). Report of the Panel on United Nations Peace Operations. A/55/305-S/2000/809.

United Nations (2000d). Report of the secretary-general on the implementation of the report of the Panel on United Nations Peace Operations. A/55/502.

United Nations (2000e). Report of the secretary-general pursuant to General Assembly resolution 53/55, titled "The fall of Srebreniça." A/54/549.

United Nations (2000f). Resource requirements for the implementation of the report of the Panel on United Nations Peace Operations. Report of the secretary-general. A/55/507/Add. 1.

Supplementary Bibliography

United Nations Documents

2001

A/55/977. Implementation of the recommendations of the Special Committee on Peacekeeping Operations and the Panel on United Nations peace Operations. Report of the Secretary-General.

A/55/713 and Add. 1. Programme budget for the biennium 2000–2001. Report of the Fifth Committee.

A/RES/55/247. Procurement reform.

A/RES/55/215. Towards global partnerships.

A/RES/55/175. Safety and security of humanitarian personnel and protection of United Nations personnel.

A/RES/55/155. Establishment of the international criminal court.

A/RES/55/135. Comprehensive review of the whole question of peacekeeping operations in all their aspects.

A/RES/55/109. Enhancement of international cooperation in the field of human rights.

A/RES/55/107. Promotion of a democratic and equitable international order.

A/RES/55/101. Respect for the purposes and principles contained in the Charter of the United Nations to achieve international cooperation in promoting and encouraging respect for human rights and for fundamental freedoms and in solving international problems of a humanitarian character.

A/RES/55/99. Strengthening the rule of law.

A/RES/55/73. New international humanitarian order.

A/RES/55/64. Strengthening of the United Nations Crime Prevention and Criminal Justice Programme, in particular its technical cooperation capacity.

S/RES/1353 (2001). Strengthening cooperation with troop-contributing countries.

United Nations Department of Public Information. Background note on United Nations peacekeeping operations, June 15, 2001.

United Nations Department of Public Information. Background note on United Nations political and peace-building missions, June 1, 2001.

United Nations Department of Public Information. Political Bulletin #3. March 19, 2001.

2000

A/54/839. Report of the Special Committee on Peacekeeping Operations (2000).

A/55/676. Implementation of the report of the Panel on United Nations Peace Operations. Report of the Advisory Committee on Administrative and Budgetary Questions.

A/54/670. Report of the secretary-general on the implementation of the recommendations of the Special Committee on Peacekeeping Operations.

A/54/549. Report of the secretary-general pursuant to General Assembly resolution 53/55, titled "The fall of Srebreniça."

A/RES/54/282. Draft United Nations millennium Declaration.

A/RES/54/82. Questions relating to information.

A/RES/55/28. Developments in the field of information and telecommunications in the context of international security.

S/2000/194. Progress report of the secretary-general on standby arrangements for peacekeeping.

S/2000/101. Report of the secretary-general on the role of United Nations peacekeeping in disarmament, demobilization and reintegration.

S/PV.4109. Verbatim Report of the 4109th Meeting of the Security Council (March 9, 2000). ("Maintaining peace and security: Humanitarian aspects of issues before the Security Council.")

S/RES/1327 (2000). Implementation of the report of the Panel on United Nations Peace Operations.

S/RES/1296 (2000). Protection of civilians in armed conflict.

Office of the United Nations High Commissioner for Refugees. Catalogue of emergency response tools. Document prepared by the Emergency Preparedness and Response Section. Geneva, 2000.

Office of the United Nations High Commissioner for Human Rights. Annual appeal 2000: Overview of activities and financial requirements. Geneva, 2000.

1999

A/54/549. The situation in Bosnia and Herzegovina.

A/54/87. Report of the Special Committee on Peacekeeping Operations (1999).

A/54/1. Annual report on the work of the organization ("Preventing war and disaster: A growing global challenge").

A/RES/53/142. Strengthening the rule of law.

A/RES/53/59. Questions relating to information.

S/1999/1257. Report of the independent inquiry into the actions of the United Nations during the 1994 genocide in Rwanda.

S/1999/957. Report of the secretary-general on the protection of civilians in armed conflict.

S/1998/883. Report of the secretary-general on protection for humanitarian assistance to refugees and others in conflict situations.

S/1999/361. Progress report of the secretary-general on standby arrangements for peacekeeping.

S/RES/1269 (1999). Responsibilities of the Security Council in the maintenance of international peace and security.

S/RES/1265 (1999). Protection of civilians in armed conflict.

ST/SGB/1999/13. Observance by United Nations forces of international humanitarian law.

1998

A/53/127. Report of the Special Committee on Peacekeeping Operations (1998).

A/53/1. Annual report on the work of the organization. ("Partnerships for global community.")

A/AC.121/42. Report of the secretary-general on the implementation of the recommendations of the Special Committee on Peacekeeping Operations.

E/AC.51/1998/4 and Corr.1. Report of the Office of Internal Oversight Services titled "Triennial review of the implementation of the recommendations made by the Committee for Programme and Coordination at its thirty-fifth session on the evaluation of peacekeeping operations: Start-up phase."

1997

A/51/950. Report of the secretary-general titled "Renewing the United Nations: A programme for reform."

A/RES/52/167. Safety and security of humanitarian personnel.

A/RES/52/125. Strengthening the rule of law.

A/RES/52/118. Effective implementation of international instruments on human rights, including reporting obligations under international instruments on human rights.

A/RES/52/12. Renewing the United Nations: A programme for reform.

Goulding, Marrack. *Practical measures to enhance the United Nations effectiveness in the field of peace and security.* Report submitted to the Secretary-General of the United Nations. New York: June 30, 1997.

1996

A/RES/50/243. Financing of the United Nations Preventive Deployment Force.

A/RES/51/207. Establishment of an international criminal court.

A/RES/51/137. Convention on the safety of United Nations and associated personnel.

A/RES/51/96. Strengthening the rule of law.

A/RES/51/63. Strengthening the United Nations Crime Prevention and Criminal Justice Programme, particularly in its technical cooperation capacity.

A/RES/51/55. The maintenance of international security—prevention of violent disintegration of states.

United Nations. *The blue helmets: A review of United Nations peacekeeping.* New York: United Nations (3rd ed.).

1995

A/50/60-S/1995/1. Supplement to an agenda for peace: Position paper of the secretary-general on the occasion of the fiftieth anniversary of the United Nations.

A/RES/50/179. Strengthening the rule of law.

E/AC.51/1995/2 and Corr.1. Report of the Office of Internal Oversight Services titled "In-depth evaluation of peacekeeping operations: Start-up phase."

United Nations, Department of Peacekeeping Operations, Lessons Learned Unit. UNOSOM I and II: Summary of Lessons Learned.

1994

A/RES/49/194. Strengthening the rule of law.

A/RES/49/189. Regional arrangements for the promotion and protection of human rights.

A/RES/49/158. Strengthening the United Nations crime prevention and criminal justice programme, particularly in its technical cooperation capacity.

A/RES/49/143. Financial situation of the United Nations.

A/RES/49/59. Convention on the safety of United Nations and associated personnel.

A/RES/49/57. Declaration of the enhancement of cooperation between the United Nations and regional arrangements or agencies in the maintenance of international peace and security.

A/RES/49/53. Establishment of an international criminal court.

S/RES/960 (1994). Endorsement of the results of free and fair elections in Mozambique.

United Nations, Department of Peacekeeping Operations, Lessons Learned Unit. ONUMOZ: Lessons Learned in Planning.

1993

A/47/277. Report of the secretary-general pursuant to the statement adopted by the summit meeting of the Security Council on 31 January 1992, titled "An Agenda for Peace: Preventive diplomacy, peacemaking and peace-keeping."

A/RES/48/132. Strengthening the rule of law.

A/RES/48/84. Maintenance of international peace and security.

A/RES/48/44. Questions relating to information.

A/RES/48/43. Strengthening United Nations command and control capabilities.

A/RES/48/42. Comprehensive review of the whole question of peacekeeping operations in all of their aspects.

S/RES/868 (1993). United Nations peacekeeping operations.

Books and Periodicals

Annan, K. (1994). Peace-keeping in situations of civil war. *New York University Journal of International Law and Politics, 26,* 623–631.

Annan, K. (1994, March 10). Peacekeeping's prospects. An address to the Archivio Disarmo, Rome.

Armon, J., Hendrickson, D., and Vines, A. (1998). The Mozambican peace process in perspective. *Accord: An International Review of Peace Initiatives, 3.*

Berdal, M., & Malone, D. M. (Eds.) (2000). *Greed and grievance: Economic agendas in civil wars.* Boulder, CO: Lynne Rienner.

Berman, E. (1996). *Managing arms in peace processes: Mozambique.* Geneva: United Nations Institute for Disarmament Research.

Butler, R. (1999). Bewitched, bothered, and bewildered. *Foreign Affairs, 78,* 9–12.

Byman, D. L. (2001). Uncertain partners: NGOs and the military. *Survival, 43,* 97–114.

Canada, Government of (1995). *Towards a rapid reaction capability for the United Nations.* Ottawa: Department of Foreign Affairs and International Trade and Department of National Defence.

Childers, E., & Urquhart, B. (1992). *Towards a more effective United Nations: Two studies.* Uppsala, Sweden: Dag Hammarskjöld Foundation.

Des Forges, A. L., & Kuperman, A. J. (2000). Shame. *Foreign Affairs, 79,* 141–144.

DeSoto, A., & del Castillo, G. (1995). Implementation of comprehensive peace agreements: Staying the course in El Salvador. *Global Governance, 1, 2.*

Doll, W. J., & Metz, S. (1993). *The army and multinational peace operations: Problems and Solutions.* Carlisle, PA: Strategic Studies Institute, U.S. Army War College.

Eriksson, J. (1996). *The international response to conflict and genocide: Lessons from the Rwanda experience: Synthesis report.* Odense, Denmark: Steering Committee of the Joint Evaluation of Emergency Assistance to Rwanda.

Falk, R. (1995). The Haiti intervention: A dangerous world order precedent for the United Nations. *Harvard International Law Journal, 36,* 341–419.

Forman, S., Patrick, S., & Salomons, D. (2000, February). *Recovering from conflict: Strategy for an international response.* New York University, Center on International Cooperation.

Frye, A. (2000). *Humanitarian intervention: Crafting a workable doctrine.* New York: Council on Foreign Relations Books.

Gardner, R. N. (2000). The one percent solution. *Foreign Affairs, 79,* 2–11.

Glennon, M. J. (1999). The new interventionism. *Foreign Affairs, 78,* 2–7.

Gordon, P. H. (2000). Their own army. *Foreign Affairs, 79,* 12–17.

Griffin, M., & Jones, B. (2000, Summer). Building peace through transitional authority: New directions, major challenges. *International Peacekeeping, 7,* No. 3.

Guéhenno, J.-M. (Winter, 1998–99). The impact of globalisation on strategy. *Survival, 40,* 5–20.

Gurr, Ted R. (2000). Ethnic warfare on the wane. *Foreign Affairs, 79,* 52–64.

Henkin, A. H. (Ed.) (1995). *Honouring human rights and keeping the peace: Lessons from El Salvador, Cambodia and Haiti.* Washington, DC: Aspen Institute.

Holm, T. T., & Eide, E. B. (Eds.) (1999, Special Winter Issue). Peacebuilding and Police Reform. *International Peacekeeping, 6.*

Jamison, L. S. (2001). *The U.S. role in United Nations peace operations.* Washington, DC: Council for a Lovable World Education Fund.

Jett, D. C. (2000). *Why peacekeeping fails.* New York: St. Martin's Press.

Kuhne, W., Weimer, B., & Fandrych, S. (1995). *International workshop on the successful conclusion of the United Nations operation in Mozambique.* New York: Friedrich Ebert Foundation.

Lehmann, I. A. (1995). Public perceptions of UN peacekeeping. *The Fletcher Forum of World Affairs, 19,* 109–120.

Lewis, W. H. (Ed.) (1993). *Peacekeeping: The way ahead?* Washington, DC: National Defense University.

Lind, M. (1999). Civil war by other means. *Foreign Affairs, 78,* 123–144.

Lipschutz, R., & Crawford, B. (1995). Ethnic conflict isn't. Policy Brief. San Diego, CA: Institute on Global Conflict and Cooperation.

Luers, W. H. (2000). Choosing engagement. *Foreign Affairs, 79,* 9–14.

Moore, J. (Ed.) (1996). *The U.N. and complex emergencies.* UNRISD.

Moore, J. (Ed.) (1998). *Hard choices.* Geneva: Lanham, Maryland, Rowman and Littlefield for the International Committee of the Red Cross.

Pugh, M. (1997). *The UN, peace and force.* Portland, ME: Frank Cass.

Rifkind, M. (1993, April). Peacekeeping or peacemaking? Implications and prospects. *RUSI Journal,* 1–5.

Rothstein, L. I. (1993). Protecting the new world order: Is it time to create a United Nations army? *New York Law School Journal of International and Comparative Law, 14,* 107–142.

Sanger, D. E. (2001, February 24). Bush tells Blair he doesn't oppose European force. *New York Times*, pp. 1, 4.

Thomas, J. P. (2000). *The military challenges of Transatlantic coalitions.* (Adelphi Paper 333) New York: Oxford University Press.

Thornberry, C. (1995). *The development of international peacekeeping.* London: LSE Books.

Tucker, R. W. (1999). Alone or with others. *Foreign Affairs, 78*, 15–21.

United Kingdom, Government of. Inspector General of Doctrine and Training (1995). *Wider peacekeeping.* London: HMSO.

Volcker, P., & Ogata, S. (1993). *Financing an effective United Nations: A report of the independent advisory group on U.N. financing.* New York: Ford Foundation.

Wallensteen, P., & Sollenberg, M. (1998). Armed conflict and regional conflict complexes, 1989–1997. *Journal of Peace Research, 35*, 345–360.

Weiner, R. O., & Aolain, F. N. (1996). Peacekeeping in search of a legal framework. *Columbia Human Rights Law Review, 27*, 293–354.

CHAPTER 7

PREVENTING TERRORISM: RAISING "INCLUSIVELY" CARING CHILDREN IN THE COMPLEX WORLD OF THE TWENTY-FIRST CENTURY

Ervin Staub

How do children become caring, helpful, and altruistic? I will discuss the socialization practices by adults and the experiences that children require to achieve this. I want to start, however, with several issues relevant to raising caring children who are unlikely to engage in terrorism.

First, it is possible for children to learn to care about others' welfare, but to restrict their caring to members of their own group. This group may be a family or extended family, a tribe, a religious or ethnic group, a nation, or defined in some other way. This makes it easier for caring children, who become caring adults, to turn against people outside the group. My concern will be with the development of caring both for members of one's "ingroup" and for people outside one's group, that is, with the development of "inclusive" caring. A strong differentiation between "us" and "them," a negative view of those outside the group, and scapegoating of others for life problems and ideologies that identify some others as enemies of the right way of life—these practices not only lead to an absence of caring for the "other," but contribute to the possibility of violence, including terrorism.

Second, caring for others' welfare develops through experiential learning. While children can be effectively instructed and guided by words, and this may even develop an "experiential understanding" that contributes to a positive orientation to self and others, caring

cannot be developed by verbal communication alone. This is especially the case when, through harsh treatment or abuse, children have
experienced other people not caring about them. Explanation and
verbal guidance must be supported by experiences in interaction with
people.

Third, for children to learn to care about other people and their
needs, it is essential that their own fundamental needs be satisfied.
Like Abraham Maslow and many other psychologists and social scientists, I have stressed in my work for well over a decade the importance of fundamental ("basic") human needs. These needs, shared by
all human beings, must be satisfied at least to a moderate degree, in
order for people to lead fulfilled, satisfying lives.

The satisfaction of these needs provides the preconditions for the
development of caring about and helping other people; frustration of
these needs generates hostility and creates a basis for aggression.
These needs include the need for security, the need for a positive
sense of self or identity, the need for a feeling of effectiveness and
some reasonable control over one's life, the need for positive connection to other people (individuals and community), the need for some
degree of autonomy, and the need for a worldview that provides a
meaningful comprehension of the world and of one's place in it. As
these needs are fulfilled to a reasonable extent, the need for transcendence, for going beyond a focus on one's own self, also becomes
important. Sometimes people in difficult times, with their basic needs
frustrated, engage in pseudo transcendence. They relinquish a bur-
densome self by giving themselves over to an ideology or movement
(Staub, 1996b, 1999, 2003, in preparation).

Some Obstacles to Raising Inclusively Caring Children and Contributors to Terrorism

It is possible to reasonably identify, on the basis of research and
theory in the last few decades, what children require to become inclusively caring persons (Eisenberg, 1992; Eisenberg & Fabes, 1998;
Staub, 1979, 1996a, 2003, in preparation). But for children to receive
that kind of socialization and experience requires adults who want to
and are capable of providing this. This is partly a matter of personality and past experience. For example, adults who have been neglected
and badly treated as children may have neither the inclination nor the
skills to provide the warmth and guidance needed (Staub, 1996a,
2003, in preparation). But the child rearing required for inclusive car-

ing is also a matter of the culture and the social and political conditions under which adults live. I will very briefly note some conditions that interfere with adults' ability to raise inclusively caring children, or that provide children with experiences that limit their caring in general, or restrict it to members of their own group.

Poverty

When poverty is not extreme, it probably does not, by itself, limit adults' ability to provide the affection, need satisfaction, and guidance (see below) required for children to become caring people. Except under extreme conditions of poverty, poor people can be as happy as wealthier people (Myers, 1992); they may also be able to be loving parents and caretakers of children.

However, when the economic condition of poor people deteriorates, this may affect their ability to fulfill both biological needs and the basic psychological needs noted above. The poor may feel less secure, less good about themselves, less effective, less able to control their lives, and so on. I have suggested that difficult life conditions—which may include severe economic decline, political disorganization, and great social change—frustrate basic needs and are one of the starting points for an evolution toward mass killing or genocide (Staub, 1989, 1999). Such conditions tend to give rise to scapegoating and destructive ideologies. They make less likely parenting that helps to develop caring, especially inclusive caring (Staub, 1996b).

Justice and Injustice, Repressive Political Systems, and Culture Change

Poverty and deteriorating economic conditions are especially likely to affect people when they see others as much better off than they are. The experience of great injustice would make less likely child rearing that gives rise to inclusive caring.

Repressive political systems make it difficult if not impossible to deal with injustice and improve the economic conditions and rights of groups that live in poverty. They create anger and hostility that, when they cannot be expressed may be channeled toward targets that are physically less dangerous and psychologically more accessible than the repressive authorities at home, which often claim they represent tradition and are carriers of cultural or religious virtues. Repressive systems also make it difficult to deal with the impact of culture change. Such systems are monolithic; they allow the expression of only limited values and beliefs and inhibit the free exchange of ideas.

To live in the modern world, to gain the material benefits, educational opportunities, and much else it has to offer, requires an integration of new and old. This is difficult under the best of conditions. The psychological demands of living with change are great. In traditional societies that have repressive systems, the struggle to reconcile tradition and change, the clash of the old and the new, engagement with discrepant values and beliefs, is especially difficult, if not impossible. The accommodation between old and new or the transformation required to integrate them may not take place. Confusion of identity, problems in connecting with other people, feelings of ineffectiveness, and especially difficulty with having a coherent understanding of reality may result. When the repressive system is highly effective, which in terms of communication and information is increasingly difficult in the contemporary world, individuals' problems may become acute if and when they encounter the outside world.

Poverty has extraordinary power, especially when combined with relative deprivation, a feeling of powerlessness to improve one's life, and great culture change—when the process of accommodation, transformation, and integration of old and new cannot take place. These factors often occur together. They may lead people to turn to ideologies, visions of a better life, that help them deal with the psychological impact of their experience. These ideologies may be nationalistic, religious, or something else. In addition to providing hope for a better future, they can give followers an understanding of the world and a sense of personal significance. But they also identify enemies of the ideology and as a result have an important role in mass killing and genocide, as well as a powerful role in terrorism—whether we look at the terrorism of Palestinians, Osama bin Laden and his supporters, Basques, or other nationalist movements.

Many of the conditions described here make it more difficult but still allow people to raise children in ways that develop caring. But they make practices that develop inclusive caring much less likely. For the latter to happen, the conditions must change. There must be greater equality, shared suffering, and mutual support in the face of life problems, integration of the new and the old, and so on. At the very least, people must create more inclusive ideologies, positive visions in the face of difficult conditions that do not create divisions between us and them—ideologies that people can strive to fulfill by peaceful means.

Important Socialization Practices

Warmth and Affection versus Harsh Treatment and Hostility

The experience of warmth, nurturance, and affection are central to the development of caring about other people and their welfare (Yarrow & Scott, 1972). An essential form of warmth and nurturance by parents and other caretakers is responsiveness to infants' and young children's needs. The satisfaction of these needs for food, stimulation, contact, interaction, and affection contributes to the development of secure attachment (Bretherton, 1992; Staub, 1996a, in preparation). Their satisfaction leads children to feel effective, to value themselves, and to feel connected to other people. It leads them to value other people.

In contrast, harshness, rejection, punitiveness, and abuse make the development of caring about others' welfare and helping others unlikely. Whatever is the adults' reason for such treatment of a child, inherent in it is a devaluation of the child. Such treatment frustrates the needs for positive identity, security, effectiveness and control, and positive connection. It teaches the child to fear and mistrust people (Staub, 1996a, 1996b, in preparation).

Warmth and affection require sensitivity in perceiving and responding to the needs of a growing child (Staub, 1996a, in preparation). For example, a young child coming home from school may be upset about something that has happened. Sensitive affection would lead a parent or caretaker both to perceive this and to consider the child's sensitivity in talking about it. The child may be ashamed of something that has happened. If it is a problem in school with other children or a teacher, the child may be concerned that parental intervention will humiliate him or her. Genuine affection and nurturance do not simply mean a certain amount of warmth, or of physical affection; they require sensitive responding to the needs and feelings of the child.

Structure and Guidance at Home and in School

Young children require predictable environments for growth and development. They require organization and structure not only in their external world, but also—with help from parents or caretakers—in their internal world. For example, parents help young children organize their emotions. They teach the child what different emotions are, help the child to modulate intense emotions, soothe the child when distressed, and reassure the child when afraid. They even help the young child to keep pleasurable excitement within controllable limits. Through all this, the parent or caretaker provides an essential structure. The parent needs also to help the child organize tasks and other activities. Such structuring—or as Vygotsky called it, scaffolding (see Rogoff, 1990)—can help the child develop internal structure, which then guides the child in his or her reactions and actions.

An important form of guidance is reasoning with children. Rules are an essential form of structure and guidance. Rules can be arbitrarily set and enforced in an authoritarian manner. Alternatively, rules can be set on the basis of values. Children can be told what these values are and how the rules relate to them. This makes it more likely that children will accept the rules, make them their own, and follow them in a cooperative manner.

An especially important form of reasoning for the development of caring and helping has been referred to as induction. Induction means explaining to the child the consequences of his or her behavior for other people (Eisenberg, 1992; Eisenberg et al., 1998; Hoffman, 1970, 1975, 2000; Staub, 1979, 1996a, in preparation). When a child says or does something hurtful—whether to strangers, peers, or parents—the painful consequences of this, the feelings of hurt and distress, physical pain, and so on, are laid out.

Actions can affect a person's body, feelings, or thoughts. Pointing out the consequences of his or her actions makes a child aware of others' inner worlds. It helps the child to see his or her own power in influencing others' welfare. It helps promote the capacity to take others' role. It helps the child develop empathy and a feeling of responsibility for others' welfare. All these have been found importantly involved in people helping others. Positive induction, or pointing out to children the positive consequences of their actions on others' welfare, is also valuable (Staub, 1979).

Another important form of guidance is modeling. The actions of adults in the child's environment, especially important adults, have great influence. So do story characters, whether in fairy tales, other types of stories, movies, or on television. Modeling teaches the child what is normal, expected, and right. It helps the child to learn the consequences of different actions on other people, as well as the reactions that different behaviors generate.

Schools are very important in all these aspects of socialization. Schools set rules for children for their interaction with teachers and peers, for attending to tasks, for living in a social world. They provide structure and guidance of many kinds. Teachers and other adults in schools can be warm and affectionate, cold and indifferent, or harsh and punitive, with consequences similar to such variations in parents.

Schools are also important in offering opportunities for participation. Children can develop a feeling of importance and responsibility by participating in significant ways in the life of the school. For example, even very young children can participate in creating rules for the classroom. In the course of discussing how various rules might affect them, their peers, teachers, and their learning in the classroom, children can learn independence of judgment.

The creation of community in the classroom is also very important (Staub, 2003, in preparation). Some children, starting at an early age, become marginal in their classroom. This is especially likely to happen with children who most need connection and community, because they have not had it in their families. Their marginality, their lack of connection to their peers and to learning in the classroom, can lead them to turn to deviant peers. This is one of the avenues through which children, as they grow into adolescents, move into gangs. When their experiences at home and in schools and their interaction with peers fail to fulfill their basic needs for identity, positive connection, and a sense of effectiveness, they are likely to turn to other groups that will satisfy these needs. These are basic needs that, starting in early adolescence, become developmentally especially important (Staub, 1996b).

A column in the *New York Times* by Thomas L. Friedman (2002) discusses the terrorists of September 11, 2001, in ways that relate to issues of socialization and experience. They were from middle-class families in the Arab world, educated young men who went to Europe for more education. There they joined a local prayer group or mosque where they became radicalized, and went off to get training in Afghanistan. The narrowness of the experience and worldview with which they grew up, the clash between that world and the world they encountered in Europe, and what Friedman described as a lack of respect that Muslims experience in Europe joined in making the influence of the mosques especially potent.

A number of factors probably all entered into the formation of these terrorists: the ideology of a strict religion, as practiced at home and as preached in the mosques to which they turned; the difficulty of integrating their past understanding of the world with their new experiences in a much different world; the lack of satisfaction of basic needs in Europe, such as positive identity (respect) and connection to the world around them; and the sharp lines between us and them that these influences would have created. However, not all young men from the same Arab countries who go to Europe become terrorists. For a more thorough understanding of them, we would also need to know the experiences of these young men in their families, and the joint influence of those experiences and the larger contexts of their lives.

The Role of Discipline

Affection, structure, and guidance go a long way in gaining children's cooperation. However, they don't always go all the way (Baumrind, 1975). While it is important to allow children a great deal of autonomy, and increasing autonomy with increasing age, it is also important to get them to abide by rules that express the values of their parents, teachers, or other caretakers.

While discipline is very important, it is essential that it not be harsh, negative, and punitive. As I have noted, children who experience harsh treatment from an early age on, who experience rejection, frequent physical punishment, and other expressions of hostility from parents, are likely to become hostile and aggressive (Dodge, 1993; Huesmann, Eron, Lefkowitz, & Walder, 1984; Staub, 1996a, 1996b, in preparation). Their basic needs unfulfilled, they will lack a positive sense of self and come to see other people in a negative light.

Moderate, positive forms of discipline are important to use but hard to devise. They can include communication to children about what consequences will follow undesirable actions. Sparingly used, they can include withdrawal of privileges. In school, getting children involved in discussing certain kinds of discipline problems and in deciding on consequences can be useful. However, children can be overly punitive to each other, a punitiveness that ought to be moderated.

Acknowledging and affirming positive behavior and ingenuity in devising mild forms of discipline techniques is important. However, the more children's needs are fulfilled starting early in their lives, and the more they are guided through explanation and other positive means, the less extensively will discipline have to be used.

Learning by Doing

A central avenue for children to learn to become caring and helpful is engagement or participation in helpful acts. In a number of studies, my students and I involved children in making toys for poor hospitalized children, or had older children teach younger children (Staub, 1975, 1979). We found that such engagement in helping increased children's later helping. There is other evidence that shows this kind of learning of caring and helpful behavior by doing (Eisenberg et al., 1998; Staub, 1979; Whiting & Whiting, 1975).

Children also learn to be aggressive through engagement in aggressive behavior. There is evidence with adults that harming people makes it easier to harm people again, and/or to a greater extent. There is also evidence, from the study of genocide, that as members of a perpetrator group harm others, they change. Increased harming of the victims, increased violence, becomes easier and more likely (Staub, 1989). This is also likely to be true of children. When children repeatedly engage in aggressive acts, they are likely to change. For them as well, aggression will become easier and more likely.

Us and Them: The Origins of Inclusive Caring

Among rescuers, people who endangered their lives in Nazi Europe to help persecuted Jews, many were found to draw a less sharp line between "us," their own group, and "them," people outside their group, than others in a similar situation who did not help. This group was composed of individuals who grew up in families with parents who, through words and actions, engaged with people outside their own group; as children, these rescuers learned to respect and value people beyond their narrowly defined group (Oliner & Oliner, 1988).

Children can learn to care about other people, but at the same time to draw a sharp line between members of their own group and those outside the group. Or they can learn to include people beyond their group in the realm of humanity. They can learn to care about their welfare and act in their behalf. Parents can promote this by the way they guide their children, including efforts to promote relationships with children belonging to different groups.

In most societies, some subgroups of society are the objects of devaluation, prejudice, and discrimination. They may be identified as a group because they are ethnic minorities, or they have a different religion, or hold currently unpopular political views, or are people who have come to occupy a lower status in society. The negative attitude and behavior toward them may have developed in the distant historical past or in response to recent circumstances in society. Almost inevitably, the cultural devaluation of a group is transmitted to children by the culture: by literature, the media, word of mouth, and the attitude and action of adults. Existing devaluation and the tendency to devalue are likely to be strengthened by the social and political conditions described earlier.

In schools, it has been found that cooperative learning promotes positive relations among children belonging to different ethnic and racial groups (Aronson, Stephan, Sikes, Blaney, & Snapp, 1978; Hertz-Lazarowitz & Sharan, 1984). For example, a group of children may be put together to work on a shared task. To fulfill this task, each of them has to learn some material and teach it to others in the group. Each child is thus a learner as well as a teacher (Aronson et al., 1978).

Deep engagement among members of groups is essential both to overcoming devaluation and to promoting inclusive, caring, cross-cutting relations (Pettigrew, 1997; Staub, 1989). Such deep engagement can take the form of joint projects, whether business projects, or members of different groups cleaning up neighborhoods together, or cultural exchanges. Schools provide extensive opportunities both for learning to care about others through participation and engagement, and for cooperative learning and cross-cutting relations.

The Development of Moral Courage

We are frequently witnesses or bystanders not only to other people's pain and suffering, but also to harm inflicted on them. This harm may be inflicted through discrimination, prejudice, or violence. Harm may be inflicted on groups of people in our society or in some other part of the world. Even in the latter case, we as individuals, our nation as a whole, and individuals and nations around the world are witnesses or bystanders to this. People can be passive bystanders or respond actively.

People often remain passive bystanders because it is difficult to speak out. Speaking or acting sometimes requires physical courage. Frequently it requires moral courage, the willingness to stand up for and act on one's values. In the course of growing up, many children suffer due to exclusion, taunting, ridicule, or other forms of persecution by their peers (Olweus, 1993). Others frequently remain passive bystanders (Staub & Spielman, 2000). Some who were initially passive get drawn in and become perpetrators. In turn, children who have themselves suffered are often passive bystanders when this is done to others. All this leaves psychological wounds, as many students in my courses have reported when encouraged to write about personal experiences in the course of exploring psychological research and theory on these issues.

The willingness of teenagers to speak out and oppose is of essential importance when a group of their peers contemplates some action that harms others or causes damage. The willingness of adults (as well as adolescents) to speak and act is crucial when a society begins to victimize a minority in its midst (Staub, 1989, 1999), or when antagonism develops toward outsiders, with the possibility of persecution, mass killing, or terrorism. The issue of bystandership is present in children's lives from an early age and remains present in their lives as adults.

How can moral courage develop, the courage to speak out and take action consistent with one's values and beliefs? Moral courage is a requirement for helping in many contexts. Teachers involving children in the creation of rules for the classroom is one important avenue to the development of moral courage. In the course of this, children can learn to express their views and beliefs, to discuss and argue, to present their points of view, to stand up for what they believe. Similar things can happen in the family as well. The example of moral courage provided to the children by parents, teachers, and other people is also central to developing moral courage of their own.

Conclusions

I have described here some central principles for raising children so that they will become caring, helpful, and altruistic people. There are no exact recipes for raising children. While the principles are important, different parents, teachers, and caretakers who want to follow such principles will do so in their own ways.

Learning about such principles and developing skills in practicing them are of great value. But they can be insufficient. Frequently, adults have had experiences in their own lives that make it difficult for them to effectively act on such principles. These experiences may include harsh treatment and abuse that they themselves have suffered. It may include current difficulties in their lives, economic problems, or lack of social support. For many adults to act on these principles may require personal transformation, that is, finding ways to change themselves and their ways of perceiving, experiencing, and reacting to events. This requires special procedures and experiences (Staub, in preparation; Staub & Pearlman, 1996).

To create conditions in which these principles can be fulfilled can also require societal changes that provide sufficient support for adults involved in raising and socializing children (Staub, 1996b). And it can require social and political changes that allow people and help develop in people a valuing of the "other" rather than restricting the focus to the self and generating hostility to people outside the group. The creation of such changes is essential for a better world (Staub, 1999, in preparation; Staub & Pearlman, 2001). The role of nations is central in this. Especially powerful nations, such as the United States, and the international community, as "active bystanders," can exert positive influence in promoting pluralistic and just societies that affirm individuals and help fulfill basic needs.

References

Aronson, E., Stephan, C., Sikes, J., Blaney, N., & Snapp, M. (1978). *The jigsaw classroom.* Beverly Hills, CA: Sage Publications.

Baumrind, D. (1975). *Early socialization and the discipline controversy.* Morristown, NJ: General Learning Press.

Bretherton, I. (1992). The origins of attachment theory: John Bowlby and Mary Ainsworth. *Developmental Psychology, 28,* 759–775.

Dodge, K. A. (1993). Social cognitive mechanisms in the development of conduct disorder and depression. *Annual Review of Psychology, 44,* 559–584.

Eisenberg, N. (1992). *The caring child.* Cambridge, MA: Harvard University Press.

Eisenberg, N., & Fabes, R. A. (1998). Prosocial development. In W. Damon (Ed.) & N. Eisenberg (Vol. Ed.), *Handbook of child psychology, Vol. 3. Social, emotional, and personality development* (5th ed.). New York: Wiley.

Friedman, T. L. (2002, January 27). The 2 Domes of Belgium. *New York Times,* p. 13.

Hertz-Lazarowitz, R., & Sharan, S. (1984). Enhancing prosocial behavior through cooperative learning in the classroom. In E. Staub, D. Bar-Tal, J. Karylowski, & J. Reykowski (Eds.), *Development and maintenance of prosocial behavior* (pp. 423–445). New York: Plenum.

Hoffman, M. L. (1970). Moral development. In P. H. Mussen (Ed.), *Carmichael's manual of child development.* New York: Wiley.

Hoffman, M. L. (1975). Altruistic behavior and the parent-child relationship. *Journal of Personality and Social Psychology, 31,* 937–943.

Hoffman, M. L. (2000). *Empathy and moral development: Implications for caring and justice.* New York: Cambridge University Press.

Huesmann, L. R., Eron, L. D., Lefkowitz, M. M., & Walder, L. O. (1984). Stability of aggression over time and generations. *Developmental Psychology, 20,* 1120–1134.

Myers, D. G. (1992). *The pursuit of happiness.* New York: William Morrow.

Oliner, S. B., & Oliner, P. (1988). *The altruistic personality: Rescuers of Jews in Nazi Europe.* New York: Free Press.

Olweus, D. (1993). *Bullying at school: What we know and what we can do.* Oxford: Blackwell.

Pettigrew, T. F. (1997). Generalized intergroup contact effects on prejudice. *Personality and Social Psychology Bulletin, 23,* 173–185.

Rogoff, B. (1990). *Apprenticeship in thinking.* New York: Oxford University Press.

Staub, E. (1975). To rear a prosocial child: Reasoning learning by doing, and learning by teaching others. In D. DePalma & J. Folley (Eds.), *Moral development: Current theory and research.* Hillsdale, NJ: Erlbaum.

Staub, E. (1979). *Positive social behavior and morality: Socialization and development* (Vol. 2). New York: Academic Press.

Staub, E. (1989). *The roots of evil: The origins of genocide and other group violence.* New York: Cambridge University Press.

Staub, E. (1996a). Altruism and aggression in children and youth: Origins and cures. In R. Feldman (Ed.), *The psychology of adversity* (pp. 115–147). Amherst, MA: University of Massachusetts Press.

Staub, E. (1996b). The cultural-societal roots of violence: The examples of genocidal violence and of contemporary youth violence in the United States. *American Psychologist, 51,* 117–132.

Staub, E. (1999). The origins and prevention of genocide, mass killing, and other collective violence. *Peace and Conflict: Journal of Peace Psychology, 5,* 303–336.

Staub, E. (2003). *The psychology of good and evil.* New York: Cambridge University Press.

Staub, E. (in preparation). *A brighter future: Raising caring and nonviolent children.* New York: Oxford University Press.

Staub, E., & Pearlman, L. (1996, November). Trauma and the fulfillment of the human potential. Workshop presented at the meeting of the International Society for Traumatic Stress Studies. San Francisco.

Staub, E., & Pearlman, L. (2001). Healing, reconciliation and forgiving after genocide and other collective violence. In S. J. Helmick and R. L. Petersen (Eds.), *Forgiveness and reconciliation: Religion, public policy and conflict transformation* (pp. 205–229). Radnor, PA: Templeton Foundation Press.

Staub, E., and Spielman, D. (2000). Students' experience of bullying and of other aspects of their lives in middle school. Unpublished manuscript, Department of Psychology, University of Massachusetts at Amherst.

Whiting, B., and Whiting, J. W. M. (1975). *Children of six cultures.* Cambridge, MA: Harvard University Press.

Yarrow, M. R., & Scott, P. M. (1972). Imitation of nurturant and nonnurturant models. *Journal of Personality and Social Psychology, 8,* 240–261.

CHAPTER 8

FROM TERROR TO TRIUMPH: THE PATH TO RESILIENCE

Edith Henderson Grotberg

Terror paralyzes. Terror intimidates. Terror makes you lose your sense of safety and security. That is its intent. It wants you to be fearful, to withdraw, to submit, to give up your dreams, your hopes, your self-confidence, and your confidence in others. Terror wants you to suffer. It certainly does not want you to become resilient, because terror fears independence, initiative, trusting relationships, self-determination.

You may well respond to terror in all the intended ways. You have had little experience, except through the unending news about terror around the world, and the inexhaustible supply of films focused on terror. You are stunned that acts of terror can happen so close. You have no background to put the terror experienced in the United States on September 11, 2001, into any kind of perspective. And having perspective is important as you begin to take the path to resilience. Resilience is a human capacity that everyone can develop to face the inevitable adversities of life and to overcome them. You can become stronger as you deal with adversities and sometimes even be transformed by them, becoming a more caring, compassionate person.

If you want perspective, turn to older people, especially resilient older people. They are the ones who can tell you how they faced, overcame, were strengthened and even transformed by experiences of terror in America. They have perspective.

In the 1940s, after the bombing of Pearl Harbor, the fear of an invasion on the mainland was so intense that it created a sense of terror everywhere. And the early failures and losses Americans experienced in the war added to the fear.

In the 1950s there was intense fear of atomic bombs being dropped on the United States by the Soviet Union. Children practiced getting under their desks at the sound of an alarm, and families were urged to dig bomb shelters in their yards, or someplace safe. Also during the 1950s, the fear of polio created an atmosphere of terror across the country. And the 1950s saw Sputnik, a phenomenon that terrified America and began a race for similar achievements and protections.

In 1963, the fear of missiles coming from Cuba put America in a state of terror requiring drastic preventive actions on the part of the American government.

In the 1980s and 1990s, mail bombs were the source of terror, as were bombings of American embassies in different parts of the world.

In 1993, the first bombing of the World Trade Center, quickly seen as a terrorist attack, sent fear throughout the nation. In 1995, the Oklahoma City bombing, at first thought to be a foreign terrorist attack, revealed that Americans also were capable of heinous crimes. Again, fear took over.

From the perspective of resilient older people, you learn that fear is important to keep you on the alert, to encourage you to take whatever steps you can to protect yourself, your loved ones, and, in some cases, your country. Fear triggers the flow of energy you need to take the necessary steps—to do a lot of thinking about what is going on, and what more you should be doing. Anger is good, too. It is the emotion that tells you something needs to be changed, and also gets the energy flowing in the resolve to make those changes.

What resilient older people can also tell you is that while fear is good for generating energy, continuing in a state of fear will get you nowhere. It will accomplish what the terrorists intended. You are paralyzed. You will do nothing. You will submit. You are an easy victim. On to the next victim!

The perspective of older people is acquired through years of experiencing events that generated reactions of intense fear and uncertainty. They learned that they would get through each one, would learn from each event, and be stronger as a result. They know that looking for and expecting guarantees of safety is futile. No one can guarantee that an engine won't fall off an airplane, as happened in New York just two months after the tragedy of the World Trade

Center. No one expected that disaster either. Life involves risk. What is more risky than driving your car every morning to join the rush hour traffic, or trying to cross a street where cars notoriously ignore stop signs and red lights? Minimize risk, yes. Totally eliminate it, no.

Does perspective diminish the tragedy we are experiencing, the loss of loved ones, the uncertainty of the future? Absolutely not! The losses are permanent. The sadness is continuous. The physical and mental damage takes its toll. But dealing with loss, sadness, and damage is the role of resilience. Resilience provides the tools and the behaviors to deal with these tragedies, these losses. It can enrich life by bringing new insight, new understanding, and new commitments to life. Transformation is the greatest result of resilience, and it inevitably involves having more empathy and compassion—not pity—for others. It results in actions to help others. Life has meaning again. One gains a deeper sense of fulfillment and comfort.

What Do We Know about Resilience?

It took time for the concept of resilience to be accepted as important in dealing with adversities. As a matter of fact, the word, as it relates to human behavior, is new to many languages. Spanish, for example, used the phrase, *la lucha contra la adversidad* (the fight against adversity) for many years before adopting *resiliencia* as the accepted word.

A major reason for this delay was the limits of our thinking. The dominant conceptual framework for studying human behavior was the medical model, a deficit, disease model, requiring studies of diagnosis and treatment. This important medical model led to attempts to diagnose "behavioral diseases" and find effective treatments. The public health model, an epidemiological model, was one variation of the medical model, counting the number of instances of a particular illness, and then supporting programs to reduce the unacceptable numbers, a kind of inoculation model. The epidemiological model, like the medical model, was applied to behavior problems. How many cases of drug-related problems? How many incidents of violence? How many teenage pregnancies? How many cases of abuse and abandonment? Have they reached epidemic numbers? The numbers determined public policy for funding of research, program, and service development, to bring the numbers down and stop the epidemic. The Centers for Disease Control keeps track of the numbers, but recently recognized that more was needed.

In 1999, the Centers added the words "and Prevention" to its title.
The purpose was to bring attention and support to efforts that prevent a condition or dangerous and unacceptable behavior from hap-
pening in the first place, with the implicit interest in promoting
behaviors that enhance life. The new emphasis included the promotion of resilience.

Another important shift in thinking came from redefining the ecological model of human behavior. The ecological model examines individual behavior within the context of the family and the
community. However, it, too, had been used within a deficit model.
The shift in thinking raised new questions: What can the community
do to help families and children deal with adversities? What can the
family do to help children deal with adversity? What can the individual do to deal with adversity? What are the separate and interrelated
roles each plays in the promotion of resilience? The redefined ecological model provides the theoretical setting for promoting resilience in individuals, families, and communities. How we think
about resilience continues to grow as new findings emerge and as
new perspectives are considered (Grotberg, 2001a).

Most of the research in the 1970s used the deficit model in studying children and families. The environment of the family was believed
to be the dominant influence in the development and behavior of the
children. Thus, if the family was dysfunctional, impacted by mental
health problems, abuse, drugs, and poverty, the assumption was that
the children would be negatively affected, even adopting some of the
undesired behaviors. The pioneer researchers of what became known
as resilience, were, in fact, studying the impact on children living in
dysfunctional families. Norman Garmezy (1974), Emily Werner
(1982), and Michael Rutter (1979), all were examining how children
were negatively affected by the family environment.

The findings were unanticipated, even shocking. About one-third of
the children were doing very well. They were happy, had friends, were
doing okay in school, and were looking forward to the future. This
was not only inconsistent with expectations, but forced a reexamina-
tion of their hypothesis. What was going on that prevented these children from being negatively influenced by the home environment? Had
the family been misdiagnosed? Were the data incorrect?

To the credit of these researchers, they began to identify what differentiated these healthy, happy children from their siblings who, indeed, were negatively affected by the dysfunctional families. They
found that these healthy, happy children reached out to neighbors,

relatives, teachers, or other adults to find help. These adults became mentors and role models for the children. The children were likable, happy to help others, and optimistic and confident that their lives would be good. They could express their thoughts and feelings, manage their own behavior, and solve problems they faced. In short, the researchers identified what are accepted today as the resilience factors. How the resilience factors were promoted, and in what dynamic interaction they were used, was not yet addressed. But identifying the factors provided the basis for future research on resilience. Grotberg (1995) organized the factors generally agreed on by the field into three categories: I HAVE, I AM, I CAN.

I HAVE are the external supports provided:

- Trusting and loving relationships within and outside the family
- Structure and rules at home and in the school (stable environment)
- Role models of behavior
- Encouragement to be independent
- Access to health, education, welfare, and social and security services

I AM are the inner strengths that are developed:

- Likable, with an appealing temperament
- Empathetic, feeling compassion for others
- Respectful of self and others
- Autonomous and responsible
- Optimistic, having faith and hope

I CAN are the interpersonal and problem-solving skills that are acquired:

- Share thoughts and feelings, and communicate
- Solve problems in school and in life
- Gauge the temperament of others
- Manage feelings and impulses
- Reach out for help

(Humor and creativity are often referred to, but have not been included in the research.)

Some studies included average and above-average intelligence and socioeconomic status as resilience factors (Masten & Coatsworth,

1998), but other studies found that resilience behavior did not rely on intelligence or socioeconomic status (Grotberg, 2000; Grotberg, 2001b; Vaillant & Davis, 2000).

The International Resilience Research Project

The International Resilience Research Project (IRRP) (Grotberg, 2000) began in 1993 and continues. The IRRP conducted research in 22 countries at 27 sites around the world, and asked two questions: How do children become resilient? What is the role of culture in the promotion of resilience? As a result of further data analysis and related research relevant to the current focus on terror, two more questions could be addressed: What is the role of the family in promoting resilience? What is the role of the community in promoting resilience?

The findings, briefly, are these:

- About one-third of the people studied are promoting resilience.
- The promotion of resilience is tied to the growth and development of each person (his or her life-trajectory).
- Resilience involves a process of behavior.
- Children are able to promote their own resilience by about the age of nine.
- Socioeconomic status and intelligence are not critical to becoming resilient.
- Boys and girls are equally resilient but with different ways of dealing with adversities.
- Cultural differences exist, but do not prevent the promotion of resilience.

These findings are addressed and integrated as they relate to the overall goal of promoting resilience. Culture plays the initial role in the promotion of resilience, and so cultural differences are examined first, to determine the impact of these differences on the promotion of resilience in children.

The Role of Culture

Culture is introduced as part of child rearing, and cultural differences are apparent from the beginning of a child's life. The differences, however, do not prevent the promotion of resilience; rather, they reflect the values of a culture that shape the styles of child rearing, as well as the promotion of resilience. The following eight differences have been noted.

1. *Pushing the rate of development versus letting it progress naturally.* The speed with which development can be advanced is important in some cultures. This push for faster development is particularly common with regard to girls. Often, they are toilet trained early, taught to become dexterous in handling food and household utensils, and trained to look after siblings. The girls are needed by their mothers to help around the house. Their brothers are not so burdened and have more time for their own pace of development.

2. *Democratic versus authoritarian family.* In an authoritarian family, children have little to say about decisions directly affecting them, and the same is usually true for their mothers. This lack of democracy is usually countered by a great concern on the part of their parents for the safety and well-being of their children.

3. *Dependence versus independence.* Probably the most notable cultural difference in families is the degree to which family members are dependent on or independent of other members. At what point can children make their own decisions? When can a family member decide on his or her own to take a certain job, or go to a certain place, or solve a problem independently? Often, girls were found to be kept dependent longer than boys, except for household chores and responsibilities.

4. *Strict versus permissive.* Setting limits for what a child can or cannot do and where a child can or cannot go varies among cultures. Sometimes, limits are set only when it appears a child will injure himself or herself, or someone else. When strict limits of behavior are set, they provide security for children but they also rob them of an opportunity to explore new places and activities. When there are no limits—permissiveness is the rule—a child who is adventurous does not know when to stop and is very likely to get into dangerous situations. On the other hand, a shy child can be so intimidated by freedom that he or she may well go off into a corner and stay alone. These extremes appeared repeatedly in the international study. Clearly, resilience is not independent of the personality and temperament of the child.

5. *Gender differences.* Cultures differ in the role of the father in the family. Major cultural differences include the amount of time spent with the children, what kinds of activities they engage in, the degree of risk they encourage their children to take, and the differential treatment of the sons and daughters.

   An important gender difference that cuts across cultures, however, involves the different ways men and women, boys and girls, deal with adversities. Girls and women tend to use empathy, faith, interpersonal relationships, and family supports to deal with adversities. Boys and men tend to be more pragmatic. They size up the adversity, make some decisions about consequences of specific actions they might take, and then act. They may or may not involve others. Violence is more acceptable to boys and men in resolving problems than to girls and women. The most basic difference between the genders may well be that girls and women cherish life while boys and men challenge death. Prepubescent boys in some cultures are taught to fight and kill, joining the military part of the society.

6. *Cooperative versus competitive.* Cultures differ in whether they tend to emphasize cooperation or competition. In other words, does the individual who is competitive, wanting to do better than someone else, violate the cultural norm of the society? A number of countries attribute their lack of creativity to the need to be part of the group and not do things independently. Their children are discouraged from acts of competition.

7. *Physical versus verbal punishment.* Discipline styles differ from culture to culture, with both physical and verbal punishments practiced. Disobeying a parent or lying to a parent (the worst offense in many cultures) often brings physical punishment. Other cultures place more emphasis on discipline through conversation (that is, helping the child understand limits of behavior). When discipline is severe, the child tends to be fearful of bodily harm, and may well become submissive or resort to lying. When discipline is verbal, there is the opportunity to talk about what happened, why it happened, and what needs to be done to make things right again. Fear is not involved, so the child can learn how to be responsible without unnecessary anxiety. Fear, as terrorists clearly know, is a powerful weapon to control people, but little growth occurs for the individual or group so controlled.

8. *Free versus utilitarian use of time.* There are cultural differences in how parents view their children's use of time. Some cultures stress the importance of play and freedom of action for their children, while others stress the importance of time being directed to "useful" activities, such as family chores or learning something related to future jobs and responsibilities. Children in the latter case are seen more as apprentices than free spirits, and they miss out on exploring their environment and enjoying the fantasy and creativity that go along with that freedom.

These cultural differences in child rearing do not prevent the promotion of resilience. About one-third of the people in each culture were

promoting resilience in their children, and engaging in resilience behavior in their families. Resilience was not compromised; instead, different resilience factors were emphasized and used in dealing with
adversities.

Resilience and the Life-Trajectory

Another major IRRP finding was the relationship between a person's stage of development on the life-trajectory and what resilience
factors can be expected to develop at each stage. The major developmental stages are trust, autonomy, initiative, industry, identity, intimacy, generativity, and integrity (Erikson, 1985). It is important to
recognize the stage of development an individual has reached in order
to determine what can be expected, and what cannot, in terms of
dealing with adversities. For example, young children cannot be expected to deal with such adversities as terrorist bombings. Young
children do not have the ability to manage or even label their emotions. They do not have the ability to analyze the intent of the perpetrators, other than to know that the perpetrators want to harm them.
They do not know what to do and they often regress to an earlier
stage of development. They rely on adults, particularly their parents,
to help them deal with extreme situations of adversity. Parents are especially important in helping children deal with extreme situations of
adversity, and in helping them become more resilient as a result
(Baruch, Stutman, & Grotberg, 1995).

The Building Blocks of Resilience

The developmental stages of life are, indeed, the building blocks of
resilience (Grotberg, 1999a). One developmental stage leads to another, while resilience factors are being built, consistent with each
stage. However, there are often gaps that prevent children, youth, and
adults from completing a stage of development and, concomitantly,
from becoming resilient. The first five building blocks are the ones
most critical to the promotion of resilience.

Trust

Trust is defined as believing in and relying on another person or
thing, and believing in and relying on oneself. The trust we develop
in our lives begins at birth. As babies, we had no choice but to trust
others to love us, feed us, comfort us, and protect us. Our very survival was at stake. Then we began to trust ourselves to work out a

rhythm of feeding, calming, and managing our bodies. This trust was tied to special people to whom we felt emotionally attached. We loved them; we were bonded with them. And, as we grew up, we learned to trust others—not necessarily to love them, but to have good feelings about them. We learned to trust ourselves—our ability to do things, have friends, and develop a career or a hobby. We even learned to trust the world. All of this trust was not blind—it was an informed trust, a selective trust.

People who do not trust others may develop certain ways of dealing with the world. Three rather common methods are the following:

- Control others. If you feel you cannot trust anyone to be loving or helpful, you may have come to see everyone as dangerous and potentially hostile. You may feel that to keep them from harming you, you need to control them. If you can control them, they cannot harm you, and trust, then, is irrelevant.

- Withdraw from human interaction. The reason for this reaction is to feel safer and less threatened by a world that cannot be trusted. You may have become self-reliant and avoided getting involved emotionally, rejecting efforts of others to develop any meaningful relationship with you.

- Become dependent. If you feel that you cannot trust yourself to achieve, then you may try to protect yourself from what you see as inevitable failure. You may let others do things for you. You may allow yourself to be manipulated because you feel certain that others are better than you are, know more, and are the most likely to protect you.

Trust is needed to promote related resilience factors. When a child trusts a parent or other adult, the child is more willing to accept limits of behavior, and imitate role models (I HAVE); be likable, empathic and caring, optimistic and hopeful (I AM); and increasingly be able to express thoughts and feelings, solve problems, and reach out for help (I CAN).

Autonomy

Autonomy is defined as independence and freedom—the ability to make your own decisions. Your autonomy began to develop when you were about two years old, and it is critical throughout your life. You first began to be autonomous when you recognized that you were separate from those around you and that you had some power over others. Saying "No!" was perhaps your first use of power. This autonomy brought a sense of independence and freedom, but it also brought new responsibilities, especially for your own behavior. You began to develop some idea of right and wrong, and to feel a sense of guilt if you did something considered wrong, like harming someone, or breaking something. You made many mistakes as you tried to become more independent. And the way adults around you—especially your parents—reacted to your mistakes determined how autonomous and independent you would become.

Autonomy is needed to promote related resilience factors. As a child becomes autonomous, accepting limits of behavior is reinforced (I HAVE); respect for oneself and others is promoted, empathy and caring are reinforced, and responsibility for one's own behavior is promoted (I AM); and managing feelings and impulses is promoted (I CAN).

To promote resilience in children around the first two building blocks, it is effective to use a dynamic interaction of resilience factors such as these:

- Balance freedom to explore with safe supports.
- Offer explanations and reconciliation along with rules and discipline.
- Give the child comfort and encouragement in stressful situations.
- Provide a stable environment for the very young child, but some novelty for the two- and three-year-old—new experiences, people, places and changes in routine.
- Change and modify the mix of freedom and safety, explanations and discipline, help and independence, etc., as the child's reactions suggest.

Initiative

Initiative is the ability and willingness to take action. Your initiative began to develop around the ages of four and five, when you started to think and do things on your own. At this age, you may have started all kinds of projects or activities that you did not or could not finish. But whether you succeeded was not important. It was the willingness to try that was important to building initiative. Creative ideas in art and science, new inventions, and problem solving in every area of life require initiative. When you face adversity in your life, you are in a stronger position to deal with it if you are able to take the initiative for finding creative responses.

Sometimes things interfere with the development of initiative. If you were stopped or criticized too many times when you started a project or activity, you felt guilty for bothering people or bad for making a mess of things. If you experienced too much rejection from those you wanted to help, you felt unworthy. Eventually, you stopped wanting or trying to take the initiative in anything.

Initiative is needed to promote related resilience factors. When initiative is developed in children, it reinforces trusting relationships, recognizing limits of behavior, and accepting encouragement to be autonomous (I HAVE); it reinforces empathy, caring, responsibility, optimism (I AM); and it contributes further to expressing thoughts and feelings, solving problems, managing feelings and behavior, and reaching out for help (I CAN).

To promote resilience in children, it is useful to draw on different resilience factors, using them in dynamic interaction. Here are some suggestions:

- Balance providing help with encouraging independence.
- Offer explanations and reconciliation along with rules and discipline.
- Accept errors and failures while providing guidance toward improvement.
- Give the child comfort and encouragement in stressful situations.
- Encourage and model flexibility in selecting different resilience factors as an adverse situation changes (for example, seek help instead of continuing alone in a very difficult situation; show empathy instead of continuing with anger or fear; share feelings with a friend instead of continuing to suffer alone).

Industry

Industry is defined as working diligently at a task. Most people develop industry during their school years, and the process may well be continuous throughout life. During the school years, your attention is focused on mastering skills, both academic and social. These skills are critical to promoting your resilience so that you have the tools to deal more effectively with experiences of adversity. It is also during the years of this developmental stage that you become able to promote your own resilience. By the age of nine, many children can promote their own resilience at the same rate as their parents; however, they reach out for help more frequently. But, if you were unable to succeed in mastering academic and social skills, you may have felt inferior and become extremely sensitive about your limitations.

Identity

The fifth building block of resilience, identity, corresponds to development during the teen years. The major questions usually on your mind at this age are:

- Who am I?
- How do I compare to other teens?
- What are my new relationships with my parents (and other authority figures)?
- What have I accomplished?
- Where do I go from here?

When you answer these questions to your satisfaction, you show skills in monitoring your own behavior, comparing your behavior with accepted standards, being helpful and supportive of others, using your fantasy to make dreams come true, and recognizing the role of idealism in thinking and planning. If you are not able to do these things, you may become self-doubting and unsure of who you really are. You may feel that no one understands you, including yourself. You may be totally confused about how to behave and about your role in life. These insecurities can lead to feelings of inferiority, frustration, and anger.

The following strategies work to promote resilience in older children during the development of industry and identity:

- Balance autonomy with available, but not imposed, help.
- Modulate consequences for mistakes with love and empathy so that the person can fail without feeling too much stress or fear of loss of approval and love.
- Communicate about and negotiate some limits to growing independence; discuss new expectations and new challenges.
- Encourage the person to accept responsibility for consequences of his or her behavior, while communicating confidence and optimism about the desired outcome.
- Encourage and model flexibility in selecting different resilience factors as an adverse situation changes (for example, seek help instead of continuing alone in a very difficult situation, show empathy instead of continuing with anger and fear, share feelings with a friend instead of continuing to suffer alone).

Resilience Is a Process of Behavior

Another important finding from the research is that engaging in re-silience behavior involves a process. The first step in the process is to identify the problem, the adversity. Often a person or group is not certain what the adversity is and there is need to clarify what is causing the problem, the risk, the adversity. The more threatening the adversity, the more difficult it is to assess it and react effectively. The second step is to determine who will be affected or who is already affected. The third step is to identify the obstacles that will need to be overcome to deal with the adversity. The fourth step is to determine who can provide help. And the fifth step is to identify the inner strengths people have and the interpersonal and problem-solving skills they have to deal with the adversity. The process takes some time, some thinking, and making changes in resilience factors used as the situation changes. People who are already resilient tend to go through this process almost intuitively and act quickly when adversity strikes.

It is important to select an appropriate level and kind of response. For children, a limited exposure to the adversity will build resilience behavior, whereas a total exposure may be overpowering or traumatic. Another kind of response is a planned one, which assumes there is time to plan for dealing with the adversity. This approach would apply in the case of planned surgery, moving, divorce, changing school, and so forth. Still another kind of response is a practiced one, which involves talking out or acting out what will be done. This approach might be used in the case of a fire drill, or a meeting with someone who has authority to make decisions affecting the person or group, or when practicing how to deal with problems such as bullying. Finally, an immediate response requires immediate reactions. This would be the case in an explosion, an accident, or an attack by terrorists.

All the resilience factors should be promoted and practiced by the end of the first five developmental stages. There are more stages, including intimacy (the need to develop sexual identity and intimate relationships); generativity (the need to provide leadership and model behavior); and integrity (the need to demonstrate values and ethics). However, the first five stages are when the resilience factors are developing and resilience behavior is practiced. Later stages strengthen the factors for increasingly mature, caring behavior in more complex situations of adversity. Practice doesn't make perfect, but it certainly helps in knowing how to respond to adversities. If you have been there, done that, you are more confident and probably more effective.

Terrorists and Resilience

There is no reason to believe that terrorists would countenance resilience in the people they need to keep in a state of fear and vulnerability. The very building blocks of resilience challenge their power. Trust, the first building block, is most at risk. Terrorists cannot trust the people they are terrorizing. They cannot expect to receive trust from the terrorized. This impasse creates a climate of fear and hatred on both sides.

This lack of trust forces the terrorists to be in a constant state of alert, adding law after law to assure their own safety. You drive at night from the airport to your place of residence and are stopped 10 times by armed patrols who check your identification papers, ask where you are going, and decide if they will let you continue to the next armed patrol. Constant vigilance is needed if you don't trust the people you are oppressing, are "governing." The oppressed, in turn, do not trust their oppressors. Distrust, even hatred, become dominant emotions. Whatever trust children develop is restricted to the family, perhaps the extended family.

Terrorists have reason to fear autonomy in the people they are oppressing. They do not want independence of thought and behavior. The oppressors will dictate what can and cannot be done, will provide the rules and punishments. Terrorists must control the people they do not trust. So autonomy, that second building block of resilience and human development, must be restricted, even crushed.

No one takes the initiative in a terrorist state. There is no room for original ideas; they might threaten the oppressors. So that third building block of resilience, initiative, is not promoted for the benefit of society.

Industry is more easily accepted, provided the terrorists control what is learned, what jobs and tasks are acceptable, and who can learn what. So, industry, that fourth building block of resilience and human development, is permitted within predetermined boundaries.

But identity is also likely to be a threat. To have a strong sense of self, to identify with anything other than the agenda of the oppressors, is to invite retaliation, even death. So the fifth building block of resilience and human development is hostage to the limits set by the oppressors, the terrorists. The punishments are severe, even fatal.

The Resilient Family and Community

The emphasis of this chapter has been on the individual. That is because it is the individual who must learn to draw on I HAVE factors of resilience increasingly over the years; it is the individual who must develop the inner strengths from the I AM factors; it is the individual who must master skills to interact with people and to solve problems and adversities of life, the I CAN resilience factors. It is the individual who must learn how to draw on these factors, use them in dynamic interaction for resilience behavior to deal with the adversities. This emphasis on the individual, however, does not imply that the individual is alone and must become resilient independent of the family or of the community. Clearly the family and the community are essential parts of an individual becoming resilient.

The Family

The family provides the setting, both physical and emotional, for resilience to be developed. Trust is not only the first building block of resilience, it is also the first factor of resilience. And that trust begins in the family. The intimacy of the family allows free expression of thoughts and emotions, with little fear of damaging consequences. It is the laboratory of life, where actions can take place, ideas can be tested, and behaviors can be experimented with. The family is the place where socialization occurs at an intimate level. There is freedom to say and do things that cannot be said or done outside the family. There is the opportunity to test social behavior with siblings and parents without the risk of social isolation. There is opportunity to experiment with such different behaviors as how and when to compete and when to cooperate. A member may be teased or ridiculed, but usually remains a valued member of the family. The family is, of course, the predominant place where culture is learned.

Role modeling is probably the most important factor in promoting resilience in children. What family members do, what they say, and how they prepare for or respond to adversities are models of behavior that influence the promotion of resilience in the children. The most powerful example of the impact of role modeling on children came from a study in Peru conducted by Giselle Silva (1999). Her study, using the resilience paradigm I HAVE, I AM, I CAN, examined the role of parents in helping their children deal with the effects of political violence, and the role of resilience in that effort. She examined the reaction of parents to the trauma, and the impact of parents as role models on the resilience of their children. Many parents became poor as they escaped the violence, moving from the countryside and the mountains to the city and lower lands. They were required to make a new life in the new setting and raise their children there. Two major reactions to the trauma distinguished families who were modeling and promoting resilience in their children from those who were not.

Some of the families focused their attention on the trauma of the violence and the necessary escape to a new environment. The focus of these families was on the violent events the family had experienced; the orientation was toward the past; close relationships in the family were negatively affected; the social relationships were affected by lack of confidence and feelings of fear and isolation; there was no adaptation to the new setting, with fantasies about returning to the former home; and deep feelings of nostalgia were experienced, with a major focus on memories.

Most children of these families did not become resilient, and, in fact, many developed severe social and psychological problems, adopting many of their parents' behaviors. In addition, the children showed lack of confidence in others, changed in negative ways their relationships with their parents, experienced frequent feelings of sorrow over the losses from the violence, frequently engaged in games repeating the trauma, and had difficulty in communicating with others.

In contrast, other families focused their attention on the new environment, sought out opportunities in the new setting (jobs, education, friends), refused to allow the trauma to affect family relationships, focused on the here and now and the future, were receptive to new relationships with neighbors, adapted and adjusted to the new setting, and remembered sad experiences of the past but used them to encourage progress. These parents were role models of resilience for their children.

The children of these families were optimistic about the future, made plans for the future, attended school for the first time, learned Spanish for the first time, helped out in the family during vacations, and talked through their experiences of violence. They sometimes showed fear and uncertainty, but they could recover. These were resilient children.

The Community

The community is in the I HAVE part of the resilience paradigm. People expect the community to protect them from harm. This involves police and fire departments and emergency services. Further, the community is expected to provide social services, health services, and education opportunities. In many countries, however, these services and protections are not available and people turn to their families and neighbors for such help. The IRRP study found fewer external supports than needed in many countries, but also found that substitutes were usually available.

The community provides for the promotion of the inner strengths in the I AM part of the resilience paradigm, especially through the church. There are few communities in the world without a church, mosque, synagogue, or other form of religious center to promote the inner strengths of people—primarily faith, hope, and confidence. The moral aspects of living are stressed in all religions.

Schools play a critical role in the promotion of the interpersonal and problem-solving skills in the I CAN part of the resilience paradigm. Teachers, administrators, and related personnel not only provide the settings for acquiring knowledge and skills of learning and performing; they also provide settings for social development. Social skills are learned and the broader social setting of the schools provides opportunities to acquire and practice them. The way you behave, the way you talk, and the way you approach people are all acquired skills. The home may be so informal that an outsider would feel uncomfortable. Some educators may feel that students should be left to socialize on their own terms as they see fit. The result, too often, is children who suffer from a lack of social skills and who have difficulty using such skills to deal with adversities. This is a particularly troubling problem for minority groups, especially immigrant groups, who face bullying, isolation, rejection, and discrimination by other children in the schools. Educators often feel they do not have the time or facilities to deal with these problems and the problems are too frequently ignored. The neglected children cannot look to the school to promote resilience, unless they find a teacher or other students to help them.

The major study of resilient communities was done by Nestor Suarez-Ojeda (2001), a former official at the Pan American Health Organization (PAHO), in Washington, D.C., a participant in the IRRP, and now head of the CIER (Centro Internacional de Investigacion y Estudio de la Resiliencia [International Center of

Information and the Study of Resilience]) in Argentina. As a result of analyzing communities that recovered quickly from disaster and those that did not, he learned what differentiated them.

Four major factors characterize resilient communities:

1. *Collective self-esteem.* The community is proud of itself in terms of cleanliness, provision of services, and caring for its citizens. It also cares about how it looks, what cultural experiences it provides, and what it is noted for.

2. *Cultural identity.* The members of the community identify themselves with the community even through changes. New companies may move in, new schools are built, new families appear, but the sense of cultural identity remains strong and can integrate the new companies and people, adding new benefits, ideas, and even problems.

3. *Social humor.* The community does not take itself too seriously and is able to engage in jokes to show its ability to recognize the humor in their lives. One community, for example, was competitive with another community, and both of them were hiding their limitations. So, a man in one community said, "Let's just keep up with them; don't try to pass them, because they might see the holes in our pants!"

4. *Collective honesty.* The community demands that all of its institutions be honest. This goal often means cleaning out corruption and voting for people who have integrity and who will not tolerate dishonesty, nepotism, or other behaviors that damage a community.

Suarez-Ojeda described nonresilient communities he studied as having these qualities:

1. *Lack of cultural identity.* Many people do not identify with their community; rather they continue to identify with the community they came from or with some concept of a foreign community. This distancing oneself or one's family from the community weakens the community, and can be especially dangerous when adversities strike.

2. *Fatalism.* When people believe they can do nothing about what happens to them, that all is predetermined, they become passive and are easy targets for those who wish to dominate and control. This leaves no room for resilience, and submission takes its place.

3. *Authoritarianism.* When there is a vacuum of cultural identity combined with fatalism, it is inevitable that authoritarian governments will take over. These communities are easy pickings—there will be no resistance. There will be no resilience.

4. *Corruption.* When no one cares about the community; when one's sense of identity exists elsewhere, or when there is passive acceptance of conditions, the community will be taken over by the corrupt, the greedy, the unsavory. You can bet your life on that. Resilience cannot be promoted in such an atmosphere.

Here are recent examples of resilient communities. One is a community after a hurricane: In 1998, Hurricane Mitch settled over Honduras and Nicaragua for days, killing countless people and creating a range of problems and tragedies for the survivors. Yet reports from the region pointed out how quickly the people began helping themselves. Because of the delays in receiving outside help, family members from other parts of the country brought supplies and food to their stricken relatives, many by walking. Teenagers got involved in the relief effort, too, carrying jugs of water on their heads.

This shows the deep pride found in many people that makes them unwilling to see themselves as victims. They want to believe they are capable of dealing with the most severe conditions and experiences, and believing it makes it true. There's no need for pity. They are strong people who will survive. They are resilient. They come from resilient families and resilient communities.

A second example is of a resilient city after the bombing of the World Trade Center: Mary McGrory (2001), a favorite columnist with the *Washington Post*, assessed New Yorkers in their response to the September 11, 2001, tragedy. She said that while New Yorkers don't want to be seen as "nice guys," that is their reputation now. She went on to say that New Yorkers overwhelmed the country with their valor and their human kindness when some 3,000 people lost their lives in the attack on the World Trade Center. She wrote about their exemplary conduct after the fall of the twin towers—especially that of the valorous policemen and fire fighters. Fellow citizens responded with heartbreaking generosity and solicitude, bringing the public servants coffee and sandwiches and socks, and hanging around Ground Zero at all hours to applaud as they came off their shifts. She wrote that New Yorkers have had their famous self-esteem ratified. They feel, with reason, they helped give one in the eye to Osama bin Laden, who did not anticipate their extraordinary resilience and resourcefulness.

Resilience Cannot Be Stopped

No one, no group, however oppressive, can kill resilience. In one occupied country where there was no trust and where there was great fear and hatred of the occupiers, groups met in special rooms late at night to share thoughts and feelings, gloat over some undetected trouble they caused the oppressors, and enjoy the moment. Here are some examples of resilient behavior.

A woman met by the writer in an airport described how she and her friends function in a war-torn country. Each morning they telephone each other and check on their safety. Then they decide where they will meet for lunch or to plan some activity. If an area where they plan to meet has been attacked the night before, they change their place of meeting, and continue with the plans. In fact, they accommodate to the situation while keeping their relationships intact and caring for each other. The woman's greatest concern was not being home to safeguard her children while she was on this necessary trip.

More than 1,100 high school students were to attend a career fair at another school on the morning of September 11, 2001, when the news of the terrorist attacks was first reported. As the students were to arrive by bus any minute, there was no possibility of canceling the fair. The concern of the teachers was for the students. What should they be told? Should the schedule be shortened or changed? Vicky Foote, reporting this event to the writer, indicated that she wanted to go home to her family and that she was frightened. But she was also responsible for the 1,100 students. She knew her demeanor would be very important to lessen the fear she was sure the students would be feeling. She was transfixed by what she saw as the students came in.

These were not the chattering, smiling sophomores from the year before who acted more like 10-year-olds than 15-year-olds, giddy with excitement about having a morning off from school. These students were somber, and painfully thoughtful. They talked in low voices, almost whispers. As I welcomed them and handed them career brochures, several leaned forward and in a hushed voice asked, "Have you heard what happened?" That was all they knew to say.

In the exhibit hall, the television booth, where students were to learn information about careers in communications, quickly became a magnet as students drew close and stared at the screen. Young eyes stared, young foreheads wrinkled, young minds tried to grasp the situation, struggling to understand.

Slowly, some began to ask questions: Will we go to war? Where? Against who? They began to express concern for relatives living near the disaster areas, and for loved ones in the military. Then, amazingly, without any answers to their questions, they moved on to other career booths and began to ask questions about job opportunities in health care, in law enforcement, in teaching, in firefighting. They were students again, trying to gain information to help them make wise career decisions. They were focusing on the future, considering, more than usual, careers in services. I could not help thinking. How brave they are. How totally resilient. I admired them. They were great role models for resilience.

Other examples of the power of resilience include two that the writer has witnessed. First, several women living in a country controlling their lives, even how they must dress, are dropped off at the hotel of the visitor, go to her room, shed the veils and go down to the restaurant, free to express themselves. No one recognizes them because they have always been seen covered. Second, women in airplanes head for the lavatory as soon after takeoff as permitted, remove their veils, and come back in the regular clothes worn beneath. They now begin to talk with passengers, both men and women. The process is reversed when they return.

Resilience shows up even in families or children alone and under constant surveillance in detention camps, far from their war-torn homes. The writer (Grotberg, 1999b) analyzed findings from a study by Margaret McCallin (1993). McCallin, of the International Catholic Child Bureau in Geneva, Switzerland, reported on the psychosocial well-being of Vietnamese children in Hong Kong detention centers. Through observations and a series of interviews, she found the worst and the best in the ways those in detention dealt with their situations.

The interviews were conducted with children and youth. McCallin identified six areas that were most damaging to the children and that did not promote or sustain resilience.

- *A pervasive sense of loneliness.* This quality was particularly true of children, regardless of their age, who had no relative with them. These children craved affection, guidance, and help.
- *A deep sense of loss and abandonment.* Much of this resulted from the loss of a parent through death or remarriage.
- *Depression.* This was characterized by a profound lack of initiative and a sense of hopelessness. It was further demonstrated by passivity, and a strong sense of powerlessness. A depressive inertia seemed to grip many of the children. This quality was adaptive in the situation of powerlessness and dependency these children faced, but it did not contribute positively in the long run.
- *Fear for personal safety.* Girls feared sexual assault and harassment. Boys feared bullying by older, more powerful males. Many children

reported a strategy of invisibility, withdrawing into reading or studying or neutralizing their appearance through dress, posture, and behavior to appear younger. This way they hoped to avoid being noticed and therefore attacked by predatory elements within the camps.

- *Current stressors.* The main stressor was the separation from their families and the constant worrying about them. A stressor of almost equal intensity was their fear of violence. They were also affected by other daily concerns, such as confinement within the detention center, lack of clothing, and monotonous and unappetizing food. Of greater concern, however, were those who reported no problems in the center at all, despite acknowledging their awareness of the existence of fights, riots, and violence against women in the camps.

- *Delays in screening.* The process for screening to determine if the detainees will be accepted to stay in Hong Kong or be sent back to Vietnam takes years. A constant finding was that this time lag has the most negative impact on the children and youth. Length of time at the center and age of the child combine to heighten the negative impact of the experience. The longer the children are detained and the older they are, the more they lose interest in life.

Evidence of Resilience

How can there be anything positive in such an experience? Surprisingly, many resilience factors were found that helped the children and youth deal with the adverse situation. For example:

- *Hope.* Even though some of the children felt the future seemed hopeless, more than 90 percent had hopes of leading a normal life. The strength of the children, in spite of their experiences, is consistent with the human capacity for resilience.

- *Planning for the future.* Access to education is consistent with planning for the future. Not only was education available at the center, it was used. The unexpected finding was that girls took advantage of the opportunity more than boys. These girls earned higher scores than girls and boys in Hong Kong, scoring two years above Hong Kong students in mean level of education. Such preparation for the future is consistent with hope and confidence. Why the boys were less interested in the opportunity was not clear. They reported spending more time in physical activities with other boys.

- *Feeling in control.* This quality completely contradicts the reality of the situation, and yet 78 percent of the children and youth said that others did not control their lives. This suggests that many of the children made adjustments in their thinking and believing in order to feel in control. They must have had certain small areas of behavior and experiences that allowed them to maintain a sense of control even when they described all the things that made them depressed and afraid. Perhaps the children maintained a sense of their own identity in spite of all that happened. This is not unlike the examples of the women living in the war-torn country or the women shedding their veils.

Resilience Triumphs

As discussed, time was needed to recognize the importance of resilience in dealing with the adversities of life. Research was primarily focused on a deficit, disease model, relying on diagnosis and treatment of identified problems. This model, basically a medical model, was enlarged by the public health model, concerned with the overall health of the nation. The public health model, an epidemiological model, involves counting the number of instances of a particular illness and then supporting research and program development to reduce the unacceptable numbers—a kind of inoculation model.

A new way of thinking was required to shift the focus of attention from disease and vulnerability to well-being and strengths. Resilience became part of the new way of thinking. But even at the beginning, it was difficult to convince groups, such as those involved in mental health, to see resilience as something needed to deal with the inevitable adversities of life. A chief of a mental health department in a government agency was certain that people in good mental health could deal with any adversity. He changed his view when he was told of a boy who was brilliant, who helped his fellow first-graders with their reading, but who could not throw or catch a ball. He was teased and embarrassed and he finally banged his head against a brick wall. He might have been saying that his brains were no good; his successes did not help him now. No one had told him he wouldn't be successful in everything. His mental health from successes and his self-confidence were no match for the adversity of failure and teasing.

The early research on resilience provided the resilience factors, and subsequent research attempted to determine how resilience is promoted and used to deal with the adversities of life. Studies of differences in culture, gender, and age of children indicated that all cultures promote resilience, but with use of different resilience factors; gender differences are mainly important in the manner of dealing with adversities; and the developmental stage of a person determines what resilience factors can be promoted at each stage. Families and the community have special roles in helping children deal with adversities, and they play an especially important role when an adversity comes from acts of terror.

Resilient people can deal with acts of terror. They become stronger as they refuse to succumb to the tragedies perpetrated by terrorists. They can be transformed as they decide to help others who have experienced similar losses. Children become resilient as the resilience factors are promoted at each developmental stage, and as they model the resilient behavior of their parents and other adults. Their resilience is enhanced as they recognize the support of the community, and indeed, the nation, in overcoming the destructive aspects of terrorism. Terrorists have good reason to fear resilient people. Resilience triumphs over terror.

References

Baruch, R., Stutman, S., & Grotberg, E. (1995). *What do you tell the children? How to help children deal with disasters.* Washington, DC: Institute for Mental Health Initiatives.

Erikson, E. H. (1985). *Childhood and society.* New York: Norton.

Garmezy, N. (1974). The study of competence in children at risk for severe psychopathology. In E. J. Anthony & C. Koupernick (Eds.), *The child in his family: Children at psychiatric risk* (Vol. 3, pp. 77–97). New York: Wiley.

Grotberg, E. H. (1995). *A guide to promoting resilience in children.* The Hague, Netherlands: Bernard van Leer Foundation: www.resilnet.uiuc.edu. (Also available in Spanish and in Polish.)

Grotberg, E. H. (1999a). Countering depression with the five building blocks of resilience. *Reaching Today's Youth, 4,* 66–72.

Grotberg, E. H. (1999b). *Tapping your inner strength.* Oakland, CA: New Harbinger Publications.

Grotberg, E. H. (2000). International resilience research project. In A. L. Comunian & U. Gielen (Eds.), *International perspectives on human development* (pp. 379–399). Vienna: Pabst Science.

Grotberg, E. H. (2001a). *Introduccion, nuevas tendencias en resiliencia* (What's new in resilience?). In A. Melillo & N. Suarez-Ojeda (Eds.), *Resiliencia: Discubriendo las proprias fortalezas* (Resilience: Discovering your inner strengths) (pp. 19–30). Buenos Aires: Paidos.

Grotberg, E. H. (2001b). Resilience programs for children in disaster. *Ambulatory Child Health, 7,* 75–83.

Grotberg, E. H. (2001c, Spring). Resilience and culture. *International Psychology Reporter,* 13–14.

Masten, A. S., & Coatsworth, J. D. (1998). The development of competence in favorable and unfavorable environments: Lessons from research on successful children. *American Psychologist, 53,* 205–220.

McCallin, M. (1993). *Living in detention.* Geneva, Switzerland: International Catholic Child Bureau.

McGrory, M. (2001, November 25). A nice change in New York. *New York Times,* p. B1.

Rutter, M. (1979). Protective factors in children's responses to stress and disadvantage. *Annals of the Academy of Medicine, Singapore, 8,* 324–338.

Silva, G. (1999). *Resiliencia y violencia politica en ninos* (Resilience in children dealing with political violence). Lanus, Argentina: Universidad Nacional de Lanus.

Suarez-Ojeda, N. (2001). Una concepcion latinoamericana: La resiliencia comunitaria (A Latin American concept: The resilient community). In A. Melillo & N. Suarez-Ojeda (Eds.), *Resiliencia: Discubriendo las proprias fortalezas* (Resilience: Discovering your inner strengths) (pp. 67–82). Buenos Aires: Paidos.

Vaillant, G., & Davis, T. (2000). Social/emotional intelligence in mid-life resilience in school boys with low-testing intelligence. *American Journal of Orthopsychiatry, 70,* 215–222.

Werner, E., & Smith, R. S. (1982). *Vulnerable but invincible: A study of resilient children.* New York: McGraw-Hill.

APPENDIX A
SIGNS, SYMPTOMS, AND
TREATMENT

Biological

The medical symptoms of a biological attack may go undetected for days. The number of casualties may increase due to the movement of infected people. In a biological attack (smallpox, plague, anthrax), there are few preventive measures aside from vaccination. A HEPA (High Efficiency Particulate Air Filter) mask, similar to a doctor's mask, may be purchased over the counter at a pharmacy as a preventive measure. Considering the immediately undetectable nature of such an attack, a mask may be ineffective; timing would be crucial. Additionally, the mask needs to be fit for initial use and each subsequent use. The masks do not fit children and have the potential to make heart and lung conditions worse.

Smallpox

Smallpox is a serious and contagious infectious disease affecting various parts of the body. Smallpox is most contagious with the onset of the rash. It is transmitted from person to person through respiratory droplets released from the infected individual by coughing or sneezing. Individuals may also be infected if they have direct contact with contaminated clothing, bed linen, or blankets. Smallpox can be fatal in a high percentage of cases.

Symptoms

- High Fever
- Exhaustion
- Headache, backache, abdominal pain
- Rash (inside the mouth, pharynx, face, forearms, trunk, legs)
- Pustules (raised bumps containing pus)

Treatment

One preventive measure that can be taken for smallpox is vaccination (which may not be available to the general public). If the vaccination is not available, avoid contact with infected individuals.

Anthrax

Anthrax is a disease that can be spread in three ways: by skin contact, by ingestion, and by inhalation. Individuals can acquire anthrax by handling an item that contains anthrax spores, an infected animal, or product of an infected animal. For example, one of the anthrax incidents following September 11 involved an individual who opened an envelope containing anthrax spores. Anthrax is not contagious. If anthrax is left untreated it can be fatal.

Symptoms

- Raised itchy bumps with a characteristic black center
- Swollen lymph glands
- Common cold symptoms
- Inflammation of the intestinal tract
- Nausea
- Loss of appetite
- Vomiting
- Diarrhea

Treatment

One preventive measure for anthrax is vaccination. At this time, it is not available to the general public. Antibiotics can be used to treat anthrax but they may be in short supply after a terrorist attack. Local authorities would need to make arrangements with the National

Pharmaceutical Stockpile to have sufficient medical supplies delivered to the area.

Plagues

Plague is a bacterial infectious disease affecting both humans and animals. Most commonly, plague is transmitted from rodents to humans by fleas. Plague can be transmitted by the release of respiratory droplets into the air and cutaneous (skin) infection. Symptoms of plague may take days to weeks to detect. Plague can be fatal if left untreated. Plague infections in humans usually occur in one of three forms: Bubonic, Pneumonic, and Septicemic.

Bubonic plague is transmitted when the bacteria infects an opening in the flesh. It is very uncommon for the bubonic plague to be transmitted from person to person.

Symptoms

- Swollen, painful lymph nodes (buboes)
- Fever
- Headache, muscle ache

Pneumonic plague is transmitted when the bacteria infects the lungs. It can be spread from person to person through respiratory droplets released by coughing and sneezing. Transmission can occur with face-to-face contact.

Symptoms

- Fever
- Headache
- Weakness
- Cough (blood, watery saliva and mucus)

Septicemic plague results when the bacteria are present in the blood and begin to multiply rapidly as a complication of bubonic or pneumonic plague.

Symptoms

- Seizures
- Shock
- Confusion

Treatment

Plagues can be treated early with antibiotics and vaccination.

Chemical Attacks

Chemical attacks can occur in three states: gaseous, liquid, or solid. Chemical agents can be transmitted in three ways: by skin contact, by ingestion, and by inhalation. Symptoms of a chemical attack may be detected within hours or days. With each of these agents, quantity and concentration determine severity.

Nerve agents (sarin, VX) disrupt the body's nervous system. Symptoms of nerve agents are:

- Runny nose
- Tightness in chest area
- Nausea, vomiting

Choking agents (chlorine, phosgene) attack the lungs. Symptoms of choking agents are:

- Coughing, tightness in chest area
- Rapid breathing
- Shock followed by death

Blood agents (cyanide) carry tissue-killing poisons throughout the body. Symptoms of blood agents are:

- Rapid breathing
- Violent convulsions
- Cardiac arrest

Blister agents (mustard gas) attack skin and eyes and cause pain and skin blistering. Symptoms of blister agents are:

- Irritation of eyes, throat, and lungs
- Redness, blistering of skin
- Skin ulcers
- Incapacitation, death

Other indicators of a chemical attack are:

- Colored residue on surfaces
- Dead foliage
- Strong odor
- Dead insects/animals

Treatment

Antidotes to reverse or weaken the effect of a chemical agent exist for certain chemical agents. However, there is no vaccination available. An individual can protect his/her body by avoiding a contaminated area. If near a contaminated area, protect the skin and cover the eyes with eye protection (tight-fitting goggles). Once away from the area, remove clothing and other articles and place them in a plastic garbage bag for safe disposal. Wash with soap and water immediately.

Radiological

Radiological attacks spread radioactive material that can contaminate the nearby area. Radioactive material can affect people if they come into contact with, ingest, or inhale it. Radiological attacks are difficult to detect because the onset of the symptoms may take days to weeks and radiological materials are generally odorless and colorless. The attack may occur by placing a non-dispersive device containing a low level of radioactive material in a public location or by detonating a "dirty bomb" containing highly toxic nuclear material such as uranium and plutonium. If left untreated, radiation sickness can be fatal.

Symptoms

- Skin reddening (burns)
- Nausea
- Vomiting

Treatment

There are two health conditions that can result from exposure to radioactive material: radiation sickness and an increased likelihood of developing cancer in the future. Radiation sickness can be treated by a physician. In any case, the following measures can be taken:

- Avoid the contaminated area by increasing the distance between you and the source of radiation.
- If you have been exposed, wash and change your clothes; wash your hair and skin with soap and water.
- Do not apply ointment to burns.
- Place clothing and articles in a plastic garbage bag for safe disposal.
- If you are outdoors, breathe through a cloth or use a filter mask to limit inhalation.

- If you are indoors, close all windows and doors.
- Do not eat or drink anything that may be contaminated with radioactive material.

An area (home, office, school, hospital) contaminated with radioactive material may remain uninhabitable for an extended period of time. Check with local authorities before returning to an area contaminated with radioactive material.

Explosive

A conventional explosive such as dynamite kills or injures through the initial blast. A "dirty bomb" is a conventional bomb packaged with radioactive material. A dirty bomb kills or injures immediately through the initial blast of the conventional explosive and later by radiation and contamination. The number of deaths and injuries from a conventional explosive or a dirty bomb explosion depend upon the sophistication of the bomb and atmospheric conditions.

Incendiary

Incendiary devices range from simple (a Molotov cocktail constructed of a bottle, rag, gasoline, and match) to sophisticated (napalm). Incendiary devices can cause loss of life and extensive property damage. Treat an incendiary attack as a major fire and get as far away as possible from the source.

Nuclear

A nuclear bomb is a weapon of mass destruction (atom bomb, hydrogen bomb). Nuclear bombs involve a complex nuclear fission or fusion reaction. The massive destruction caused by a nuclear bomb is the result of the initial blast or shock, the heat that irradiates immediately after the blast, and the residual radiation emitted from the explosion. The loss of lives and the destruction and contamination caused by a nuclear bomb would be devastating.

(Source: National Strategy Forum, 2002, "Prudent Preparation" at www.nationalstrategy.com, reprinted with permission.)

Appendix B
Personal Preparation

There are various ways to prepare for a mass casualty incident. For example, first aid classes and regular evacuation drills could make the difference between incurring minimal and serious injuries—even life and death. As you actively consider taking precautions, you may discover other like-minded individuals with whom you can cooperate to provide information to friends and neighbors.

Develop a Personal Disaster Plan

Some basic things to be included in this plan are:

- Determination of multiple evacuation routes out of your home and office.
- Identification of two meeting places (one near home, one that is distant from home in case that area is affected) with friends and loved ones in case of separation.
- Designation of an emergency contact person to assist in the process of notifying friends and family.
- Recognition that phone lines may be tied up.
- Recognition that computers and other electronic equipment may be inaccessible.

Create a Personal Disaster Kit

Some suggestions for what to pack in a disaster kit:

- A large plastic trash bin with handles for transportation to store your supplies

- Garbage bags

- Supply of drinking water (1 gallon per day, per person, for three days)

- Supply of non-perishable food that does not require cooking (a three-day supply per person)

- Blankets

- Household chlorine bleach

- A change of clothing, including sturdy boots

- First aid kit

- Medicine dropper

- Flashlight w/spare batteries

- Battery powered radio w/spare batteries

- Essential medications/prescriptions (Consider: What do you do if you do not have a sufficient supply? Where can you get a supply.? What would you do if you could not get medications for a week or more? Ensure that you or your family members have necessary medical supplies for diabetes, incontinence, low blood pressure, etc. Ensure you or loved ones have Medical Alert Identification if needed.)

- Extra pair of eyeglasses/contacts/contact solution

- Local maps

- Sanitation goods (toilet paper, personal hygiene products, feminine products)

- Basic tools (tape, compass, pen/pencil, wrench, pliers, hammer, needle and thread, duct tape)

- Non-electric can opener

- Inexpensive filter mask

- Eye protection (goggles, safety glasses)

- Gloves (disposable/rubber)

- Car/house keys

- Whistle
- Child care items if applicable: diapers, baby wipes, formula, bottles, toys
- Pet care items, if applicable (food, ID tags, litter, veterinarian records)
- Photocopies of important personal/financial documents (driver's license, passport, will, stock certificates, birth and marriage certificates, tax returns, insurance policies, proof of residence, social security)
- Cash
- List of telephone numbers of friends, family, business associates, banks, physicians

Communication

Plan on being out of contact with family and friends after an event, at least temporarily. On September 11, 2001, in New York City, phone lines, cellular phones, and the Internet were jammed and inaccessible. However, out-of-state phone calls worked best and Internet access via DSL lines was not interrupted.

Discuss and plan with your family, friends, and others what alternative means of communication might be, what alternate locations for regrouping might be, and over what period of time.

Learn now what emergency radio channels are available in your area from which you might get important information until normal communication is restored

Dependents

Ensure that people you are responsible for are taken care of (e.g., elderly people, children, or those with special needs require continuing care during your absence).

Ensure that an alternate care giver is available in your absence.

Ensure that someone is monitoring his or her meals, water, and environmental conditions. (Make these preparations in advance rather than relying on communication by phone, E-mail, or other modes of communication during emergencies.)

Temperatures in homes during periods of power outages can be deadly, hot or cold. People who are elderly, handicapped or otherwise unable to care for themselves may not realize that they are be-

coming dehydrated or experiencing excessively cold or hot temperatures that can kill them.

If you have left children or minors with friends or relatives, ensure
that custodians are able to authorize routine care if such becomes
necessary. This commonly overlooked requirement causes lost time
and sustained discomfort. Check with a doctor or the local hospital
before the need arises.

If you have relatives in nursing homes, check with the nursing
home administrator to determine the need for special authoriza-
tions, consents, or orders and alternative points of contact if you are
out of communication.

Consider continuing services such as Meals on Wheels, which may
be disrupted in an emergency situation. Keep the phone number of
the agency providing this service handy.

Plan on keeping some easily prepared meals in that person's freezer.

Schools

Parents may wish to contact schools (and School Boards) and day-
care centers attended by their children to determine the status of
planning for a mass casualty incident, and how schoolchildren and
their parents will receive appropriate guidance.

(Source: National Strategy Forum, 2002, "Prudent Preparation" at
www.nationalstrategy.com, reprinted with permission.)

Appendix C
Personal Response

Terrorist attacks are executed to inflict personal and structural harm to disorient the public and spread fear. It is critical to know how to respond to immediate and long-term dangers.

Space

Attempt to assess your proximity to the attack. If danger threatens, try to get as far away as necessary using planned evacuation routes, etc. Do not use short cuts because passage may be blocked.

Routine

The goal is to survive a mass casualty incident and its immediate aftermath and return to daily routine as soon as possible. Disruption of services you rely on is likely.

Time

Attempt to assess the length of the attack and prioritize your actions in accordance with that assessment. Should you be unable to leave an attack area immediately, attempt to minimize the time that you are in the hazardous area.

Exposure

Attempt to assess your susceptibility to and defenses from the attack's effects. Respond by taking available precautions to limit the degree of exposure to harm. This step is especially important if space or time considerations are unavailable.

Person

Attempt to assess your condition. Try at all times to remain calm and optimistic. Conserve your energy. Detect any injuries and address them according to their nature and extent. Attempt to determine if you are able to help others and what inherent risks you might undertake should you decide to do so.

Water Shortage

Your home hot water tank, ice cubes, and water from streams, lakes, and rivers can serve as additional sources of water. Sterilize any water that is taken from a source that may be unsanitary. Boiling the water or treating the water with a small amount of household chlorine bleach (5 drops per gallon) may be necessary. If chlorine bleach is used as a sterilizer, make sure the water does not smell like chlorine before ingesting it. Store water in a plastic container such as a soda bottle. A milk jug will decompose and a glass bottle can break. Change stored water every six months.

Fire/Debris

If confronted with a fire, distance yourself while staying low to the floor to avoid smoke and heat. Cover your nose and mouth with a wet cloth to avoid the inhalation of smoke or toxic fumes. Cover your nose with a dry cloth to avoid inhalation of particulates in the air after an explosion. If trapped in debris, tap on a pipe or wall to attract attention of rescuers or use a whistle if available. Avoid movement or prolonged shouting since both actions can interfere with breathing.

Evacuation

In case of evacuation, remain calm, move, and have your lightweight traveling disaster kit with you. Wear full-length protective clothing. Utilize evacuation routes you have tested which are government/business approved, unless these options are unavailable. Ensure that your business has an emergency evacuation plan that is regularly practiced including an emergency evacuation kit for each employee.

Psychological Aspects

A terrorism attack can cause great psychological and physical trauma. The loss or injury of friends and loved ones or the stress of an attack can cause emotional harm. Understanding your feelings is as much part of the recovery process as rebuilding your home and finances. The National Center for Post-Traumatic Stress Disorder recommends several things that you can do:

- Spend time with other people.
- Talk about how you are feeling.
- Get back to your everyday routine as soon as possible.
- Take time to grieve.
- Ask for support from friends and family.
- Eat well and take time to exercise.
- Get enough sleep.
- Find enjoyable things to do.

Professional assistance is available for those who find themselves unable to cope with events on their own. Following are suggested places to start should you feel that you or someone else needs further help: National Institute for Mental Health, *www.nimh.nih.gov*; American Psychological Association, *www.apa.org*; National Association of Social Workers, *www.naswdc.org*.

Pediatric Vulnerabilities and Potential Remedies

Small children, especially infants, have higher metabolic rates, breathe relatively more air per minute for their body weight, and have a larger relative skin surface for weight. These factors translate into increased susceptibility to airborne particles or chemicals, increased risk of rapid dehydration, and increased risk of hypothermia (low body temperature), all of which can be life-threatening. Several responses may mitigate some of these differences. Children should be among the first victims to be sheltered and decontaminated, if possible. Water used to wash contaminated small children should be warm, as you would use for a baby's bath. Ill children with decreased feeding and/or vomiting or diarrhea must be encouraged to drink small volumes of fluid frequently, watched carefully for signs of dehydration, and may require earlier institution of intravenous fluids.

Young children have less capacity to escape attack or take evasive actions without parental guidance. Planning ahead for parental surrogates or shared child care in the event of crisis may be crucial for young children's survival after an attack.

Children will likely have fewer coping skills if a loved one is injured or killed, and may experience greater anxiety over reported incidents (even hoaxes) and media coverage. Children and adolescents may manifest this anxiety in subtle ways for which parents will need to be alert. Younger children may become more clingy, less playful, or regress developmentally (thumb-sucking or bed-wetting). School age children and adolescents should be monitored for disturbed sleep, fatigue, decreased pleasure in usual activities, isolation from former friends, decline in school performance, and new onset substance abuse.

Parents may be able to mitigate some of this anxiety and post-traumatic stress with some common sense approaches. These might include:

- Communicating with children, as much as possible, that they are safe. Indicate willingness to discuss their concerns and fears.
- Avoiding repetitive exposure to TV coverage of traumatic incidents, especially by young children watching alone.
- Professional counseling for older children with evidence of significant stress response may be needed.

Community Response Capabilities

Emergency medical services and hospital bed capacity may be particularly stressed by a large influx of pediatric patients. Ordinary referral patterns (transfer of critically ill or injured children from community hospitals to children's hospitals) may be limited or inoperative.

Individual parents may feel that they have little to offer in minimizing these problems, but together they can advocate on a community-wide basis for robust planning for pediatric patients in the event of a tragic incident. Parents can raise questions about adequacy of pediatric preparedness with their physicians, local hospitals, regional pediatric society, and health departments. Such advocacy would also help address other scenarios such as natural disasters, infectious disease epidemics, or large-scale accidents (such as a school bus crash) involving multiple children.

(Source: National Strategy Forum, 2002, "Prudent Preparation" at www.nationalstrategy.com, reprinted with permission.)

Appendix D
Resources

Publications

American Academy of Pediatrics, Committee on Pediatric Emergency Medicine (2000). Disasters, mass casualty events, and disaster preparedness. In: J. M. Seidel, J. F., Knapp (Eds.), *Childhood emergencies in the office, hospital, and community: Organizing systems of care* (pp. 217–246). Elk Grove Village, IL: American Academy of Pediatrics.

American Academy of Pediatrics Workgroup on Disasters (1995). *Psychosocial issues for children and families in disasters: A guide for the primary care physician.* (DHHS Publication (SMA) 95–3022). Washington, DC: U.S. Department of Health and Human Services.

Broad, W., Engelberg, S., and Miller, J. (2001). *Germs: Biological weapons and America's secret war.* New York: Simon & Schuster.

Ehrenreich, J. (2002). *Coping with disaster, a guidebook to psychosocial intervention, for any discipline in helping survivors of a disaster,* at www.mhwwb.org/disasters.htm.

Ehrenreich, J. (2002). A guide for humanitarian, healthcare, and human rights workers, a guidebook for staff of humanitarian aid, healthcare, human rights, organizations and others working day-in-day-out with disaster survivors. Sections on the effects of trauma, ways of dealing with traumatized people without retraumatizing them, and the problem of secondary or vicarious traumatization of humanitarian workers, at www.mhwwb.org/disasters.htm.

FBI Academy, (2002, February 28). *Countering terrorism: Integration of practice and theory*, American Psychological Association, at www.apa.org/ppo/issues/ct.pdf.

Federal Emergency Management Agency (2002, September). *Are you ready? A guide to citizen preparedness*, available on Web site: www.fema.gov.

Frist, W., M.D. (2002). *When every moment counts: What you need to know about bioterrorism from the Senate's only doctor.* Lanham, MD: Rowman & Littlefield.

Lindell, M., Tierney, K., and Perry, R. W. (2001). *Facing the unexpected: Disaster preparedness and response in the United States.* Washington, DC: Joseph Henry Press.

Pickering, L. (Ed.) (2000). *Red Book 2000: Report of the Committee on Infectious Diseases.* Elk Grove Village, IL: American Academy of Pediatrics.

U.S. Government (2001, September). *21st century complete guide to bioterrorism, biological and chemical weapons, germs and germ warfare, nuclear and radiation terrorism—military manuals and federal documents with practical emergency plans, protective measures, medical treatment and survival information.* (CD-ROM) U.S. Government.

Venzke, B. N. (Ed.) (2002). *First responder chem-bio handbook.* Alexandria, VA: Tempest Publishing.

Web Sites

Aftermath of Terrorism (Parent Materials)
    http://www.nccev.org/resources/terrorism/aftermath_index.html

American Academy of Child and Adolescent Psychiatry
    www.aacap.org/publications/facts-fam/disaster.htm

American Academy of Pediatrics
    www.aap.org/advocacy/releases/disastercomm.htm

American Psychological Association, Science Directorate
    www.apa.org/ppo/issues/terrorhome.html

American Red Cross

www.redcross.org

American Veterinary Association

www.avma.org

Bioterrorism preparedness and response: use of information technologies and decision support. Agency for Healthcare Research and Quality, Evidence report/Technology Assessment, No. 59.

www.ahrq.gov

Center for Civilian Biodefense Studies

www.hopkins-biodefense.org

Centers for Disease Control and Prevention

www.bt.cdc.gov

Citizen Corps

www.citizencorps.gov

Department of Homeland Security

www.ready.gov

www.dhs.gov

Federal Emergency Management Agency

www.fema.gov

Illinois Homeland Security

www.Illinois.gov/security/athome.cfm

Local Emergency Planning Committees

http://yosemite.epa.gov/oswer/ceppoweb.nsf/content/index.html

Medical NBC Online

www.nbc-med.org

Mental health and mass violence, Evidence based early psychological intervention for victims/survivors of mass violence 2002

www.nimh.nih.gov/research/massviolence.pdf

National Center for Children Exposed to Violence

http://www.nccev.org

Shelter in Place

http://cseppweb-emc.ornl.gov/SIP/SIP.htm

U.S. Department of Health & Human Services Office of Emergency Preparedness

http://ndms.dhhs.gov

U.S. Postal Service

www.usps.com/news/2002/epp/emerprepplan.pdf

Bioterrorism Resources

General Web Sites

CDC: Updated Web page devoted to Public Health Emergency Preparedness and Response to Bioterrorism

> http://www.bt.cdc.gov/

Johns Hopkins University Center for Civilian Biodefense

> http://www.hopkins-biodefense.org/index.html

St. Louis University, Center for the Study of Bioterrorism and Emerging Infections

> http://www.slu.edu/colleges/sph/bioterrorism/index.html

U.S. Army Medical Research Institute of Infectious Diseases, Fort Detrick, MD

> http://www.usamriid.army.mil/

Professional Organization Web Sites

American Academy of Pediatrics (AAP)

> http://www.aap.org/advocacy/releases/cad.htm

American College of Emergency Physicians (ACEP)

> http://www.acep.org/1,4634,0.html

> American Academy of Child and Adolescent Psychiatry (AACAP)

> http://www.aacap.org/publications/DisasterResponse/index.htm

American Medical Association (AMA)

> http://www.ama-assn.org/ama/pub/category/6206.html

Articles of Interest

AAP Materials

The Child with a Suspected Anthrax Exposure or Infection

http://www.aap.org/advocacy/releases/anthraxsusp.htm

Talking to Children About the Recent Crisis
http://www.aap.org/video/schonfeldspeech.htm

Testimony Before the Senate Committee on Health, Education, Labor & Pensions Subcommittee on Children and Families about Special Needs of Children in a Bioterrorist Attack
http://www.aap.org/advocacy/washing/dr_wright.htm

AAP Policy Statements

Chemical-Biological Terrorism and its Impact on Children
> www.aap.org/policy/re9959.html
> http://www.aap.org/policy/re9959.html

How Pediatricians Can Respond to the Psychosocial Implications of Disasters
> www.aap.org/policy/re9813.html
> http://www.aap.org/policy/re9813.html

The Pediatrician and Childhood Bereavement
> www.aap.org/policy/re9917.html http://www.aap.org/pol
> icy/re9917.html

Pediatricians' Liability During Disasters
> www.aap.org/policy/re0026.html http://www.aap.org/pol
> icy/re0026.ht

Emergency Medical Services for Children (EMS-C)

After the emergency is over: Post-traumatic stress disorder in children and youth fact sheet
> http://www.ems-c.org/downloads/pdf/ptstress.pdf (PDF file)

Journal of the American Medical Association (JAMA) Consensus articles

http://jama.ama-assn.org/issues/v285n8/ffull/jst00017.html

(1999). Anthrax as a Biological Weapon. *JAMA, 281*, 1735–1745.
> http://jama.ama-assn.org/issues/v281n18/ffull/jst80027.
> html

(2001). Botulinum Toxin as a Biological Weapon. *JAMA, 285*, 1059–1070.

http://jama.ama-assn.org/issues/v285n8/ffull/jst00017.html

(2000). Plague as a Biological Weapon. *JAMA*, *283*, 2281–2290.
 http://jama.ama-assn.org/issues/v283n17/ffull/
 jst90013.html

(1999). Smallpox as a Biological Weapon. *JAMA*, *281*, 2127–2137.
 http://jama.ama-assn.org/issues/v281n22/ffull/jst90000.
 html

(2001). Tularemia as a Biological Weapon. *JAMA*, *285*, 2763–2773.
 http://jama.ama-assn.org/issues/v285n21/ffull/jst10001.
 html

Morbidity and Mortality Weekly Report (MMWR)

(2001, November 30). Adverse events associated with anthrax prophylaxis among postal employees—New Jersey, New York City, and
the District of Columbia metropolitan area, 2001. *MMWR*,
50(47):1051–1054.

 http://www.cdc.gov/mmwr/preview/mmwrhtml/mm5047a2.
 htm

(2001, November 9). Considerations for distinguishing influenza-
like illness from inhalational anthrax. *MMWR* 50(44):984–986.

 http://www.cdc.gov/mmwr/preview/mmwrhtml/mm5044a5.
 htm

(2001, November 9). Interim guidelines for investigation of and response to *Bacillus anthracis* exposures. *MMWR*, 50(44):987–990.

 http://www.cdc.gov/mmwr/preview/mmwrhtml/mm5044a6.
 htm

(2001, November 16). Interim recommendations for antimicrobial
prophylaxis for children and breastfeeding mothers and treatment
of children with anthrax. *MMWR*, 50(45):1014–1016.

 http://www.cdc.gov/mmwr/preview/mmwrhtml/mm5045a5.
 htm

(2001, November 2). Interim recommendations for protecting
workers from exposure to *Bacillis anthracis*. *MMWR*, 50(43):961.

 http://www.cdc.gov/mmwr/preview/mmwrhtml/mm5043a6.
 htm

(2001, November 9). Investigation of bioterrorism-related anthrax
and adverse events from antimicrobial prophylaxis. *MMWR*,
50(44):973–976.

http://www.cdc.gov/mmwr/preview/mmwrhtml/mm5044a1. htm

(2001, November 2). Investigation of bioterrorism-related anthrax and interim guidelines for clinical evaluation of persons with possible anthrax. *MMWR*, 50(43):941–948 (contains diagnostic algorithm).

http://www.cdc.gov/mmwr/preview/mmwrhtml/mm5043a1. htm

(2001, October 26). Investigation of bioterrorism-related anthrax and interim guidelines for exposure management and antimicrobial therapy. *MMWR*, 50(42):909–919.

http://www.cdc.gov/mmwr/preview/mmwrhtml/mm5042a1. htm

Vaccination Information

U.S. Public Health Service Advisory Committee on Immunization Practices (ACIP)

Recommendations on anthrax vaccination

http://www.cdc.gov/mmwr/preview/mmwrhtml/rr4915a1. htm or

http://www.cdc.gov/mmwr/PDF/rr/rr4915.pdf (PDF file)

Recommendations on smallpox vaccination

http://www.cdc.gov/mmwr/preview/mmwrhtml/rr5010a1. htm or

http://www.cdc.gov/mmwr/PDF/RR/RR5010.pdf (PDF file)

Web Casts

To view these programs, you will require Real Player, Microsoft Windows Media Player, or C-NetDownload.com.

Anthrax: What Every Clinician Should Know

http://www.sph.unc.edu/about/webcasts/bioter_10-18_ stream1.htm

Anthrax: What Every Clinician Should Know Part II

http://www.sph.unc.edu/about/webcasts/2001–11–01_ Anthrax/Current/

Index

ABOUT THE SERIES EDITOR AND ADVISORY BOARD

CHRIS E. STOUT, Psy.D., M.B.A., holds a joint governmental and academic appointment in the University of Illinois College of Medicine and serves as Illinois's first chief of Psychological Services. He served as a nongovernment special representative to the United Nations, was appointed by the U.S. Department of Commerce as a Baldridge examiner, and served as an advisor to the White House for both political parties. Dr. Stout was appointed to the World Economic Forum's Global Leaders of Tomorrow. He has published and presented more than 300 papers and 27 books, and his works have been translated into six languages. Dr. Stout has lectured across the nation and internationally in 16 countries, visiting more than 60 nations. He has been on missions around the world and has summated three of the World's Seven Summits.

BRUCE E. BONECUTTER, Ph.D., is director of Behavioral Services at the Elgin Community Mental Health Center, the Illinois Department of Human Services state hospital that serves adults in greater Chicago. He is also a clinical assistant professor of Psychology at the University of Illinois at Chicago. A clinical psychologist specializing in health, consulting, and forensic psychology, Dr. Bonecutter is also a longtime member of the American Psychological Association Taskforce on Children & the Family.

JOSEPH FLAHERTY, M.D., is chief of Psychiatry at the University of Illinois Hospital, a professor of Psychiatry at the University of Illinois College of Medicine, and a professor of Community Health Science at the University of Illinois at Chicago College of Public Health. He is a founding member of the Society for the Study of Culture and Psychiatry. Dr. Flaherty has been a consultant to the World Health Organization, the National Institutes of Mental Health, and the Falk Institute in Jerusalem.

MICHAEL HOROWITZ, Ph.D., is president and professor of Clinical Psychology at the Chicago School of Professional Psychology, one of the nation's leading not-for-profit graduate schools of psychology. Earlier, he served as dean and professor of the Arizona School of Professional Psychology. A clinical psychologist practicing independently since 1987, his work has focused on psychoanalysis, intensive individual therapy, and couples therapy. Dr. Horowitz has provided Disaster Mental Health Services to the American Red Cross. His special interests include the study of fatherhood.

SHELDON I. MILLER, M.D., is a professor of Psychiatry at Northwestern University, and director of the Stone Institute of Psychiatry at Northwestern Memorial Hospital. He is also director of the American Board of Psychiatry and Neurology, director of the American Board of Emergency Medicine, and director of the Accreditation Council for Graduate Medical Education. Dr. Miller is also an examiner for the American Board of Psychiatry and Neurology. He is founding editor of the *American Journal of Addictions*, and founding chairman of the American Psychiatric Association's Committee on Alcoholism.

DENNIS P. MORRISON, Ph.D., is chief executive officer at the Center for Behavioral Health in Indiana, the first behavioral health company ever to win the JCAHO Codman Award for excellence in the use of outcomes management to achieve health care quality improvement. He is president of the Board of Directors for the Community Healthcare Foundation in Bloomington, and has been a member of the Board of Directors for the American College of Sports Psychology. Dr. Morrison has served as a consultant to agencies including the Ohio Department of Mental Health, Tennessee Association of Mental Health Organizations, Oklahoma Psychological Association, the North Carolina Council of Community

Mental Health Centers, and the National Center for Health Promotion in Michigan.

WILLIAM H. REID, M.D., M.P.H., is a clinical and forensic psychiatrist, and consultant to attorneys and courts throughout the United States. He is a clinical professor of Psychiatry at the University of Texas Health Science Center. Dr. Reid is also an adjunct professor of Psychiatry at Texas A&M College of Medicine and Texas Tech University School of Medicine, as well as a clinical faculty member at the Austin Psychiatry Residency Program. He is chairman of the Scientific Advisory Board and medical advisor to the Texas Depressive & Manic-Depressive Association, as well as an examiner for the American Board of Psychiatry & Neurology. Dr. Reid has served as president of the American Academy of Psychiatry and the Law, as chairman of the Research Section for an international conference on the Psychiatric Aspects of Terrorism, and as medical director for the Texas Department of Mental Health and Mental Retardation.

About the Contributors

HENRY BREED has worked more than a decade in the United Nations, having been a humanitarian affairs officer, assistant to the undersecretary-general for peacekeeping, and assistant to the special representative of the secretary-general to the former Yugoslavia and to NATO. He is currently political affairs officer in the Office of the Iraq Programme. In past posts, he has been called on to go to Mozambique, Rwanda, and the former Yugoslavia. In his current post, he has been closely involved in a broad range of international activities within Iraq. He has worked as a consulting editor for UNESCO on issues including education, development, and cultural preservation, and he has been actively involved in a range of environmental activities related to the Earth Summit. Born in Norway and raised in New York, he received undergraduate degrees in music and fine arts from Indiana University in Bloomington. He also holds a master's degree in public administration from Harvard University, a diplôme in international history and politics from the Graduate Institute of International Studies in Geneva, and a master's in international affairs from Columbia University. A member of the Council on Foreign Relations and of the International Institute of Strategic Studies, he was awarded the Beale Fellowship at Harvard and was admitted to the academic fraternity Pi Kappa Lambda at Indiana University. He is also a Fulbright Scholar, a *boursier de la Confédération Suisse*, and a Regents Scholar. He lives in New York.

JOHN M. DAVIS is professor of psychology at Southwest Texas State University. He completed advanced work at two German universities and received his Ph.D. in experimental/social psychology from the University of Oklahoma. He has lived and worked as a psychologist in Germany, China, England, and the United States. He has researched and published in the areas of interpersonal relations, refugee stress/adaptation, health psychology, and international psychology. Recent publications include a book chapter (1999) on health psychology in international perspective and an invited article (2000) on international psychology in the prestigious *Encyclopedia of Psychology* (APA/Oxford University Press). His current research interests include (1) international terrorism from the perspectives of social and international psychology, and (2) the influences of ethnic self-identity and attitude similarity on interpersonal and intergroup attraction.

STEPHEN D. FABICK is a consulting and clinical psychologist in Birmingham, Michigan. He is past president of Psychologists for Social Responsibility (PsySR), past chair of the PsySR Enemy Images program, and current chair of its Conflict Resolution Action Committee. He is also chair of the Conflict Resolution Working Group of The Society for the Study of Peace, Conflict and Violence (Division 48 of the American Psychological Association). His interest has been in conflict transformation and prejudice reduction. He authored *US & THEM: The Challenge of Diversity*, a workshop presenter's manual. The program was included in President Clinton's Initiative on Race Relations and selected by The Center for Living Democracy as a model program in their book, *Bridging the Racial Divide*. The program focuses on transforming group prejudice and conflict.

TIMOTHY GALLIMORE is a certified mediator, facilitator, and third-party neutral in conflict resolution. He researches and writes on trauma healing and reconciliation and on violence prevention. He earned a Ph.D. in mass communication from Indiana University in 1992. He was a consultant to the United Nations Development Program for Women and on the USAID Rwanda Rule of Law project to institute a community restorative justice system for trying genocide suspects.

EDITH HENDERSON GROTBERG, a developmental psychologist, works for the Civitan International Research Center at the University of Alabama, Birmingham, and with the Institute for

Mental Health Initiatives, George Washington University, Washington, D.C. As she questioned the focus on deficits and diseases as the critical concepts to understanding and enhancing human health and behavior, resilience seemed a promising new focus. Through the International Resilience Research Project, she found many answers to the role of resilience in understanding and enhancing human health and behavior. Her articles, books, workshops, and radio and television shows present the findings and their applications. Her articles appear in the *Ambulatory Child Health* and *The Community of Caring* journals, and some of her books on resilience have been translated into other languages.

CLARK McCAULEY is a professor of psychology at Bryn Mawr College and serves as a faculty and codirector of Solomon Asch's Center for Ethno-Political Conflict at the University of Pennsylvania. He received his Ph.D. in social psychology from the University of Pennsylvania in 1970. His research interests include stereotypes and the psychology of group identification, group dynamics and intergroup conflict, and the psychological foundations of ethnic conflict and genocide. His recent work includes a new measure of intergroup contact, "the exposure index."

ERVIN STAUB is professor of psychology at the University of Massachusetts at Amherst. He has published many articles, book chapters, and several books about the influences that lead to caring, helping, and altruism and their development in children. His most recent book is *A Brighter Future: Raising Caring and Nonviolent Children*. He has also done extensive research and writing about the roots and prevention of genocide and other group violence, including his book *The Roots of Evil: The Origins of Genocide and Other Group Violence*. Since 1999, he has been conducting, with collaborators, a project in Rwanda on healing, reconciliation, and other avenues to the prevention of renewed violence. His awards include the Otto Klineberg International and Intercultural Relations Prize of the Society for the Psychological Study of Social Issues. He has been president of the Society for the Study of Peace, Conflict and Violence: Peace Psychology Division of the American Psychological Association and of the International Society for Political Psychology.